Barrington J. G
42 Fanshawe St.
Benger-

Hertford

SG1 4 3AT

tel : 01992 558889

TWENTIETH CENTURY MAVERICK

THE LIFE OF
NOEL PEMBERTON BILLING

Also by Barbara Stoney

Enid Blyton

Sibyl, Dame of Sark

Henry Ford, The Motor Man

TWENTIETH CENTURY MAVERICK

THE LIFE OF

NOEL PEMBERTON BILLING

Barbara Stoney

TWENTIETH CENTURY MAVERICK—THE LIFE OF NOEL PEMBERTON BILLING

First published 2004

ISBN1-904408-09-5

Printed and bound by Lightning Source

Layout, repro and typesetting by

BANK HOUSE BOOKS
PO Box 430
East Grinstead
West Sussex
RH19 4PU

For my Husband and Family

CONTENTS

ILLUSTRATIONS

FOREWORD

When Barbara Stoney first told me that she was writing a biography of Noel Pemberton Billing, I was stunned. Either she had little idea of the formidable task facing her, or she was made of sterner stuff than I. As this admirable book demonstrates, the latter proved to be the case.

As an aviation historian I had become fascinated by the aircraft designed by 'PB', both actual and projected, and by the manifold aspects of his irregular involvement in aviation from the pioneer years up to the 1940s. That specific theme was enough to keep me occupied for some time, and in the process of endeavouring to sort out fact from fiction (much of the latter being of PB's own creation), I inevitably learnt all manner of things about the myriad other matters in which this great eccentric had become involved. There were so many that it was difficult to believe they were all centred on a single person.

Luckily, in addition to helping Barbara with the very specialist aviation aspect, I was able to help in other ways. During my own investigations I had made contact with a variety of people who had either worked for PB or had researched his work in other fields, and were keen to share their memories and discoveries. I was delighted to put Barbara in touch with them, thereby ensuring that other aspects of PB's life were adequately recorded. Billing was obviously one of those larger-than-life characters who, once encountered, was never forgotten. Usually he was remembered with fond affection, but there were those who regarded him scornfully, as an opinionated, bigoted and butterfly-minded meddler in matters of which he knew too little. But PB was one of those people who could get things done and stir the apathetic into action; often by upsetting the apple cart.

In many ways, he was his own worst enemy. As this long-overdue biography shows, time and again he would energetically embark on some ambitious project in a burst of enthusiasm, only to drop it when the next brainwave washed it away. Moreover, he inevitably had several different projects on the go simultaneously, all at different stages of development. How his ever-tolerant wives put up with this constant state of flux is beyond me; they must have been saints. But, for all his faults, there was evidently a side to the man that endeared him to intimates and friends.

He was never a 'great man' in any of his many spheres of interest, and his sometimes outrageous behaviour and intolerance of bureaucracy and petty-mindedness won him enemies in high places. Then there were the rather more questionable affairs in which PB became involved. These included the accusation of 'murder' levelled against the Royal Aircraft Factory during the First World War and the notorious 'Black Book' affair and the action brought against him for criminal libel by the actress, Maud Allen, episodes which served to keep him in the public eye, but did not present him in a particularly favourable light. Even so, despite his shortcomings, it is impossible to ignore his numerous accomplishments in so many different fields. Most of us would be pleased to have just one of these to our credit.

Recording the life of a person having such manifold interests would pose a major challenge to any biographer. Both PB and the readers of this book can count themselves fortunate that Barbara Stoney took up the gauntlet, for her reputation in this field stood her in good stead. She has saved a great British eccentric from undeserved obscurity and, possibly, oblivion. In an age when individualism and eccentricity are increasingly discouraged, suppressed and frowned upon, both in industry and society, it is refreshing and enormously entertaining to be able to take an intimate look into the eventful life of a great adventurer. If this book helps to restore appreciation of individuality, I for one will be delighted.

Philip Jarrett
22 January, 2004

ACKNOWLEDGEMENTS

Any attempt to chronicle a life as varied and full as that of Noel Pemberton Billing would have been impossible without the help and encouragement of his family and those experts in the many fields of his activities who have placed at my disposal much interesting technical material and helped to clarify matters which, in some cases, would have been totally unintelligible to me.

I am particularly grateful to his daughter Noel and her husband Bernard who gave me such great help and encouragement throughout the writing of this book and to her brother Robin and his wife Maggie who, together with PB's niece Mrs Rosemary Nicholls and sister-in-law Mrs Nina Cann, also provided me with valuable family reminiscences, information and photographs. Of great assistance, too, in piecing together much of the personal and working life of this extraordinary man, have been the unpublished memoirs and diaries of Charles G. Grey, so generously lent to me by his daughter, Mrs Beverley Grey Davis, who was also able to add her own memories.

Aviation historian, Philip Jarrett, has been chief among those whose technical expertise has been particularly helpful. He has guided me through my subject's many—often confusing—aeronautical ventures and provided me with a wealth of interesting photographs. My special thanks also to Ian Richardson, whose father worked with Supermarine in the early years and who was able to supply me with pictures of those days, and to Albert (Bert) Tagg who lent me the, now rare, illustrated silk-paged brochure PB had produced for the 1914 exhibition at Olympia. Mention must also be made, with gratitude, of Adrian Rance for the loan of his notes on the diaries of Hubert Scott-Paine; of Mike Sutcliffe and Chris Long who supplied material and photographs to help me with my research into the Australian side of PB's sound recording enterprises and Reginald Cox, who was of great assistance with his memories of record-making with PB in England, as was Edward S Walker, who provided me with his *Catalogue of World Records.*

My thanks, too, to all those people in PB's old constituency of East Hertfordshire, who have contributed photographs or other information for the book, in particular, Cyril Heath, Alan Greening, Mrs G. Howes, Mrs L. Carter, Tony Bell and the Hertford librarians and museum staff.

Among those living at Burnham-on-Crouch who were particularly helpful and I would like to mention are: Mrs Maureen Owen, Mrs Warwick Smith, Owen Bowton, Arthur Cole, Murray Prior, George Clarke, and Grenville Lewis.

Others to whom I would like to show my appreciation for help in their various ways include: The Rt Hon Merlyn Rees, PC, MP; Miss H.R.Martin at the Ministry of Defence; Dr David Styles, keeper of the Riley car records; R.A.

Storey, Archivist of the Modern Records Centre, Warwick University; Patricia Gill of the West Sussex Record Office; Lynda Springate, Librarian of the National Motor Museum; the Archivists at EMI, National Film Library and Royal Court Theatre; Public Record Office; British Library and Newspaper Library; Patent Office Science Library; Chris Burlace; Lettice Curtis and the Twyford Branch Librarian and her assistants. I am also very grateful for the skilled help I have received from Margaret Body and from Ted Aubury, Tony Barham and Brian Read. Special thanks are also due to my husband for his constant encouragement and belief in the task I had set myself, particularly on those occasions when the gathering together of the many diverse parts of PB's incredible life seemed almost too arduous to pursue.

INTRODUCTION

Parliament has always had its fair share of eccentrics but the life and career of Independent Member Noel Pemberton Billing must still rank among the most bizarre. He was an extraordinary, far-sighted polymath of events on the world scene during the first half of the last century yet the range and value of his activities have never been fully appreciated. During his 67 turbulent years he was a prolific inventor, an aircraft designer, a pioneer aviator and motorist, yacht broker, gun-runner, spy, soldier, sailor, author, playwright. newspaper proprietor – and much more besides. His appearance was as striking as his lifestyle for he was well over six foot tall, wore a monocle and clothes made to his own design. Women found him irresistible and he, being a highly-sexed man himself, was equally susceptible to their charms. It was once said that his main fascinations in life were 'fast aircraft, fast boats, fast cars and fast women.' Yet, despite his many infidelities and impulsive, often outrageous behaviour, his two marriages were long and successful.

I came across his name, quite by chance, some years ago while sorting out family papers after the death of my mother-in-law. She was a great hoarder and we did not want to destroy anything that might be of historic interest. Among a large bundle of Northern Ireland newspapers were some which caught my eye as they included long reports of a remarkable six-day trial for criminal libel held in London at the Old Bailey in the early summer of 1918. The defendant had conducted his own case and, seemingly against all odds, was acquitted - much to the delight of those in the public gallery and the crowd gathered outside. I was intrigued by the unusual situation of a layman conducting his own defence in such a prestigious court of justice, and also why this trial should have received such nationwide coverage at a particularly crucial period of the First World War when the Germans were subjecting the Allies to what turned out to be their last major offensive on the Western Front. I decided to research further and discovered that the full life story of the man at the centre of the trial was infinitely more interesting than I could ever have visualised - a gift for any biographer but one that was to involve me in several years of fascinating work exploring the various aspects of his colourful career and personality which, in the following pages, I have tried to convey.

Barbara Stoney

CHAPTER ONE

Noel Pemberton Billing was born on 31st January 1881, at 6 College Villas, Finchley Road, a large Victorian house in North London. He was the sixth child of Charles Eardley Billing and his wife Annie Amelia (née Claridge) but one daughter died shortly after PB's birth. The family employed a governess, nurse, cook, housemaid and under-nurse and, being an attractive child with an elder brother and three adoring sisters, it is easy to see how PB, on his own admission, soon became very spoilt. His father, an inventor with iron foundries in London and Birmingham, was usually far too preoccupied with business affairs to spend much time at home, so the small boy very quickly learned how to use his charms on the rest of the household when he wanted to get his own way. It was an art he was never to lose, certainly as far as women were concerned.

PB spoke little of his father in later life and he remains a shadowy figure. All that is known of Charles Eardley Billing is that he was a dreamy eccentric, who shopped for his own food in the London markets and owned 364 pairs of shoes. His favourite phrase, remembered with amusement by his family, was 'business will always accrue' – something which apparently did not happen as often as he would have liked. His inventions, manufactured in his own foundries, were mainly concerned with gas and oil burners for heating and cooking but he also registered a patent for a coin-operated machine which supplied clean towels and registered 'empty' when it ran out. Other designs included an assortment of unusual brush, bottle and umbrella holders. His wife Annie was extremely proud of her husband's skills and accepted his idiosyncrasies with great equanimity, making sure he was kept as free as possible from household worries. He did, however, take some part in directing the education of their lively younger son.

PB loathed school from the moment he began his first lessons, at the age of seven, at the High School in Finchley Road. So mischievous and awkward was he in class that after only a year his father decided to take him away and send him instead to Cummings College, a boarding establishment at Boulogne in northern France, noted for its discipline. Cummings, the headmaster, had his own methods for dealing with boys who had a will of their own. According to PB's recollections, he was 'a man with a way, a way that was chiefly manifested by beating faithfully with many rods'. The young boy ran away three times but only once did he succeed in getting across the Channel. When he did eventually manage to get home, he was in such a state of distress his parents were forced to believe his stories of the headmaster's cruelty and he was allowed to leave.

His stay at a third school, Westcliff College at Ramsgate, was equally brief for it was not long before his antics here, which culminated in setting fire to the headmaster's study, resulted in his expulsion. He claimed later that the fire was a protest at having been wrongly accused with a fellow-pupil of a mere schoolboy prank. His parents were by this time beginning to despair of him ever settling down to a regular pattern of education. They nevertheless tried once more and he became a pupil at Craven College, Highgate, at which he claimed later to have spent the happiest years of his short schooling, despite learning little in return for the heavy fees his parents paid. Sitting at a desk was, he felt, a boring occupation when there was so much else he wanted to do.

When he was barely twelve years old and spending a summer vacation with his parents at Folkestone, he set up a small business on the sea front, teaching young women to ride bicycles for a moderate charge. A few months later he played truant from school and found himself a job in the City of London as an office boy but after throwing an inkwell at what he termed 'an offensive clerk', the company quickly dispensed with his services.

By the time he reached his thirteenth birthday the routine of school life had become so irksome he could stand it no longer. Early one morning he stole out of the house and made his way to the East India Docks where, being tall for his age, he had no difficulty in signing up as a deck hand on an 800-ton sailing ship, the *Bampshire*, bound for South Africa.

'My outfit,' he was later to write,[1] 'though not extensive, was peculiar and characteristic, comprising what I then considered to be the sheer necessities of life—to me, anyhow'. He took two feather pillows, to satisfy his desire for physical comfort, a cornet to indulge his passion for music, a revolver to protect himself, and his pet kitten, snugly buttoned up within his jacket.

His family's reaction to his disappearance was naturally one of shock. He was, after all, only thirteen years old. Police were alerted and searches were made, but all to no avail and it was to be many years before news of him reached his home in North London.

Years later he described the voyage to his friends, telling of how he was thrown from one of the yards onto the deck during a gale, resulting in fractures to his leg, which were set so crudely he was lame for months afterwards. He also suffered greatly at the hands of the first mate and on one occasion was driven to flourishing his revolver at him, which caused quite a disturbance on board. When the ship reached Lourenço Marques (now Maputo) he decided he could no longer stand the harassment and went ashore. There was a coastal steamer at the quay, bound for Durban and he boarded it.

By this time his small stock of belongings had been greatly reduced: the pillows had been stolen by the steward, his kitten by the captain's wife and his clothes had become so threadbare they flapped in ribbons about his lanky, rapidly-growing body. He had managed, however, to keep his cornet and

1. In a biographical booklet published in 1917 by *The Imperialist*

revolver—his 'sound and fury', as he termed them—and was able to exchange these for fresh clothes and a few shillings.

On arriving at Durban, he heard that fruit-growing was a profitable industry at Pinetown, seventeen miles inland, and decided to go there, seeking shelter or work where he could. After several days tramping through the dusty terrain, he arrived, hot, dishevelled, hungry and in some pain from his injured leg, only to discover that there was, after all, no work to be had. He journeyed hopefully on through Natal but soon realised that, as far as employment was concerned, there was no alternative but to retrace his steps to Durban.

There then followed a two-week period in that city, which he later recalled as being of such privation he could never look back on that episode of his life without it assuming nightmarish proportions. 'The worst privation the Lord can send,' he wrote afterwards, 'is that which one endures alone in a city—far worse than dying in the open as so many nameless pioneers of Empire have died'.

He found himself a job at last sweeping up wood shavings in a furniture workshop attached to a sawmill. But he did not remain a sweeper for long, for he took to watching the carpenters at work and found he had a natural aptitude for woodwork. He persuaded the manager of a cheap furniture factory that he was skilled enough to help make cabinets and in due course became a reasonably efficient carpenter. When, after only a few months, he felt that he had learned all he could of this trade, he decided to try his hand at others.

It so happened that the building industry in Durban was flourishing for it was a period of great growth in the city. PB took advantage of this and managed to find himself a job as an assistant bricklayer and was soon allowed to work on his own.

During this time, a building strike led to workers being imported from India at an exceedingly low rate of pay and a massed protest march was organised by the strikers. PB viewed the fighting that then broke out with horror, particularly as many of the immigrants were killed. Always on the side of the underdog, he disliked the way the whole affair was handled and let it be known that his sympathy lay with the immigrant workers whom he felt had been exploited and, through no fault of their own, had then suffered from the wrath of the pickets.

Whether the incident that followed was the result of his outspokenness there is no way of knowing but later, while working from a wooden scaffold, a plank mysteriously gave way and he fell several feet to the ground. He was badly concussed, injured his back and when he finally left hospital, found that he had temporarily lost his head for heights.

He soon discovered, however, that working in humid, stifling conditions as a conductor on the trams, was by no means an ideal alternative. The job became even more arduous when the Hottentot drivers went on strike and he had to work for a pittance with extra trailers on the trams, from six in the morning until midnight, and he took it upon himself to confront the manager with his grievances. Such brazen criticism from one so young (he was barely sixteen) infuriated his employer and a fight ensued. Fortunately, PB had height (he was already well over six foot) if not years on his side and he emerged from the confrontation relatively unscathed, albeit without a job. Such experiences later led him to claim that those days in South Africa had taught him 'How exceedingly cruel Capital can be to Labour when Labour is too compliant.'

His next job was a locomotive cleaner on the Natal Railway. This soon led to him becoming first a shunter and then a stoker. Tinkering with the engines intrigued him and he learned a little about engineering in the process. But within a few months he was on the move once more. Durban, he considered, had become too 'civilised' and he longed to see more of what was going on outside the confines of the railway. He left his safe situation and with what money he had managed to save set off on foot to trek through Natal and Zululand, living frugally and picking up what work he could along the way, revelling in the sense of freedom this offered.

Many years afterwards he recalled the joy he had felt each morning at dawn on seeing freshness and beauty around him while working for a spell on a mountainside as a quarryman. This pleasure, he claimed, was heightened by knowing that he was there of his own free will and that his 'good right arm' was providing him with all his needs. Such a carefree life, however, was to end when he reached Pietermaritzburg for by then he had decided to follow yet another occupation. During his travels he had encountered a troop of Natal Mounted Police and was instantly attracted by the excitement and variety that service with the Force appeared to offer. He was not quite seventeen and officially under age but his height, manner and general appearance—plus the fact that the adjutant's family lived in Hampstead and knew of the Billing family—persuaded the officer in charge to take him on.

He enjoyed his service as a trooper and became a fine horseman. He also became a useful boxer for his company, for by this time he had grown into a wiry young man, six foot four in height and with a strong physique. His good looks and easy charm fascinated the few women he met in this predominantly male society and he sometimes found himself succumbing to their attractions, although he always made it a rule to steer clear of any serious attachment.

He was stationed on the Orange Free State border when the first rumours of a possible war with the Dutch settlers reached the Force and all the outstations were ordered to mobilise at the Natal Mounted Police headquarters at Newcastle. In the weeks before the outbreak of the Boer War, in October 1899, PB's detachment was ordered to patrol the border from Charlestown and a few shots were exchanged but these were fired, according to his own account, 'more in sport than animosity'. His first experience of real war came later when he was with a small band of outnumbered police which was forced to retreat from Newcastle to Dundee.

At Dundee, he was directed to General Penn-Symons staff, under Colonel Dartnell, and took part in the battle of Talana Hill and also acted as a guide during the retreat to Ladysmith. With the troops he endured four traumatic days of blistering sun or drenching rain, with little time for sleep or food. He also pressed on with them through the Helpmakaar Pass and across Sunday's River only to find on arrival at Ladysmith, exhausted and caked in mud, that the garrison town was even hotter, dustier and typhoid-ridden. He found it difficult to believe that over the hills and ridges that surrounded the base, was the fresh green veldt he remembered so well from his trekking days. There was little time to reflect further on his situation for, almost immediately after his arrival, he was ordered to conduct some Boer prisoners to Pietermaritzburg and left on what proved to be almost the last train out of Ladysmith before the famous siege began.

When General Redvers Buller arrived to plan the relief of Ladysmith, PB was detailed to accompany him as a bodyguard and later as one of his gallopers. As such, he was at the battle of Colenso and crossed the Tugela River and entered Ladysmith with the relieving troops in February, 1900. By this time he had been slightly wounded on two occasions and had seen horrendous and bloody battles in which many of his friends and acquaintances had been killed or maimed and he was beginning to wonder if the war was achieving anything, other than tearing apart the country he had grown to love.

In the autumn of 1900, he became ill with dysentery and enteric fever and it was while he was convalescing in Durban that he heard of a hospital ship about to sail for England. This gave him a sudden desire to see his family and home again. He persuaded the officer in charge to let him help with the stretcher cases and finished up working his passage back as a member of the ship's company.

After an interval of some six years, the sudden appearance at the Billing's Hampstead home of the tall, tanned young man of nineteen—still a little emaciated after his illness—came as something of a shock. His mother had died just over a year earlier and his father was being cared for by PB's sisters, Mabel, Hilda and Mary. He stayed with them for a few weeks, amusing himself by drawing up plans for a gun carriage and designs for tunics, stirrups and other military equipment which he subsequently submitted to the War Office. However, when the officials appeared disinterested in his designs, he succumbed to his usual restlessness and searched for new ways to spend his time.

He heard that a touring theatrical company needed young men to take part in a patriotic drama entitled *Serving the Queen* and was given the part of a young soldier who died on stage an hour or so after the curtain rose. It was an unpromising theatrical debut for a young actor but PB extracted every bit of drama he could from the role.

Among the innovations he had noticed on his return to London was the appearance of a number of motorised vehicles on the streets. This new form of transport fascinated him and he resolved that when the tour of the play came to an end he would learn to drive. This did not prove quite as easy as he had anticipated. No-one of his acquaintance possessed a car and to buy one was far too expensive. His chance came when he noticed that a Mr von Lehr was advertising for someone to drive him to the City each day. Investing in a suitable leather uniform and with his usual self-confidence, PB applied for the job. Much to the astonishment of his family and friends, he was taken on without his employer realising that his new chauffeur had no knowledge whatsoever of either cars or driving.

The vehicle was a 4½ hp Phoenix Panhard and, with determination and a certain amount of natural ability, it did not take him long to learn the basic mechanics and to drive well enough to satisfy his employer. For the two pounds a week he was paid, he was expected to keep the vehicle in pristine condition but he felt he had better things to do with his time and hired a man for twenty-five shillings a week to carry out the cleaning for him and spent the remaining fifteen shillings on getting to and from his employer's home by cab. For him, it was enough just to drive this splendid machine around the streets of London and was the beginning of what he later described as one of the 'infinite pleasures' of his life.

When one of his friends, Guy Lewing, something of a motoring pioneer himself, suggested that PB join him in a scheme to open a garage he planned to run at Kingston-upon-Thames, it was an offer not to be refused. PB gave up his chauffeuring job and plans were made for the launch but his personal involvement proved to be short-lived. Within a few weeks he had managed to talk himself into being engaged to manage the Orient Express stand at the first Crystal Palace Motor Show in November 1901 and with his brother, Eardley, he took part in a commemorative drive to Portsmouth to celebrate the anniversary of the Locomotives on the Highway Act.

As Brussels and Paris then appeared to be the centres for so much that was going on in the European motoring world, he figured they might be the obvious places in which to study motor engineering which would prove a useful asset for when the garage got under way. Of course, it never did.

After a spell in Brussels, he went on to Paris and began training for one of the big races being held there but this needed more capital than he had anticipated and predictably he soon ran out of money. He returned to England as a stowaway on a small steamer from Le Havre and as the boat pulled into Southampton he spotted another about to depart for South Africa. Impetuous as ever and without going through any of the usual formalities, he hopped aboard and, by fair means or foul, was somehow allowed to work his passage to Durban. Soon after landing, he became involved in a spot of horse dealing, buying unwanted cavalry re-mounts for a bargain price, fattening them up and then selling them very profitably. So successful was this venture, that he put his newly-acquired capital and what small knowledge of motoring he had into yet another scheme—to introduce cars to South Africa.

At that time, ox-wagons were still the most common form of transport on Durban streets and cars were almost unknown, so he set about educating the public by producing a newspaper devoted exclusively to motoring topics. Unfortunately, the small capital he had recently acquired was insufficient on its own to set this up, so he looked around for other ways of raising the money.

He had noticed that the building industry in Durban was still thriving, so it seemed a good idea to make use of his early experiences in the trade and he managed to obtain a contract to build new houses on the outskirts of the city. Meanwhile a friendly tea-broker gave him the nightly use of his office from which to launch his motoring paper, which he planned to run in tandem with his building business.

He called his paper, which he compiled entirely on his own, the *British South African Auto-car* and worked on it for most of each night, visiting the printers and dealing with advertisers on the half day he took off each week from his bricklaying. Not surprisingly, after a time his health began to suffer from his self-inflicted, gruelling workload and he found it increasingly difficult to cover his costs. As a result, on completion of his housing contract, he gave up the building business altogether and devoted all his energies towards getting his paper properly established.

Despite all his efforts, sales remained poor, which was not surprising since it dealt exclusively with something which most of the South African public had never even heard of—let alone seen at that time. When, inevitably, publication ceased, he settled all but one of his debts and even this he managed to pay off by working for the creditor, a prosperous bill-poster.

Shortly afterwards, much to his surprise, he was approached by the touring manager of George Edwardes' and Wheeler's Musical Comedy Company who had heard him sing in an amateur concert in Durban, liked his voice and was prepared to offer him an engagement. This he promptly accepted although the salary was less than he was earning with the bill-poster but the lure of the footlights was too strong for him to resist. The idea of travelling through the rest of South Africa in the comfort of a first-class railway compartment was also very appealing for, now that the Boer War was over, he thought it would be interesting to see the changes that had taken place in the country since his trekking days.

He sang several minor parts in popular musicals for the company, appearing on the programme as 'Noel Pemberton', to avoid confusion with an actress in the cast whose surname also happened to be Billing. When the tour came to an end at Cape Town, he joined another travelling company, Sass and Nelson, and this time understudied most of the male roles. It was all highly enjoyable and he basked in the attentions of the many attractive women he encountered on and off stage. By the time the tour ended at Johannesburg and the rest of the company had returned to England, PB had already made other plans.

He had met some businessmen who offered to back him in starting up an illustrated paper to specialise in sport and drama, neither of which he thought were adequately covered by other Johannesburg publications. Within a few months of his twenty-first birthday, he therefore set himself up as editor and proprietor of what (always the optimist) he felt sure would eventually be a flourishing enterprise. The first issues certainly sold well and as the weeks went by he even managed to build up a reasonably substantial bank balance. He bought himself a comfortable flat, an auto-steam car and a dog-cart and all seemed set for a golden future. Few young men of his age had packed such a variety of experiences into so short a space of time. If they had, most would probably have been content to enjoy the fruits of their hard work, but this was not PB's way. The accumulation of wealth as such was never his main ambition. His goal was always to have enough money to explore each interesting new experience or project that came his way.

As had always been the case, after the initial enthusiasm his interest began to fade—as did that of the general public. The journal's slow decline happened to coincide with PB sustaining an incapacitating injury to his right hand which inevitably hastened the paper's closure. The injury came about late one evening in Johannesburg when he saw what he later described as 'a big bully dishing out injustice to a diminutive person' and he decided to spring to the smaller man's defence. After a short scuffle, he knocked the assailant out but in the process smashed his own knuckles. The wounds became infected and PB became extremely ill—amputation of his hand even being considered at one stage—but he slowly recovered after several months with his arm in a sling.

Having scraped up enough money for his fare, he thought it an opportune time to return to England and arrived there on a cold winter's day in the early months of 1903. Although he was never again to return to South Africa, he often looked back with pleasure at the years he had spent there and maintained that, despite what he considered the many injustices he had encountered in that country, he sometimes longed for the 'smell of the veldt'. 'To know South Africa as I knew her,' he wrote years later, 'is to forgive her everything, to love her always'.

CHAPTER TWO

England seemed harsh, cold and unsympathetic during his first few days at home and he wondered if he had, perhaps, been too hasty in leaving South Africa when he did. He cheered up a little, however, when he ran into a friend from his theatrical days who took him to dinner and reminisced about their days in that country. His friend was currently resident manager of the Richmond Theatre but was about to resign and go on tour. When he suggested that PB might like to take over from him it seemed a wonderful idea and by the following afternoon all had been arranged.

At first he enjoyed being so closely involved with plays and actors but after a while he found the routine of being a theatre manager tedious. To break the monotony he began writing a play—*Memory*—which was subsequently performed at a small theatre in Greenwich but it proved to be an abysmal failure and sank without trace after only one performance.

When he was offered a part in *The Geisha* with the Number One Northern Touring Company, he gladly accepted for by this time he was ready to move on again. He enjoyed being back on the stage once more but the weather that spring was appalling and the northern climate did not suit him after the warmth of South Africa. He caught a severe cold which developed into a chronic throat infection and resulted in his voice giving out completely, obliging him to leave the company. He returned to London, found himself a small, if expensive, flat in the Adelphi and began searching for an interesting alternative occupation.

The newspapers were full of stories about Britain lagging behind the rest of the world in the promotion and marketing of new ideas and machinery. American typewriters, motor-cars and the new gramophones were all well advertised and selling well, whereas in England, previously known as the workshop of the world, there appeared to be a reluctance to invest capital in developing new products or modernising the old. He knew from the experiences of his inventor father that this was so and it seemed an opportune moment for him to get to work on several ideas of his own, which he had been mulling over for some time, confident that he would be able to interest businessmen in marketing them for him.

Thus began PB's new persona: Noel Pemberton Billing, inventor. What he had not envisaged, however, when he made these plans was that within a few weeks he would embark on a venture of a very different kind—one that would have an even more far-reaching effect on his life.

In the autumn of 1903, his father and sisters invited him to dinner at their new London home at Hyde Park Mansions and, full of enthusiasm, he took along the prototype for a design he was about to patent, a powder puff attached to a handkerchief. Sitting quietly in the flat with Mary, the youngest of his three sisters, was a small, dark-haired woman with a sweet expression and the most remarkable eyes he had ever seen. She was by no means as beautiful as some of the women he had met in his short life but he was attracted to her immediately. Her name was Lilian Maud Schweitzer, Dot to her friends. She had been born in Bristol and, although PB was not aware of it at the time, was ten years older than himself. Her father, Theodore Henry Schweitzer, was of German parentage and a retired ship's chandler. Her mother, Sarah, was a Scot from Edinburgh.[1]

Altogether Dot seemed an interesting person and PB was determined to know her better but this proved to be more difficult than he expected. Up to now he had been accustomed to attractive women responding quickly to his charms, but this time his usual overtures made little impression and he sensed that behind this intelligent woman's quiet, placid manner was an intriguing strength of character.

Three weeks later, after only a few further meetings, PB came to a decision. Following a sleepless night, he arrived at the local telegraph office at half past eight the next morning and handed the startled clerk a telegram which read:

'Will you marry me? Wire reply Adelphi'.
The reply came back promptly:
'No'.

It was not in PB's nature to be put off that easily, however, and despite protests from both families, who thought the courtship too short and their joint income too little, the pair were married at St Marylebone Register Office in London, on 12th December 1903. His father was too ill to attend the ceremony and, in fact, died later that same month but his two elder sisters, Hilda and Mabel, acted as witnesses. On the marriage certificate PB appears as 'Noel Pemberton Billing, otherwise Noel Pemberton' and his occupation is recorded as 'Journalist'. Dot is shown as being only twenty-eight, four years younger than she actually was, although her youthful appearance lent credence to this understandable subterfuge.

Despite PB's impetuous, mercurial temperament, the marriage worked. Dot remained a faithful, loving wife and he never lost his deep love and respect for her. One lifelong friend of them both described her as 'a most intelligent and wholly admirable little lady', while another spoke of her as being among 'the cleverest and bravest women' he had ever known. Maybe she needed to be all these things, having taken on PB for a husband.

At first the couple continued to live in his flat at the Adelphi. Dot had a

---

1. Dot was also the cousin of Albert Schweitzer, already making a name for himself in philosophical and theological circles.

small amount of money but this soon went, helping her husband to pursue his various inventions which never seemed to progress beyond the outline drawings. Debts began to mount up and now that he felt responsible for someone else, even PB was beginning to lose his habitual confidence. Fortunately, quite by chance, he met the managing director of a small South London paraffin lamp company, who told him of a technical problem his firm was having, which PB's skill with machinery was able to solve and for which he was well rewarded. On the strength of this, the couple were able to pay off their debts and move to a larger flat in Hampstead. Predictably perhaps, this happy state of solvency and stability was destined not to last.

PB had greatly enjoyed his flirtation with print in South Africa and when a friend, Gordon Lawes, agreed to join him in producing a weekly journal to be called the *Hampstead Social Review*, he began looking around for suitable premises. These were found in Hampstead but the landlord, uncertain as to whether the old building would stand up to the heavy machinery involved, had a clause written into the contract specifying that, should the structure appear to be suffering, work must be stopped immediately. When a crack did appear in the basement ceiling, the landlord understandably insisted on sticking to the terms of the contract and told PB that the machinery must not be used until the repairs had been carried out. As the paper was on the point of going to press, PB and Gordon Lawes decided to take a chance and go ahead anyway with the printing.

Although no further harm befell the building, the furious landlord brought an injunction against the two young proprietors which forbade any further printing the following week. With no alternative premises available at such short notice, the journal could not be printed in time. The advertisers refused to settle their outstanding debts and the *Hampstead Social Review* was no more. Gordon Lawes helped as far as he was able but any savings the Pemberton Billings had managed to scrape together quickly disappeared in winding up the business. Dot, who was never strong physically, then became ill and PB's health began to break down under the strain.

Dot soon recovered but PB continued to look and behave in a way that was completely foreign to all who knew him. The normally ebullient young man sank into a state of acute depression and despair, became thin, pale and unable to eat or sleep. His doctor ordered a complete rest to give his over-active brain time to recover. His sisters and friends were very sympathetic and supportive and helped move him and Dot out of their London flat and into a small furnished cottage near Crawley in Sussex. Here he gradually recovered but as his physical strength returned, so did his desire to occupy himself with some creative activity.

He took a lease on an adjoining ten-acre field and constructed, with Dot's help, a small bungalow with its own dairy and outhouses. He then set about digging a well and making furniture for what Dot hoped might become their permanent home. Together they bought a pig, some hens and a cow and did their best to cultivate the heavy clay soil. But the hens refused to lay, the cow took to chasing the pig and in the process lost the calf on which they had set so much store. Added to which, their efforts at trying to run the small-holding were treated with wry amusement by their farming neighbours, most of whom considered that the tall, bearded man with a monocle who lived with his wife in what they considered to be 'the doll's house in the middle of a field', were only playing at being farmers. PB was never one to care what others thought of him so did not bother to explain that he had only grown his beard in the first place because he had been too ill to shave. As for his monocle, it was not—as he knew some of his neighbours thought—merely an affectation, but had become a necessity since an injury to his right eye, during his boxing days with the Natal Police, made it difficult for him to focus without its aid.

During the bleak winter of 1904-5, he had ample time for what he later described as 'sad, cynical thoughts' and, although he was barely twenty-four years old, he felt like an old man. It was at this period, having already had experience of being both employer and employee, that he first began thinking seriously about what he termed the 'interdependence of capital and labour' and he started mulling over ideas for some form of employees' insurance scheme. This was set aside with the coming of spring, but many years later he was to pursue the idea further.

Fired by the reports he had read of the Wright Brothers' experiments with powered flight, he built a glider in one of the outhouses and launched himself in it from the roof of the bungalow. The glider fell apart on hitting the ground but he fortunately escaped injury. He tried again and again but the result was always the same and he claimed later that he had buried in his garden many of these 'lost endeavours'.

By the end of the summer he was feeling more like his old self and the restlessness returned. Acting once again on impulse and much to Dot's dismay, for she had grown to love the bungalow and the small-holding, he sold up, bought a car on the proceeds and set off in search of a new home. They found it not far away at East Grinstead and here he continued with his experiments into flying machines and later claimed to have built a man-lifting glider, which had the appearance of a large, kite-like, triangular box. As with his previous efforts, this did not stay in the air for more than a few seconds.

He also patented other designs, including one for a complicated 'Digit Typewriter' operated by the index finger only, but the cost of all this was such that within a few months the capital from the sale of his small-holding was almost exhausted. There was nothing for it but to move back to London and try to find cheaper accommodation.

Their new home consisted of one small room at 30, Seymour Place. In it PB installed a lathe and bench and here, for several months, he and poor, long-suffering Dot lived and worked. On one occasion he stayed in the room for sixteen days and, despite Dot's protestations, existed on tea and cigarettes while he sought to perfect a design for another typewriter which he was convinced would be more successful than his earlier model.

One by one, Dot saw her wedding presents pawned and her few bits of furniture disappear in order to raise enough money just for their rent and food while her husband was continuing with his experiments. By the time the typewriter was finally designed to his satisfaction and was ready for demonstration to an interested businessman, the contents of their room had been reduced to three old sugar crates, a bed, bench and lathe. While he was waiting for the would-be buyer to decide whether or not he was interested in the typewriter, PB found himself a four-week engagement with a touring theatrical company's production starring Mrs Patrick Campbell. The part was a minor one but the money he earned at least helped Dot retrieve some of the smaller articles from the pawnshop.

There had been a boom in rifle-shooting and miniature ranges since Lord Roberts had issued warnings about the unprepared state of the country should it be attacked and PB had taken note of this. On returning from his theatrical tour, he and some friends founded Shots, a small rifle club in Regent Street which proved very successful.

At about the same time the businessman interested in the typewriter decided to launch a company for its manufacture. This encouraged PB in the summer of 1907 to found the Pemberton Billing Patents Company for his other inventions. Although he did not register all of these at the Patent Office, his designs at that time included an automatic petrol gun, a machine for measuring unrolled bales of cloth (for use during stock-taking) and a 'calculating pencil' which supposedly worked out calculations as it wrote down figures. None of these designs survive but his descriptions do give some indication of the range covered by his fertile mind.

Despite its complex design, there were interested buyers for the typewriter in Canada and America and PB made his first voyage across the Atlantic to demonstrate his machine to the American Typewriter Trust and to register his patent in the United States. But while he was there, the wheel of fortune appeared to be once again bringing him down.

The ex-sergeant-major he had left in charge of the rifle club had begun drinking heavily, the co-founders had not been supervising his activities and by the time PB returned, membership had dwindled and the club was in danger of closing down. He immediately sacked the ex-sergeant-major and did his best to put the club to rights again, but it never regained its initial success. Meanwhile, he began work on the model of a petrol turbine engine and of a cycle car he was hoping to show at a forthcoming exhibition but, as the money for his typewriter design was slow in coming from the manufacturers, he was forced to sell his share in the rifle club in order to cover his mounting debts.

This was the first of many such experiences which later caused him to write: 'It is the Capitalist who reaps the harvest which has been sown by the brains of labour, at the cost of stern sacrifice.' By this time he and Dot had moved to a furnished cottage at Burnham-on-Crouch, in Essex. His lathe and bench, however, he kept in the cellar of a house in the City for he intended to use it as a London workshop to continue his experiments.

CHAPTER THREE

PB's interest in flying had by no means abated over the past few years, rather the reverse in fact. In the summer of 1908, Wilbur Wright sailed across the Atlantic, with his aeroplane packed up on board, in order to demonstrate to Europe how he and his brother Orville had achieved the powered flight which many others were now trying to emulate. PB read the reports and told Dot that the Wrights' conquest of the air had captured his imagination more than anything had ever done before and that he could see all the possibilities that would evolve now that man could fly. At the same time he feared this achievement would make the country no longer an island, protected by its seas, and that its security in the future might well depend on its supremacy in the air.

The enthusiasm with which he passed on these views to a wealthy acquaintance resulted in this man putting up £150 towards the construction of an experimental aeroplane which PB planned to build, subject to finding a suitable site at which to begin work.

A few miles up river from his cottage at Burnham-on-Crouch was a flat, bleak piece of reclaimed marshland on which stood the semi-deserted village of South Fambridge, the few remaining buildings being grouped around a disused hydraulic crane factory. When PB first set eyes on the village, his quick mind immediately saw far greater possibilities than he had originally envisaged. Here, he thought, would be the perfect place not only for his own experiments but for other would-be aircraft designers and manufacturers to build and fly their own machines undisturbed. While doing so they might also be able to contribute in some way to the nation's defence. This would, he knew, be his most ambitious scheme to date and he could hardly wait to put it into operation.

When an idea came to PB, the lack of capital to see it through was generally the least of his worries. Somehow or other, he would convince himself, he would manage to find a way round such a tiresome detail. This proved to be the case at Fambridge.

The owners of the factory and the deserted village were not willing to sell the two separately but were prepared to give PB an option on the whole. As luck would have it, he happened to hear of a buyer for the village and sold it to this man for the price the owners had already agreed for the complete site. With the factory and its surrounding land now his, virtually for nothing, he was all set to go ahead with the rest of his plans.

In February 1909, after an interview at his Burnham home, the *Essex Weekly News* reported:

> Dagenham land has already been secured by the Aero Club for trials of

airships and according to other reports, another well-equipped station is likely to be established in Essex on about 3,000[1] acres of land near South Fambridge. In the latter project the military side of aeronautics will be considered as well as mere sport. Indeed, the founders have the idea of establishing and training aeronautical volunteers who would be able to give practical training assistance to the authorities. The proposed site at South Fambridge is well adapted for the purpose. An uninterrupted run down to the coast could be obtained and flights of over twenty miles could be attempted. Another advantage is that on the proposed grounds are several large factory buildings which could readily be converted into aeroplane erecting shops and stores while various bungalows in the neighbourhood would give housing to the experimenters.

PB's enthusiasm for his new project had obviously been imparted to the reporter and there is little doubt that he had great hopes for its success. With a total capital of less than £100, gleaned partly from friends and partly from delayed income from a cigarette-making machine he had invented several years earlier, he collected some local boat-builders as staff and began work on his 'Colony of British Aerocraft'.

He had noted that the two main sheds of the disused factory had concrete floors and were fitted with travelling cranes. The larger, measuring 125 feet by 110 feet, had doors at one end thirty feet high by 48 feet wide and he saw this building as being perfect for his 'aerodock', where aircraft could be made, housed and wheeled out for testing. An electrical generating plant and water tower were already installed and the four-roomed bungalows on the site could, he felt, be renovated for the resident airmen to rent. The general stores, post office and hotel nearby were all conveniently placed for visiting aviators and there was ample mooring on the Crouch for members' boats and garages for their cars.

In March, in order to publicise his aerodrome, he founded a monthly magazine, *Aerocraft*, which he subtitled 'The official organ of the Colony of British Aerocraft' and put on sale for sixpence. As proprietor, editor and main writer he was able to keep his readers informed of the progress being made at Fambridge and in his first editorial set out his main purpose in founding his aerodrome and magazine:

> So rapid has been the advance made during the past year in matters appertaining to the science of aerial locomotion and the problem of human flight, the proprietors of *Aerocraft* make no apology in issuing to the general public, and those interested in aviation, the first English Monthly Review of the world's progress and practice in Aerial Navigation. In doing so, they have prepared a journal dealing exhaustively with every branch of the subject, from the box kite and balloon to the aeroplane and dirigible.

1. In fact it was 1,600 acres and the Dagenham site was acquired by the Aeronautical Society of Great Britain, not the Aero Club.

He then gave a brief outline of his plans for the contents of the new publication and issued a warning regarding the possibilities of aviation in time of war and the need for adequate defence.

Among other items in this first issue were 'Aeroplane Clubs—their use and abuse'; 'The Laurel List', which gave details of prizes, cups and medals for aeronautics throughout the world; snippets of information on what was going on in flying circles internationally and a large section devoted to the founding and functions of the 'Colony of British Aerocraft'.

In his description of the aerodrome as it then was, it is apparent that since he had acquired the site PB had put in a considerable amount of work. He had divided his aerodock into twelve smaller units on either side of a central aisle, with access to and from the main hall through sliding doors. These, he wrote, were for experimenters wishing to work privately on their machines and the weekly rental for these units would include the use of machinery and other amenities of the aerodrome. For an extra 10 shillings a week the services of the boat-building staff he had engaged could also be used.

The two-storey building behind the main aerodock, he told his readers, housed the general offices, together with a print department, and close by were workshops for carpentry, covering and varnishing. There was a petrol store, forge, steam bending plant and an engine and boiler house. Plans for a club house had already been approved. To ensure the privacy he considered essential for the commercial side of aeroplane construction, he had erected an eight foot high wooden fence round the whole complex and entrance to the aerodrome could only be gained by a special, non-transferable pass, signed by himself.

According to PB, he had already received numerous enquiries about the aerodrome and was convinced that a great future was in store for Fambridge, 'both as a school for the advancement of aeronautics and as a colony to whom patriotism will not appeal in vain'. He had already proposed to the War Office that an 'Imperial Squadron of Aviators' should be formed, not necessarily under the jurisdiction of the Army but available should any crisis arise. He hoped that his colony of aeronautical enthusiasts would not only be anxious to accomplish flight but also have the interests of their country at heart, placing at the disposal of the Government, should the need arise, any experience they might acquire.

Elsewhere in the inaugural edition of his magazine, he gave notice of the first Aero and Motor-Boat Exhibition about to be held at Olympia at which he intended to exhibit a scale model of his aerodrome. This he duly did and also put on display a working model of a petrol turbine engine designed some years earlier, together with copies of his new magazine. Among those who approached him at the Exhibition was a young man whose enthusiasm for aircraft, PB was quick to note, seemed to match his own.

Eric Cecil Gordon England was never to forget this first meeting with

PB for it was to change the whole course of his life. Many years later he wrote of how he had been trying to persuade his father to let him leave his training at the Great Northern Railway Works in order to learn something about aviation. So persistent was he that in the end his father had reluctantly agreed, providing the young man first found himself a paid job in that field. As the Aero and Motor-Boat Exhibition appeared to be the best way of meeting people who might be prepared to take him on, the would-be airman set off for Olympia with high hopes.

Before encountering PB he had already approached two other exhibitors who, although sympathetic, had told him they could not afford to take on any more employees. The reaction from PB was different. He listened intently to the young man's story before telling him enthusiastically that he had the right spirit and to step into his office and he would write him a letter of engagement. The delighted Gordon England asked in what capacity he would be employed and was told, in typical PB fashion: 'Rest assured, by the time I get down to typing the letter, I'll have thought of something'. In less than ten minutes a bemused Gordon England emerged having been appointed Manager of Fambridge Aerodrome at a provisional salary of 25 shillings a week.

Neither lived to regret the arrangement and Gordon England's father was as good as his word. To seal the arrangement, on the morning the young man began work at Fambridge, he and his father were treated to lunch by PB at the local hotel. This proved to be such a riotous affair that according to Gordon England it led to his father having a lasting admiration for his son's new employer: 'One cannot help liking that old pirate PB,' he would often tell people afterwards. 'He is a unique character'.

By the close of the show at Olympia, the future of PB's Colony looked rosy. There had been numerous enquiries and two other exhibitors had already chosen Fambridge for further aeroplane trials. Richard Lascelles, well-known in motoring circles, and his partner, Beny, had also decided to establish a parts supply service at the aerodrome.

The first machine to arrive was a tailless, swept-wing monoplane from the Handley Page stand. It had been designed and built by Jose Weiss, a talented landscape painter who had been experimenting with gliders. The second was a biplane with a forty-foot span and an unusual undercarriage, which had been built by Howard T. Wright at his Battersea works and had already been described, with drawings, in the first edition of *Aerocraft*. Unfortunately, this biplane, which had been sent to Fambridge by its new owner, a Mr Seton-Kerr, was badly damaged in transit. It first became jammed in a railway arch and then suffered further damage on arrival when its tailplanes were broken as it was being pulled over a ditch on the airfield. PB was undeterred by these disasters, however, for he was confident that the biplane would soon be repaired and ready for flight.

In the April edition of *Aerocraft* he reported on all that had taken place during the past month and said that such was the success of his aerodrome he found it necessary to broaden the scope of his Colony. He therefore proposed to change its name to The Association of British Aerocraft and to administer it in a businesslike manner, with an entrance fee that would not prevent a 'man of moderate means' from joining but at the same time would prevent the possibility of the Association becoming the home of 'importunate cranks'. What was needed from now on, he wrote, was 'less talk and more men in the air'.

Within a few months, affairs at Fambridge were looking less optimistic. When Blériot crossed the Channel in July, PB thought that the aviator's achievement would spur more would-be airmen into building their own machines and filling his aerodocks—most of which still remained empty—but this did not happen. To add to his worries, even those pioneers who had already installed their machines at the aerodrome were not finding the going easy.

The weather for most of that summer was wretched and the reclaimed marshland could not stand up to the frequent heavy rain. Added to which, PB had not taken into account the several deep drainage ditches close to the take-off areas. At the beginning of May, the Howard Wright biplane owned by Seton-Kerr met with another disaster, even before it had left its shed. The repairs from its encounter with the railway arch had been carried out and its engine was being given a trial run, prior to testing on the airfield, when the propeller shaft suddenly broke and its blades shattered. The fragments narrowly missed the men gathered round and one large piece hurtled clean through the iron roof. No-one was injured but the whole of the rear part of the chassis was badly buckled and extensive repairs were again necessary.

Weiss, who had decided to begin his trials a few days later, was more fortunate. He took his monoplane out for routine testing and achieved a series of long runs and short hops, at one stage reaching a satisfactory 25 mph. Before he could begin further tests in the air, he was offered some good painting commissions and any further trials had to be postponed.

In his May issue of *Aerocraft*, PB made an offer to budding designers: the inventor who could send the magazine the greatest number of votes in support of his proposed aeroplane could have his machine built free of charge and be allowed a month's trial of it at Fambridge. Handley Page had offered to supervise the construction and other manufacturers had offered materials but the conditions PB imposed were far too restrictive. Fifty backing votes were required from each inventor and the cost of building the machine was not to exceed £100, exclusive of the engine. The last clause of the competition read: 'In the event of fewer than 100 entries being received, the Editor reserves the right to postpone the date of closing the competition until such a number is qualified to compete'. Evidently this happened, for instead of announcing the winner in August as planned, he did not close the offer until September and announced in the October *Aerocraft* that there had not been sufficient support.

Weiss had returned to the aerodrome in July to carry out further trials on his monoplane but the original cycle wheels on his machine invariably stuck in the marshy ground. He therefore decided to replace them with a new skid undercarriage which he ran off a greased twin rail using a weight and derrick catapult launch system. Towards the end of August he again encountered problems with the machine's engine which had to be sent to Paris for repairs. Another was tried but this proved unsatisfactory and by the time the original engine returned from France, Weiss was busy building an entirely new aeroplane embodying detachable wings and other improvements. Sadly, Fambridge was not to see this in action for by October Weiss had decided to return to his former testing site in Sussex and with him went the young aerodrome manager, Gordon England.

PB had previously invited the young man to stay for a weekend with Dot and himself at their Burnham cottage. Here he reluctantly told Gordon England that he could no longer afford his weekly salary and suggested he transfer himself to 'one of the more worthwhile Fambridge Fledglings'. Both agreed that Weiss would be the obvious choice. Almost from the start Gordon England had found that his duties as manager of the aerodrome had been too few to occupy all his time and he had often given his help as a skilled fitter to the experimenters. Weiss had recognised the young man's talent with engines and, since Gordon England always enjoyed working with his team, both parties were happy when PB suggested they make this a permanent arrangement. His departure from the aerodrome was nevertheless tinged with a certain amount of regret at leaving the employer for whom he was always to retain the greatest respect and admiration throughout his subsequently successful career in aviation.

Seton-Kerr had already decided—two months before Weiss left—G37 that he would take the Howard Wright biplane and its shed to Camber Sands at Rye, in the hope that this new site in Sussex would offer a more congenial setting for its further trials. The biplane had been dogged by bad luck ever since its arrival at Fambridge from Olympia. Even the shed that housed it had been blown down while the latest repairs were being carried out. Despite this, work continued and by early June its original contra-rotating propellers had been replaced by a more conventional two-bladed unit, its main undercarriage had been strengthened and all appeared to be ready for trials to begin. But although successful taxi runs and even short jumps of thirty feet were made, its monowheel undercarriage combined with the general condition of the ground, made it difficult to keep the aeroplane on an even keel for any length of time. Consequently its owners decided it would be better to move the machine elsewhere before any further tests were attempted.

In the August *Aerocraft* PB had cryptically reported that a number of applications had been received to visit the aerodrome and to lease workshops but all had to be refused because of 'certain important constructive operations which necessitate the greatest privacy being observed'. No further explanation was given and the particular construction he had in mind remains a mystery. There was a newcomer to the aerodrome at that time: Robert Macfie, an American who had plans to design and build his own monoplane. He managed to complete this by mid-September and began trials but, as with his predecessors, the lack of smooth ground and the deep ditches were to prove too hazardous. After crashing his machine four times he, too, left Fambridge in early November for testing grounds elsewhere.

Long before this, PB had been forced to admit that the project which he had begun with such high hopes was not going to succeed. No reference to the aerodrome was made in either the November or December issues of *Aerocraft* and even PB's enthusiastic plans for forming a volunteer 'Imperial Flying Squadron' had not been taken up by the War Office, despite some officials showing interest. When the January/February 1910 *Aerocraft* appeared he officially announced that he had severed all connections with the magazine. The March number, which proved to be the last, was edited from new offices by another proprietor.

Even the three aeroplanes he had built for himself at Fambridge had proved a disappointment and in the autumn of 1909 he decided to take them for demonstration purposes to Park Royal, where Lascelles and Beny had by then set up their own aerodrome. The first was an open cockpit tailless pusher monoplane, powered by a valveless rotary petrol engine of his own design and in this he claimed to have made his first successful attempt to fly—although the machine had barely lifted when one of the wheels hit a hummock and it fell to pieces. Undaunted, he installed a two-cylinder JAP engine into a second machine but after making several short hops, this met a similar fate to the first. This time he did not come out of the accident unscathed and was in hospital for over a month with injuries to his knee and back. His third aeroplane, which he considered by far his best, with its forward elevator and 40 hp four-cylinder NEC Aero motor, he never had an opportunity to test.

When he was finally discharged from hospital, he discovered that one of his creditors had taken him to court and by order of the sheriff, his third machine and the remnants of the others had been seized and auctioned to settle the £8 debt. As the London auctioneers were only able to raise £28 from these and £20 of this went in costs, nothing remained for PB from his whole Fambridge venture but a great deal of heartache and a multitude of debts.

CHAPTER FOUR

After winding up his affairs at Fambridge, PB had less than £100 to his name. Scanning the newspapers for ideas to replenish his funds, he came across a story of a Canadian who had broken the bank at the Casino in Monte Carlo and the thought that he might be able to evolve a similarly rewarding system was appealing. He invested some of his precious capital on a miniature roulette table and began to work out what he hoped would be a foolproof winning scheme. After all, he reassured himself, things could not be much worse and he might just strike lucky. Desperate conditions, he told the apprehensive Dot, demanded desperate remedies. Within a few weeks, he achieved what he considered to be the perfect system and, having given Dot half of his remaining money, sent her to stay with her sister and took himself off to Monte Carlo.

Needless to say, the enterprise proved a dismal failure. He did not win once and travelled home in the way most ruined gamblers were then repatriated—'on the Casino'- mentally bruised by the whole experience. He dreaded the prospect of telling Dot that he had once again failed her and, on arrival at Newhaven in East Sussex, decided not to go home directly but to break his journey at Lewes and go instead for a tramp across the Downs to think things out. He made it as far as Lancing but his leg, injured in his crash at Park Royal, was by then paining him so much he sat down on the beach to rest. Watching the winter waves breaking on the shore, he began a mental stocktaking of all that had gone before and tried to assess how best he could utilise what talents he had for the future.

After tossing these thoughts around for a while, he got up from the beach and, as he did so, caught sight of a large board advertising the fact that the whole foreshore on which he had been sitting was up for sale. As he turned and looked inland at the pretty village, it occurred to him what a serious business it would be for Lancing if some enterprising person purchased that beach and either built over it or closed it to the public. He took note of the seller's name and address—George Cecil Buller, Managing Director of the Shoreham and Lancing Land Company—and that same afternoon presented himself at Mr Buller's office. He took an instant liking to the businessman who, he later told Dot, was one of the shrewdest and straightest he had ever encountered. From their conversation, PB gathered that the land in question was considered of little value and Buller willingly agreed to give him, without any money being exchanged, a three-month option of purchase, with permission to take any reasonable steps to enhance its value. It is from this point onwards that PB's later account seems to be at variance with the facts.

According to his version, within twenty-four hours he had painted a new advertisement on the original board: 'The Summerland Extension and

Development Company. Proposed site of casino and pleasure gardens. For full particulars apply Pemberton Billing, Shoreham'. He then set up twenty smaller boards on all the paths leading to the beach which read that it was private and that trespassers would be prosecuted.

Within a day of the boards going up there was a protest meeting of the Lancing Parish Council which led to his involvement in what became known to the popular press as 'the Foreshore Fight'. But this version was by no means the full story.

As far as can be ascertained, he did, as he claimed, get an option for the development of the foreshore but on 30th January 1910 began surveying, measuring and pegging out sites for bungalows which he actually started to build the following day. It was then that irate local residents began to protest. On 7th February the *Sussex Daily News* carried a letter from the Secretary of the Lancing Ratepayers Association, claiming that the residents had been thrown into a state of alarm by the threatened destruction of their sea front 'with its quiet promenade and beautiful uninterrupted sea view'.

There was, however, another greater cause for concern. The letter went on to explain that the cost of providing and maintaining three sets of groynes with a double protecting seabank was met by the ratepayers of South Lancing and it was on this very bank that the erection of the first of PB's thirty proposed bungalows had commenced. 'Can our sea defences be quietly taken away from us in this way?' asked the writer. The other ratepayers apparently decided they could not and that evening a well-attended public meeting of protest was held at the Home Hall in South Lancing.

In his opening address the chairman referred to the damage done by the sea in the Lancing area, prior to the provision of the present defence barriers, which were paid for and maintained out of the rates. He considered that, as they were paying for the maintenance, residents had certain rights over the foreshore and that it was their duty to see that these were not infringed.

PB then introduced himself as the acquirer of the land in question and with his usual charm told the audience that it was not his intention to build on the beach. He intended to erect bungalows of a 'Colonial structure' on the green to the north of the sea defences and to strengthen the sea wall with concrete to make it a permanent defence, instead of 'a more or less shifting bank of shingle'. After a great deal more opposition from the floor, the meeting ended with a resolution to make a public protest against PB's plans to the Steyning West Rural District Council.

Shortly afterwards, another letter appeared in the local newspaper drawing attention to the fact that the pegging out and first 'cowshed-looking' structures had already been completed on the upper dam of the actual defences, which made nonsense of PB's statement at the meeting that he did not intend to touch them: 'If this is not utilising, or interfering with our sea defences it is hard to understand what would bear this description'.

In March, the District Council, having agreed with the residents' protests, applied to the Local Government Board for the foreshore to be included in a town planning scheme under the new Town Planning Act which came into force that year. It was only then that PB decided to place his notice boards beside the pathways leading from the main road to the sea, stating that the whole of the foreshore would be closed to those not in possession of special permits. Payment would also be required for bathing facilities and pleasure boats drawn up on the beach which, according to a correspondent in the *Worthing Gazette* on 9th March: 'seems to be the sequel to the collapse of the scheme for the erection of bungalows thereon... though some of us have had to laugh in our sleeve for our spasmodic panic with reference to the backwoods scheme which was to flout our Building By-laws and erect human tenements on poles, high in the air, over waterlogged land!'

Exactly what transpired between Lancing Parish Council and PB after that is not clear but the Chairman of the District Council, a local JP, evidently advised the parish to accept PB's offer to give up his interest for the sum of £2,000. From that time onwards, which also happened to coincide with the end of PB's three months option with Mr Buller, his name no longer appears in connection with the site and there is every indication that he received this payment. He admitted as much in a later account: 'suffice it to say that long before my option of purchase had expired, the Shoreham and Lancing Land Company had fully awakened to the real value of what I think Mr Buller at least had regarded as a "white elephant". Also, as a result of what I will describe as a brain-wave...I found myself in possession of sufficient of what this world so unhappily misnames wealth, to enable me to carry on'.

He claimed that he had then settled down at Shoreham where, 'more as a hobby than a business', he went on to design, build and sell a number of bungalows on another site, 'really artistic, comfortable, attractive little places' for which he obtained a better price than the neighbouring bungalows, 'ramshackle affairs, of the disused and converted railway carriage order that was the popular idea then'.

One of these bungalows he gave to his sister Mary but it was washed away by heavy seas in January 1912 and, judging by photographs which show how close these also were to the shore, the probability is that the others met a similar fate.

Although (or was it, perhaps, because) he made a great deal of money out of this rather dubious affair, certain feelings of guilt remained with PB, for years later he wrote of the incident: 'sometimes I have said to myself that morally I was wrong. I have asked myself what right has a man, practically penniless, to apply for and take an option the fulfilment of which would require considerable capital?'

Once his housing project had got under way and money began to come in, his thoughts turned to other matters. He bought himself a small steam yacht,

Violet, for £50 and he and Dot derived a great deal of pleasure from sailing it around the coast. Ever since his early experiences at sea, he had enjoyed 'messing about in boats'. He delighted in the freedom a boat afforded and there were rumours circulating among the south coast yachting fraternity that he often took beautiful women on board, for days at a time, without either Dot or a suitable chaperone being present. But PB could never resist a pretty face, especially when it smiled in his direction.

Although he appreciated Dot's sterling qualities and appeared to love her deeply, his sexual needs were such that his affairs with other women were as many and transitory as his numerous schemes. But it was to Dot that he always returned, apparently needing the security of her presence, whatever the excitement of his current infatuation.

As he now had more time to spare at Shoreham, he decided to take another look at the insurance plan he had begun working on while he and Dot had been living on their small-holding at Crawley. He visualised it as a sort of National Insurance, Old Age Pension and National Health scheme all rolled into one and was attracted to the idea of becoming a Member of Parliament and presenting his plan to the House of Commons himself. The more he thought about entering Parliament the more appealing the idea became and, as it appeared to him that the public was more inclined to vote for a man with a profession, he mulled over the possibility of studying for a suitable qualification.

It so happened that a lawyer friend came to stay the following weekend and to his astonishment PB told him he had just decided to become a barrister. The friend pointed out that, as he had not been to university and obtained a degree, he would first need to pass a special Bar Preliminary Examination and, as this means of entry would no longer be available after the end of the year and it was already November, it seemed unlikely that PB would ever see this particular idea realised. But the lawyer was obviously not aware of the lengths to which his friend was prepared to go in order to achieve an ambition.

The very next morning they travelled to London together and PB visited the Middle Temple. Here he discovered that there were in fact two more of these examinations, the first in a week's time and the second on Christmas Eve. He immediately got in touch with Dot and told her that he would be remaining in London and engaging a private tutor to help him with his studies, for he was determined to sit for the examination. He told friends afterwards that, filling in his entry form, he was particularly amused by the question: 'What have you done since you left school?' The two dotted lines allotted for the reply seemed, he thought, hardly adequate to describe all that he had managed to pack into the eighteen years since he had first boarded that ship in the East India Docks with his pet kitten.

His faith in his own abilities must have been profound. The subjects for the examination were dictation, ancient and modern history and Latin composition (Virgil, or Caesar's Civil and Gallic Wars). His formal education had been minimal, he had never studied Latin, knew little of history and yet was still prepared to be examined in these subjects less than a month after signing the entry form. He was fortunate indeed in being able to engage a particularly clever crammer, a Dr Symons, who taught him as much Latin and history as he could in six hours of intensive study each day. Another teacher took over for a further six and PB worked on his own for another four.

It was a gruelling timetable but he stuck it out, ignoring Symons's comment after four days of study that he would never be a Latin scholar and that there was no point in him attempting to sit for the examination. PB's answer to this had been to pay his entrance fee to the earlier examination. He knew he had no hope of passing but thought he might be able to pick up a few tips and gauge the atmosphere.

It is hardly surprising that he could not answer a single question but he turned his frustration and disappointment into an optimistic gamble. He told Symons afterwards that as Virgil had been set for that particular examination it seemed more than likely that Caesar would be chosen for the next and went on to back that idea by memorising 306 of the 612 chapters of the Civil and Gallic Wars—missing out alternative chapters for he superstitiously believed that odd numbers brought him luck. He tackled the set books on English History in a similar way and crammed his brain to such an extent that he woke up on the morning of the examination with his mind a complete blank.

His friends, who had been taking odds of up to thirty to one against his passing, were now confident of winning their bets but this did not deter PB from presenting himself for the examination at the appointed hour. To his surprise he was able to remember more than he thought and managed to answer most of the questions in the history paper. His luck held, too, in the Latin examination. Each student was asked to translate certain chapters from the works of Caesar and the odd numbered ones he had chosen to concentrate on during his crammer's lessons turned out to be some of those he was given. Against all the predictions, of the sixty who sat he was one of only fourteen who passed and duly gained entry as a student to the Middle Temple. He took chambers at 3, Essex Court, and set aside what he considered would to be sufficient money to see him and Dot through his next three years of compulsory reading for the Bar.

Early in 1911, between lectures and dinners, he settled down to working out the details for his 'Endowment by Increment Scheme', as he now called his insurance project, and engaged an accountant to check his calculations. He also enlisted the help of a friend, H.E. Raynes of the Society of Actuaries, to verify the feasibility of the scheme, and when it was reasonably complete, submitted it to the Conservative politician, Austen Chamberlain. He listened for several hours to PB's enthusiastic interpretation and then wrote a charming letter suggesting that as the scheme sounded so promising PB should take immediate steps to make it public.

Although ideas for some form of national insurance had been widely discussed, both in and outside Parliament, nothing had yet been officially formulated. Encouraged by Chamberlain's reaction, PB took the idea to George R. Sims of *The Referee*, who published several articles about it. *The Daily Graphic* also brought out an illustrated supplement and PB was commissioned to write pieces about his scheme for both the *19th Century* and *The Fortnightly* magazines.

Basically his idea was that the scheme should eventually abolish all other forms of taxation and at the same time provide for sick benefit, accident insurance and a State pension at the age of fifty for every worker. There was already a pension in existence for seventy-year-olds as a result of the 1908 Act but PB saw no reason why the age for this should not be lowered. Another aspect of the scheme, which he thought particularly valuable, was that it provided a complete national register of every man, woman and child in the British Isles.

His proposal was that at birth everyone would be a card-holder and throughout life stamps were to be bought and stuck upon these cards—PB's theory being that by the time of death each person's contribution would have covered the nation's liability to the stamper. He thought the project would be simple to operate, only one card being involved, but the general feeling of those who studied it was that, as it stood, it would only benefit those not yet born. Even so, there were many who thought that Lloyd George's 'Ninepence for Fourpence' insurance proposals put forward some months later, bore certain similarities.

From the moment he began to pursue his Endowment by Increment project, the money he had originally set aside for his law studies began to dwindle, for PB was never one to present his ideas on the cheap. To illustrate the scheme and to show how it would affect everyone, he had a series of books and coloured linen cards prepared, together with a variety of specially engraved stamps. The die, engraving and printing alone were expensive and most of his friends thought he had been over-lavish for what, after all, was only an outline proposal.

As he had so often done in the past when short of money, he sold what he could of his personal effects but left until last the little steam yacht *Violet* which he kept at Burnham-on-Crouch. He knew there was no chance of selling the yacht there for most people at Burnham were more interested in sailing craft than steam vessels. Southampton or Cowes, in the Isle of Wight, he decided, were far more likely places in which to find a buyer. With Dot and a young friend, Dorothy Dewar, he therefore set off from Burnham one grey morning in late summer, despite warnings from local sailors that a storm was brewing.

The yacht had barely reached the open sea when it met the full force of a gale and three days later was off the coast of France near Le Havre, with its decks awash, one dinghy battered and only enough coal left for three hours steaming. As *Violet* had a top speed of around 7 knots, the situation looked critical. Dot remained courageously at the wheel—lashed to it for safety most of the time—while PB, with the assistance of Dorothy Dewar, tried desperately to keep up steam by ripping to pieces anything he thought might burn after the coal ran out.

At one point he took over the wheel to give Dot a much needed break and on going below she noticed that the paraffin lamp in the saloon was swinging perilously and quickly extinguished it. Seconds later it was torn away from its fixture and smashed, its oil leaking onto the wooden boards of the deck. Had it not been for her prompt action, a serious fire would almost certainly have resulted. Dorothy Dewar was full of admiration afterwards for the manner in which Dot had dealt with this and with the voyage as a whole. At the height of the storm, while PB, excited by the danger and obviously in his element, had rushed hither and thither attending to a multitude of tasks, Dot had remained calm and in control, never doubting for a moment that they would reach their destination safely.

Having weathered the storm, the yacht finally reached Cowes later that third day but it was in urgent need of repairs and PB knew that this would be a costly business. Fortunately, he managed to sell one of the two motorised dinghies which had somehow escaped unscathed and with this small sum he was able to buy the materials he needed to make the yacht seaworthy again. He then laid in stores and took on a boy to act as crew and stoker and steamed in great style to Southampton to look for a likely buyer. Within a few days of arriving, he managed to sell the vessel for £275—more than twice the amount he had originally envisaged and a considerable advance on the £50 it had cost him originally.

To complete the transaction, he travelled to London with the purchaser, who was arranging the details of sale with a ship-broker. During their conversation he discovered that there was a very profitable world-wide trade in the buying and selling of boats and that the prerequisites for success in this field were a knowledge of the sea, an ability to reach rapid decisions and, above all, the nerve to take risks—attributes which PB felt he already had in abundance. He decided there and then that he would not, after all, return to his rooms at Essex Court to continue his law studies but instead would try his luck as a yacht-dealer. If this should prove as profitable as the broker had led him to believe, he could always return later to finish his studies or embark on any other ideas his darting mind might produce, with adequate financial resources to carry such plans through.

His first move was to introduce himself to a large yacht-dealing firm in Southampton and, through this company, begin what he later termed his 'buccaneering' or 'ship-running' period. One of his life-long friends, Charles Grey, always referred to this as 'the time PB bought luxury yachts with money he hadn't got, in order to sell them for cash to people who didn't really want them'. This description was a constant source of amusement to PB, who countered by telling Grey that it was one of the best compliments he had ever been paid.

Charles Eardley Billing. father of PB   **Anne Amelia Billing, his mother**

PB aged 7

Gerald Leake (left) and José Weiss with the Weiss Pusher monoplane at Fambridge

The Aerodock and other buildings at Fambridge Aerodrome, 1909

PB's sister, Mary, outside one of the bungalows at Lancing, 1910

SS Utopia

PB on board *Hildegarde* to meet George V

From the late autumn of 1911 to the summer of 1913 he went on to buy, sell, charter and captain all manner of yachts, sail and steam, to and from the British Isles, France, Spain, Italy and the Middle East, experiencing many exciting adventures along the way. He handled crews of several nationalities and encountered his fair share of rogues and ruffians but his size, personality and dominating presence enabled him to cope with most situations aboard.

In January 1912 his steam yacht *Hildegarde* was chartered by the *Daily Mirror* to go out from Southampton to meet the liner *Medina*, bringing King George V back from his State visit to India. A blizzard off the Needles prevented the planned rendezvous in the Channel but the newspaper carried photographs of PB out on deck with his small crew, muffled against the falling snow and battling with the elements. Later in the year, in a specially fitted boat, he took on the dangerous mission of running guns from Marseilles to Turkey, then at war with Italy in Cyrenaica, and largely due to his ingenuity and daring somehow managed to escape interception.

In the early summer of 1913, his boat-dealer in Southampton asked PB if he would be willing to attempt the recovery of his steam yacht *Clara*, which had been chartered—but not paid for—by a German officer. The officer had registered the vessel as a unit of the German Navy's Volunteer Fleet, loaded it with cases of good Rhine wine and set off for a spree along the Riviera to Monte Carlo where the dealer understood it was still tied up. PB did not need much persuading to take on the task. He knew the Principality well for he had recently purchased the *Princess Alice* a splendid steam yacht that had once been the pride and joy of the Prince of Monaco.

With a picked crew he set sail in the *Princess Alice* and on arriving at Monte Carlo was able to berth close enough to the *Clara* to be able to study the movements of her German crew. Choosing an evening when he knew their captain would be away gambling at the Casino, he instructed his men to invite the German sailors aboard the *Princess Alice* and lace their drinks. When they became too drunk to stand up, PB and his crew gently carried the sailors ashore and laid them out in rows on the quayside. The *Clara* was then untied and, with PB's second-in-command and several other members of his crew on board, the vessel was towed out to sea by the *Princess Alice*.

Putting both yachts into Marseilles for refuelling, he came face to face with an irate German Consul who charged him with stealing a ship belonging to the Kaiserliche Naval Reserve and demanded that he be arrested. Having no wish to spend what could be weeks explaining the situation, PB managed to escape under cover of darkness, slipping the tow rope and putting both yachts out to sea again, after arranging a rendezvous in Spain with his men aboard the Clara. When the yachts became separated during a storm and while PB was waiting at Barcelona for the other vessel to arrive, he was again confronted by a German consular official and once again was forced to make a quick getaway.

At Gibraltar a Royal Navy picket boat came alongside and the young midshipman in charge told him that he was under arrest at the request of the German Consul. Thinking fast, PB haughtily demanded that he first be shown some printed authority for his detention and when the officer confessed that he did not possess such a document, PB insisted that one be instantly obtained. He could be very intimidating when the occasion warranted and no sooner had the inexperienced young officer left, than he did the same.

Halfway up the Portuguese coast *Clara* ran out of coal and had to be lashed alongside *Princess Alice* in the open sea while it was refuelled. When they eventually entered Southampton Water, with PB triumphantly towing his prize, the grateful dealer paid him handsomely for the vessel's return and presented him with the large stock of Rhine wine that the Germans had stowed aboard the chartered boat.

With PB on this and most of his other seafaring adventures went the ever-faithful Dot and Hubert Scott-Paine, a stocky, red-haired young man in his early twenties, who had first met PB in 1910 on the beach at Shoreham. In those days there was no footbridge linking the bungalows on the beach to the main village and if the residents should miss the ferry it meant walking an extra mile. PB was in a hurry to catch his train to London one morning and seeing the young Scott-Paine with his bicycle delivering paraffin for his family's store, had shouted: 'Hey, boy! Can I borrow your bike? I want to get to the ferry quickly as I'm late for my train'.

The nineteen-year-old lent him the bicycle and from then on the two families, who both had bungalows on the beach, became friends. Scott-Paine's mother was a widow, with three sons and a daughter, and was only too happy for her youngest son to give occasional help to PB, who had quickly recognised in the young man not only a reflection of his own adventure-seeking temperament but also that of their similar interests.

Both liked tinkering with machines and the young Scott-Paine had always preferred a spanner and an oily rag to academic work at school. When still quite young he had constructed with his brothers a single-seater car with motor-cycle wheels, belt-driven by a JAP engine, and over the years had taken every opportunity to increase his knowledge of mechanics.

He was, thought PB, the ideal man to join him on his seafaring venture. At the beginning of his diary for 1912, Scott-Paine wrote: 'Joined Billing on Wednesday, December 20th, 1911. Left home, amidst much weeping, for Southampton with my little hat and bag and stayed until just before Christmas.' 'No doubt he wondered just what kind of life lay ahead on the boats acquired by his unpredictable employer, whom he subsequently referred to as 'the Governor'. PB, for his part, later described Scott-Paine as being 'chief of the little bodyguard of faithful fellows who sailed the seas with me.'

By 1913, PB's wealth—thanks to the profits of his boat-trading—had accumulated considerably. He added the three-masted schooner *Gleniffer* to his collection of yachts, re-named it *Utopia* and converted it into a floating home for Dot, himself and Scott-Paine, who by then was more than willing to participate in any scheme that might fire his Governor's interest.

CHAPTER FIVE

Nearly four years had elapsed since PB's involvement with the aerodrome at Fambridge and other matters had occupied his time, but developments in the world of flying were never far from his thoughts. In the summer of 1913, with *Utopia* safely berthed at Southampton for a spell, he decided to drive to Hendon Aerodrome near London, to seek out some of his friends from the Fambridge days and catch up on all that had been happening to them since.

He was delighted to find three of his old acquaintances there, including Frederick Handley Page—now a well-established figure in the aviation world— who joined the others in some good-humoured teasing over PB's own lack of success in that field. This culminated in Handley Page asking when he was proposing to take to the air again. Slightly needled, PB answered: 'At the first opportunity.' To which Handley Page jokingly retorted: 'But first you've got to learn *how* to fly. The damned things get *off* the ground nowadays.'

His remarks caught PB at a time when he was already feeling at a distinct disadvantage, seeing evidence all around him of the progress that had been made since he was last involved. Adjusting his monocle with a flourish and drawing himself up to his full height, he glowered down at his tormentor: 'Mr Handley Page, sir,' he said icily, 'when I *want* to fly an aeroplane, I shall just get into one and *fly* it'.

There were several pilots standing round by this time and all joined in the mirth his statement evoked. This riled PB even more. When Handley Page then claimed that in his 'automatically stable machine'- his Type E 'Yellow Peril' monoplane—'*anyone* could learn to fly in twenty-four hours', PB decided he had had enough. With as much authority as he could muster, he asserted that he did not believe in 'automatic stability' but rather in the skilful handling of the machine and that '*any* man who had enough sense to come in out of the wet could learn to fly *any* machine in one summer's day'.

Carried away by the obvious impression he was making on his audience, he then rashly made a five hundred pound wager with Handley Page that he would not only learn to fly before him but would also qualify for his Royal Aero Club certificate within twenty-four hours of getting into any machine of his choice—and he challenged Handley Page to do the same in his Yellow Peril.

Since up to that time neither man had ever truly flown, beyond making a few trial hops, the wager created considerable interest in flying circles, particularly as most pilots took several months to qualify. In those days the weather alone was an important factor, as the machines then available were lightly-powered and reacted sensitively to the slightest wind. Most flying schools only possessed one or two aeroplanes and if one should crash, the whole training programme could be delayed, proving costly both to the school and the would-be pilot. It was therefore not surprising that few attempted to qualify before spending some weeks in preparation.

To obtain the RAeC certificate in 1913, it was necessary to make two flights of at least two kilometres over a closed circuit, marked by two posts about five hundred metres apart. As each post was circled, the pilot was required to change direction so as to make an uninterrupted series of five figures of eight. An altitude flight with a minimum height of fifty metres then followed and, on all three landings, the motor had to be stopped at, or before, the moment of touchdown. The aircraft had also to be brought to a halt within fifty metres of a specified point.

In the circumstances, it is understandable that PB found it difficult to persuade anyone either to give him the necessary tuition or to provide an aeroplane. F. Warren Merriam of the Bristol School was willing to instruct PB but his employers were less happy to let him do so in one of their treasured machines. The Vickers School reacted in the same way when Merriam introduced him to their instructor, Robert Barnwell. However, after some persuasion on PB's part, Barnwell agreed to give him intensive private tuition if his prospective pupil could find a suitable aeroplane.

As 17th September, the date fixed for the wager, drew near PB seemed no closer to finding anyone willing to lend him a machine and in desperation he was obliged to buy an old Henry Farman biplane, powered by a 50 hp Gnome rotary engine. Barnwell sportingly agreed to keep his promise to instruct him: 'I know my man', he told a newspaper reporter who commented on his pluck at taking on the job.

PB decided to make his attempt from Brooklands—the Surrey motor racing track which was also used as an airfield—while Handley Page favoured Hendon. At a quarter to six on the morning of the appointed day, the biplane was wheeled out in a fine drizzle of rain and under an overcast sky. Normally the instructor would take over the controls at the start while the pupil watched or reached over to the controls from the rear seat but as time was all-important, PB sat in the pilot's seat from the first, with Barnwell behind.

After taxiing for about four minutes while the instructor explained the procedure, Barnwell signalled to PB to take off. The biplane lifted steadily to two hundred feet and made a dozen or so circuits of the field as the instructor took his pupil through several figures of eight, volplane (power-off descent) landings, and a few landings under power. As it was by this time raining steadily and the machine was becoming sodden and sluggish, this was no easy matter with two thirteen-stone men aboard and some of the landings were, in PB's own words, 'rather speedy.' Even so, after a rigorous twenty-five minutes of further instruction, Barnwell decided to get out and leave PB to it. Watched nervously by those below, including Dot and his sister Mary, the intrepid airman gave the engine full throttle and shot into the air again, rather faster than he had intended. Looking down with some apprehension at the green pocket-handkerchief that was Brooklands, he skirted some trees, did a half circuit, landed, took the machine up again, circled and landed again.

Taking off for the third time, he had intended to execute twelve circuits but after five the engine began to misfire and the agitated spectators below signalled with petrol cans that he needed to refuel. On landing, as the rain had now become even heavier, he was advised to wheel the aeroplane into a hangar to let it dry off a little. After half an hour, as the weather had improved slightly, Barnwell again went up with him to test his pupil's right-hand turns, before allowing him to attempt the figures of eight on his own. He managed this manoeuvre successfully three times, but startled himself at one juncture by the angle at which he took the right-hand turn[1]—despite Barnwell's warning that this needed to be executed with care—and he hung grimly on to the struts for safety. 'strangely enough,' he commented later, 'while I was on the ground my one fear was of the air; but as soon as I was in the air my one fear was of the ground'. He was next instructed to practise his volplanes from an altitude of one hundred feet with the engine cut off. Meanwhile Barnwell had set off in search of the official observer from the Royal Aero Club who, not expecting anyone to be foolhardy enough to attempt a test on such a day, was proving difficult to find. When the official arrived an hour later, he was still dubious about the advisability of going ahead with the idea but he eventually relented and PB again took to the air, rising in a steep climb to a height of two hundred and fifty feet, far higher than he needed but, as he later put it, 'so as to make sure of the altitude test once and for all'.

He next made a left-hand turn and began the first of five figures of eight. All went well until, on the fifth right turn, he happened to catch sight of an anxious Dot and in his usual expansive manner gave her an encouraging wave. This unfortunately took his attention from the controls and, to the horror of those watching below, the machine immediately shot steeply upwards, jerking him backwards and throwing him completely off balance. To make matters worse, he continued to hang on to the joystick, which caused the machine to stall about two hundred feet up before falling rapidly tail-first. Dot and Mary clutched each other in fear and those with them held their breath as the small plane plunged to within fifty feet of the ground before PB, thinking that the control wires had broken, had the good sense to throw his whole weight forward, which caused the plane partly to right itself. It nevertheless continued to dive, nose first this time, until—with only twenty feet left between him and the ground—he managed at last to regain control.

Although he feared he had spoiled his chances of a certificate, he decided to climb to one hundred and sixty feet and perform an extra figure of eight and followed this with a volplane landing. Not surprisingly, Barnwell

---

1. With rotary-engined machines, the gyroscopic moment of the spinning engine caused the nose of the aircraft to rise as the turn was made and caution was always needed.

greeted him with what PB later referred to as 'illuminating and very forcible remarks on right-hand turns,' but even so he was allowed to take up the aircraft once more to complete the rest of his test. This he accomplished successfully, finishing off with a volplane from one hundred feet with the engine switched off and bringing the machine to rest without switching on again.

Despite his hair-raising performance, the Royal Aero Club's observer was apparently satisfied and after less than three-and-a-half hours in the air, PB proudly claimed his RAeC certificate, No. 632. When the Press arrived half an hour later he was having breakfast with Dot, Mary and the others in the well-known Blue Bird restaurant—run by his brother Eardley and his wife.[2] The photographers wanted pictures so, without more ado and with his usual showmanship, he climbed back into the aircraft and went through the whole procedure again before Handley Page had even left the ground at Hendon in his Yellow Peril.

His exploit, however, did not meet with approval in all quarters. The *Pall Mall* magazine commented: 'Freak matches in aviation are, in the opinion of leading authorities, best left alone. They demonstrate no useful quality of machine or man, and call for the taking of quite absurd risks.'

Other aviation experts agreed and said that although it may have proved PB's 'unusually quick reflexes and exceptionally steady nerves,' his achievement did not necessarily indicate that he was a capable pilot. Even Barnwell was reported as saying afterwards that his pupil had doubtless shown great aptitude but that 'if he thinks he knows anything about flying—God help him!'

Such comments did not worry PB one iota for nothing could dispel his joy at having achieved his certificate and won his wager. As he and Dot drove back to their floating home at Southampton—in his Brooklands Napier 'Mercury', known to his friends as the 'Birdcage'—his ever-fertile brain was already engaged on plans for another project, towards which he had earmarked his newly acquired five hundred pounds.

He realised that if he were to stay with his boat-dealing business it could provide him with all the financial security he would need for the rest of his life, but since his encounter with his old flying friends at Hendon, his thoughts had been directed almost entirely towards the idea of once again constructing aircraft of his own. What he had in mind would, he felt sure, be revolutionary and on his return to *Utopia* he discussed the whole matter with an equally enthusiastic Scott-Paine.

The result of their deliberations was that, within the month, PB had found what he considered to be ideal waterside premises on the River Itchen at

2. Eardley was one of Brooklands' first and ablest mechanics, a designer and inventor. As early as 1910 he brought out a static ground trainer, later used by the services for instructing new pilots and, in association with N.S. Percival, he built a biplane known as the 'Oozely Bird' because of its sound and quaint appearance. In 1915, a year after the popular Blue Bird restaurant had been commandeered by the Army (on the outbreak of war), Eardley died suddenly, aged 44.

Woolston, near Southampton and had set about converting an old coal wharf into a factory. It was here that he intended to build what he termed his 'supermarine' aircraft—'boats that would fly, rather than aeroplanes that would float'. He chose the name because he felt it was more descriptive for what he had in mind. Just as 'submarine' was the word for a boat that operated *below* the sea, so should 'supermarine' be the natural antonym for one that would fly *over* the water and an abbreviated form—*Supermarin*—would also be used for his new company's telegraphic address.

The patent for his first flying boat was applied for on 28th October 1913. In his application he explained that, as aircraft at rest upon the open water were always at the mercy of the weather, his designs incorporated wings that would be safe in flight but could also be shed, if necessary, to convert the aircraft into a motor-launch. Such a machine would, he asserted, be ideal for rescues at sea for it could fly to a ship in distress, land beside it, shed its wings and become a lifeboat.

By the following month, PB's activities at Woolston were attracting attention, both in the aeronautical world and in the local press. On 1st November the *Southampton and Hampshire Express* devoted a column to the 'Flying Factory at Itchen Ferry' where, it reported, workmen were busily engaged preparing premises for the establishment of a factory for the construction of 'super-marines'—vessels of the seaplane type: 'Mr Pemberton Billing...is the proprietor of the venture, which is expected to be in full swing before Christmas.'

Despite this optimistic forecast, the buildings were still not completed by the end of February 1914, when a journalist from *Flight* magazine visited Southampton to view what he understood to be the first batch of flying boats being constructed at Woolston. PB, Dot and Scott-Paine (introduced as the company's secretary and chief mechanic) entertained the visitor to dinner aboard the *Utopia*. PB described the kind of aircraft he intended to produce and his plans for using a floating aerodock as a base for regular passenger services to the Isle of Wight but the only completed aircraft visible in the factory were PB's old Farman biplane from Brooklands and the Radley England twin-float seaplane which PB had bought, with other stock, from his old employee, Gordon England, whose own aircraft company had just been wound up. Work was, however, being carried out on the wooden hull of what was to be the very first flying boat—the PB.1—although this machine was not, after all, designed with his much-discussed detachable wings. The hull, which owed its fine structure to Linton Hope, a brilliant marine architect who brought his advanced theories of yacht design into its construction, was built of laminated wood in circular section, to give it the necessary strength and lightness for what PB had in mind.

Within a few weeks the aircraft was miraculously completed and on display (albeit without its engine) in London on 16th March at the Aero,

Motor-Boat, Marine and Stationary Engine Exhibition. PB was the first to give credit for this to the efforts of Scott-Paine and his small team of boat-builders, metal-workers and others, who had worked all hours in a desperate attempt to have it ready in time.

The Globe reported next day: 'Three examples [of a flying boat] are on view in Olympia, of which one of the most striking is the Pemberton Billing "super-marine". This is a peculiarly racy-looking white machine, with a central hull of fish-like form in which the pilot sits, and at the side of and above which the biplane-lifting surfaces are mounted. Between the latter the engine and propeller are separately carried, and the motor, a Gnome, is almost entirely enclosed.'

The curious tilted nacelle, in which the 50 hp engine from his old Farman biplane and its fuel tanks were to be fitted, was designed, in PB's words, 'to create a maximum up-thrust on take-off,' but it proved to be the source of much amusement at the show. His friend, Charles Grey, later commented in *The Aeroplane* magazine that there was 'certainly something of the comic in the tip-tilted nose and round goggly face of the egg-like engine casing' and added that he had been assured that the machine had not been sold to the well-known comedian, Mr Harry Tate. Another visitor to the exhibition, intrigued by the fact that the nacelle appeared to be empty, asked PB what it was used for, to which he replied, 'That is where we keep the coffee'.

Those who knew PB's lavish ways were not surprised to find that he had produced, specially for the exhibition, an expensive illustrated silk-paged brochure, which described his plans for the company in words as extravagant as some of the claims he made for his aircraft and the dates he gave for his own early involvement with flight. After a brief description of the PB.1, with a drawing of the side elevation, he went on to elaborate on its successor, the PB.2, a squat, two-seater monoplane flying boat powered by a 120 hp Austro-Daimler engine; and the PB.3 'aerial cruiser' with its 90 hp Austro-Daimler engine, neither of which had, as yet, gone into production.

The brochure also mentioned a possible seaplane school between Southampton and the Isle of Wight. On another page were his drawings and a description of his 'supermeter', an instrument which could be used 'to facilitate the landing of aircraft at night or when conditions rendered it impossible for a pilot to estimate his height'. He had taken out a patent for this some months earlier and *Flight* magazine had published a piece about it only two days before the exhibition, describing it as 'decidedly simple and ingenious'. The basic idea was that the pilot lowered a rod below the aircraft which, when the machine was fifteen feet above the ground or water, operated a gong and electric bulb simultaneously—the former to attract the attention of the pilot and the latter to project a beam of light to aid his vision for landing.

By the time the show closed on 25th March, PB was well pleased with the interest his stand had evoked. King George V and Winston Churchill, then First Lord of the Admiralty, had both been among those who had viewed his PB.1. There had also been enquiries about the possible production under licence of his 'Trinity' propellers (a three-bladed airscrew, which PB claimed was of unique construction) and some German military representatives had told him that they proposed to visit the factory at Woolston with a view to placing an order.

Feeling quite optimistic about the future, he went off to take part in the Monaco motor-boat races and managed to steer his *Frigidi Pedibus* into first place in the Prix des Dames, a handicap race over fifteen and a half miles. Meanwhile Scott-Paine, who had expected to accompany him to Monte Carlo and act as his mechanic, stayed behind to manage affairs at the factory.

Soon after PB's return, buoyancy tests were started with the PB.1 on the Itchen and these proved reasonably successful, but getting the machine airborne was another matter. Try as he could to raise it from the water, taxiing frantically up and down the Itchen like a mad thing, PB could not achieve even a short hop and it was obvious that drastic modifications would have to be made. First to be scrapped was the peculiarly shaped nacelle, which appeared to be hindering rather than assisting the initial thrust. The old Gnome engine from the Farman biplane, which was increasingly losing the power it once had, was mounted instead on top of the hull, to drive two of PB's 'Trinity' three-bladed propellers as pushers. The position of the cockpit was also changed so that the pilot was in front of the wings, not behind as previously; the fuel tank was placed beneath the top wing centre section and ailerons were added to the lower wings.

All these alterations, with a few extra features, appeared in another of PB's patents for a slip-wing flying boat which he registered on 28th May. Despite Scott-Paine's fears that the machine was still too heavy for flight, it was arranged for Howard Pixton, Sopwith's test pilot, to try and get it into the air on 30th May. Earlier that month PB had leased part of his large shed to Tommy Sopwith[3] and on 17th May, with Scott-Paine beside him, had ruefully witnessed Sopwith's float plane—the *'Bat Boat'*, which had taken part in the *Daily Mail* Round Britain Air Race a month earlier—take off with ease from Woolston. But PB's hopes of his own flying boat doing the same were not to be fulfilled.

On the appointed day, in front of a crowd of interested spectators, Howard Pixton made several unsuccessful attempts to lift PB.1 into the air. More modifications were made and there was another test on 7th June, but the result was still the same. PB blamed the ancient Farman engine for the failure, commenting later that 'an aeroplane with an under-powered engine is like a knife with a blunt blade'. Whatever the reason for its lack of success, he was bitterly disappointed and infuriated by the fact that he now had to admit that the PB.1, the first of his much-publicised 'flying boats', would never be capable of

3. Later Sir T.O.M. Sopwith. He founded the Sopwith Aviation Co. Ltd. at Kingston-on-Thames in 1912.

living up to its name.

Eric Blay, one of the staff, was working on the slipway soon afterwards when PB approached and, much to his surprise, asked him to fetch an axe. On providing it, Blay was appalled to see his employer wield it angrily over the wings and hull of the ill-starred machine, demolishing its frame piece by piece. He then threw down the axe and walked away in disgust from the remains. The company records at the close of that year estimated the loss of what was now termed the 'dismantled PB.1' as being £368 2s 1½d, but for PB it represented what he later termed 'yet another sacrifice on the altar of aviation'.

CHAPTER SIX

Since the beginning of April 1914, PB had realised that the general running costs of his factory, including the wages for the forty-five men he employed, were far more of a drain on his purse than he had expected. Once again he had been spending money extravagantly and, with no return as yet on his enterprise, he knew he must somehow recoup his losses.

His share in the heavily mortgaged *Princess Alice* was the first to go. The yacht was towed off its mud berth where it had lain for the past year and put into dry dock in Southampton. It was later sold to Lord Inverclyde for £13,000—a gift at the price, according to PB. This money, added to the income from leasing the shed to Sopwith and some motor-launch building he had undertaken (including a twenty-seven foot boat for Prince Carl of Russia), enabled him to keep things ticking over for a few months but more was obviously going to be needed. Fortunately, a wealthy friend, Alfred Delves Broughton, was also interested in aeroplanes and decided to invest money in the concern. 'Pemberton Billing Limited' was therefore inaugurated on 27th June 1914, with Broughton as one of the directors. *Flight* magazine, reporting this in July, quoted the capital of the company on its formation as £20,000.

Although documentation covering those months is sketchy, it is known that during the early summer of 1914, in addition to the work on the PB.1, other aircraft were being built in the factory. Scott-Paine recorded in his diary that there was a large 'char-a-banc' under construction, which could have been either the PB.3, the 'aerial cruiser' mentioned in the Aero Exhibition brochure, or the PB.5, both of which PB later claimed to have laid down at Woolston during this time. These were both flying boats with 'slipping wings' which, he said, 'rendered them capable of operating without wings as armed high-speed boats'. There is no evidence, however, that either of these was completed.

In early June, new hulls were laid down for another slip-wing aircraft, the PB.7, two of which had already been ordered by the German officials who had shown an interest in the PB.1. at Olympia. The hull of this aircraft was again constructed as a motor-boat, with a cabin for pilot and passengers, but it also had a rear section incorporating wings, tail surfaces and propellers, all of which were detachable from the main body should an emergency landing be necessary. The boat section was estimated to have a speed of 35 knots and the complete aircraft to be capable of flying at between 45-70 mph. PB intended to start water trials with the hull at the end of July but there were delivery delays over the engine that was to power the machine and before he could fit an alternative, the world was at war, the German order was cancelled and work on the PB.7 came to a halt. The eventual loss to the company was £527 15s 8d for the three hulls[1] and a number of wings that had already been built for the machines.

July was an eventful month for PB. He appeared in court at the Old Bailey on the 2nd, seeking damages from a small magazine *Modern Living* which, he claimed, had published a paragraph in October of the previous year that was totally untrue. Headed 'Things Ladies Would Like to Know...' it asked if Mr Pemberton Billington [sic] the airman had weathered his 'stiff matrimonial breeze over some girl's earring which chanced to come into the possession of his wife...' Although his name was spelt wrongly, most people understood it to refer to PB, particularly as it appeared barely a month after his Brooklands wager, and he complained to the paper, which replied: 'Airmen nowadays are public characters, and although we maintain that the paragraph was harmless, we have no hesitation in expressing our regret that it has in any way caused annoyance'.

Apparently this was not good enough for PB and, despite the defendants pleading that the piece had been true in substance and in fact, he was awarded £500 damages. Whether the story had really been true, only the loyal and ever-faithful Dot could confirm, but the outcome raised some quizzical eyebrows among his friends. Certainly the extra £500 was more than welcome for he had just moved his home from the *Utopia* to a large country house, Steep Hill Park, at West End near Southampton. He had also bought himself another car, a Rolls-Royce.

During that summer of 1914 he had become increasingly convinced that war was inevitable and on 31st July travelled to London in his spanking new car to see Murray Sueter, Director of Air Services at the Admiralty, in the hope that he might be able to obtain further orders for his PB.7 or other work for his factory. He could not interest Sueter in the PB.7, but by the time he returned home he had already formulated plans for what he thought would be a more acceptable machine. If, as he had been led to believe at the Admiralty, the Royal Navy needed land-planes rather than sea-planes, then he would design and build a fast little single-seater to be used for scouting purposes, a machine which could be assembled easily and quickly.

Ever since his Fambridge days he had preached the importance of air supremacy in time of war and the need for the country to maintain a large reserve of aircraft. He had reiterated these views many times over the previous few months, to both the War Office and the Admiralty and was infuriated by the response from one Government department that, if war came, 'any damned joiner' could build aeroplanes.

The day after his visit to London he drew rough sketches of the aeroplane he had in mind and discussed the whole project with Scott-Paine late into the night,

1. Two were later believed to have been used by Scott-Paine for motorboats, and there is a possibility that one could have been converted for towing the Supermarine 'Sea Lion' in the 1919 Schneider Trophy race, under the name of *Tiddlywinks.*

firing his young Works Manager with such enthusiasm that Scott-Paine wrote excitedly in his diary the following day that he thought the aircraft they planned to build would be 'of great note and moment in the world'.

In several later books and publications, PB claimed that he had sketched on the walls of his factory, in chalk that very night, the design for his PB.9— later to be termed 'the Seven Day Bus'. He also described how Scott-Paine and all his men had stood by him throughout the aircraft's construction, 'working without ceasing for seven days, and seven nights, feeding as we worked'. A gramophone, with a boy in attendance, was kept going all night 'to stop us going to sleep'[2] and 'on the seventh day we brought her out into an adjacent field and she not only flew without mishap, but broke all world records as to speed, climb and stability for her horsepower... That was indeed a red-letter day. We forgot to be tired!'

This was a romantic story indeed. The fact that an aircraft was built—if not flown—within the week, was an achievement in itself, but PB appears to have been carried away (by no means for the first time) and in his enthusiasm chose to exaggerate the amazing exploit. Scott-Paine tells a slightly different tale.

According to his diary, on 2nd August 1914, after working on the project all night at Steep Hill Park, Scott-Paine handed PB's rough sketches of two elevations to the company's talented young draughtsman, Carol Vasilesco[3], to make the final drawings. Thirty new carpenters were engaged and work began on the actual structure on Tuesday 4th August—the very day that war was declared. It has been suggested by some historians that it might have been at this stage that PB made his chalk drawings of the machine, but that these were more likely to have shown the positioning of the various sections on the factory floor than the designs on the wall, as he later claimed.

By the following day, the plate work was well under way but as most of the company's mechanics had by that time been called up to serve at various air stations, it was left to Scott-Paine to install the Gnome engine himself. His diary noted that PB chose this moment to visit London to try to secure orders for the new machine and his young manager was left in charge. At the end of the next day, the fuselage was up and wired with engine plates mounted, the fin and rudder were completed and the oil and petrol tanks installed. By Saturday 8th August, the wings were erected and covered, all the fittings of the chassis were finished and the main controls completed. Work continued, however, throughout the night and on Sunday the wings were ready for mounting. It was only at lunchtime on this day that PB returned to Southampton and on Monday, when the machine was finally completed, he arranged for its testing to take

2. This gave PB the idea he was to patent the following year for a simple mechanism by which the playing of a record could be repeated automatically.
3. Vasilesco was a Rumanian immigrant who was to die of a heart condition, aged only nineteen, on Christmas Eve, 1914

place next day at Netley, three miles from Woolston.

Early that morning, on Tuesday 11th August, a little procession left the factory. First came PB in the Sheffield Simplex car he used most days, towing the wing cellule of his PB.9, then followed Scott-Paine in the works lorry loaded with equipment needed for the test flight and with the fuselage of the machine hauled along behind. Waiting at the field was Howard Pixton and Sopwith's chief mechanic and pilot, Victor Mahl, both of whom had agreed to help launch the machine into the air.

The aircraft was assembled and Victor Mahl climbed into the cockpit and started to taxi. In the process he clipped one of the wing tips on a fence and immediate repairs had to be made but these were soon executed and the engine was re-started. After a short take-off run Mahl turned the PB.9 into a steeply-banked climbing left-hand turn, at a speed which an observer from *Flight* magazine estimated at 75 mph, with a rate of climb of about 500 feet a minute. PB, Scott-Paine and the rest of the team could not contain their excitement. At last the Woolston factory appeared to have produced an aeroplane that actually flew and one that Mahl, after a fairly long test flight, pronounced not only easy to fly but 'blessed with exceptionally good stability'.

It certainly looked a neat little machine—a single-seater biplane with an engine mounted in a wide cowling at the front of its fabric-covered fuselage. To have put the machine together so quickly and to fly it in so short a time was something of which the team felt justifiably proud. At the end of that magic day at Netley, PB's team, headed by Scott-Paine, decided to celebrate. After some liquid refreshment, they visited a cinema, where they took over the two front rows and persuaded one of their number to commandeer the piano and play wildly inappropriate music to accompany the silent film being shown. So boisterous did their behaviour become that the manager was summoned and they were all evicted from the cinema, but their celebrations continued well into the night. Meanwhile, PB had returned to a private party at Steep Hill with Dot, Delves Broughton and two of his sisters who happened to be staying at the house.

On 17th August, another small procession left the factory at Woolston, this time for Brooklands, where PB had arranged for the PB.9 to have military trials. On this occasion he used his new Rolls-Royce to tow the fuselage, while Scott-Paine drove the Sheffield Simplex which pulled the wings. The next day, Jack Alcock[4] took the aircraft up for a test flight and it appeared to function reasonably well. But he damaged the tail on landing for the second time and Scott-Paine and a mechanic had to make a quick repair—using a replacement landing skid Scott-Paine had found on a scrap heap. However, after two further flights, Alcock became increasingly apprehensive about its safety. 'Alcock suffers from cold feet', wrote Scott-Paine in his diary, but he had to admit later that he had worries himself for he also recorded that the previous night he had

4. Five years later, with Arthur Whitten Brown, Alcock made the first transatlantic flight.

'dreamt the PB.9 broke in the air'.

On the 21st, Alcock again took the machine up before taking it to Farnborough but after only a short circuit he landed and refused to attempt another flight. H.C. Miller, a Sopwith mechanic, later wrote an account of what happened next. He was at Brooklands and had examined the PB.9 himself after Alcock had voiced his fears that it had 'some peculiar fault'. Miller agreed that the construction was not good enough to stand up to military trials and was with Alcock when PB arrived that afternoon in a large sports car, 'gloved and coated in great style and wearing a monocle'.

PB asked Alcock if he was ready to fly the machine and when the pilot politely answered that he would not be taking her up again because of various deficiencies in its performance, PB's temper flared: 'Damnation,' he roared, 'bring her here and I'll fly her myself'. Alcock brought out the machine and swung the propeller. PB settled himself at the controls and began taxiing.

'He won't fly it,' Alcock said quietly, 'You'll see!'

According to Miller, the machine then turned out-of-wind, the motor roared and the aircraft spun round, buckling the undercarriage as it did so. PB was furious. He got out of the cockpit with as much dignity as he could muster and waving his hand towards the wrecked machine, instructed the onlookers to 'Put the damn thing away!' He then leapt into his car and disappeared in a cloud of dust, while an equally disappointed Scott-Paine was left to take the damaged PB.9 back to Woolston, piling the wings on top of the Simplex car and towing the fuselage.

As for PB, this was yet another disappointment to add to those he had encountered over the previous weeks. For the past month he had haunted the War Office and Admiralty, placing his factory and services as an aircraft designer at their disposal. He had even offered them the use of his cars—a real sacrifice, this—but all had been rejected. There was, he felt, only one course now open to him. His friend and co-director, Delves Broughton, had already joined up as an officer in the Hussars and PB decided that he, too, would go into the Services. His decision was not a happy one for Scott-Paine, left behind to sort out matters at the factory where, with no work in the offing, seventy-two workers had already been laid off and the remaining fourteen—including himself—had been put on half pay. 'My aunt,' he wrote in his diary, 'what a blag Billing is!'

It is not surprising that the relationship between the two was never quite the same again. Scott-Paine's brother had just been injured in an air crash, his mother's income had been depleted by the war and the young man felt that PB was deserting him just when he was most needed at Woolston. When a job in Russia presented itself in September, he was ready to hand in his notice but on hearing this, PB came up with an idea for turning the factory over to the production of light cars, 'the Rolls-Royce of light buses', which he thought could sell for around £500 each. Scott-Paine looked at the designs for this

'King Car', as PB dubbed it, but decided that, like so many of his employer's schemes, it was just not feasible.

When there was still no work by October and PB's offer to get him an 'important post in the Army' turned into the suggestion that he become a mechanic in the Royal Navy, the fiery young works manager wrote in his diary: 'I told him some things, I can tell you. Billing must think that I'm a fool to go out as a sort of chauffeur to him!'

Luckily, Scott-Paine managed to gather in some repair work from Sopwith, who still leased the adjoining shed, and also to put the PB.9 back into sufficient order for it to be requisitioned as a training machine. It was moved to Hendon early the following year and proved very useful at that station for the Royal Naval Air Service, as *Flight* magazine noted on 5th February 1915: 'The little seven-day bus is doing quite a lot of air work at Hendon and seems to be very fast, considering that she is fitted with an engine of only 50 hp'. But despite this favourable report, its active flying came to an end the following June when it was badly damaged in a crash at Chingford. PB was to have a brief reunion with his 'seven Day Bus', however, when he later brought it back to serve him in quite a different capacity. That occasion was still far off, however, when, in October 1914 he was granted a temporary commission as a sub-lieutenant in the Royal Naval Volunteer Reserve to carry out duties of a special nature.

CHAPTER SEVEN

Winston Churchill, then First Lord of the Admiralty, was strongly in favour of an offensive air policy and was convinced that destruction of the German Zeppelin bases was essential. The airship sheds at Düsseldorf and Cologne were attacked unsuccessfully in September. During a second raid early in October a Zeppelin was destroyed in its shed and this had encouraged the idea that the next attack should be on the major hydrogen and Zeppelin factory at Friedrichshafen, on the shores of Lake Constance. Because of the distance, however, the only possible way for aircraft to reach such a target was from a base in France and the most suitable was the airship station at Belfort, 125 miles from the German factory. The French reluctantly agreed to the idea but were understandably anxious to keep the whereabouts of this lightly defended base secret, for they feared German retaliation. Absolute secrecy for the operation was therefore essential.

It was at this stage that Murray Sueter approached PB with the suggestion that he should organise the whole operation, which seemed tailor-made for the intrepid adventurer, requiring as it did great ingenuity and daring. He was told that, providing top security was maintained, he would be given a free hand and all necessary help.

PB could scarcely contain his excitement. He first contacted a friend, Flight Lieutenant F.A. Brock, a member of the Brock firework family (then serving in Naval Intelligence and knowledgeable about bombs and incendiaries) and dressed in civilian clothes, the two set off in mid-October to drive through France to Switzerland. Apart from PB's driving, which was hazardous at the best of times, the journey was made more dangerous in those early months of the war by the French sentries who were prone to fire nervously at anyone or anything that looked suspicious. They reached the Swiss frontier and, having convinced the Customs authorities that they were commercial travellers, were allowed to journey on to Romanshorn on the south bank of Lake Constance, opposite the Zeppelin works on the far shore.

Here PB bought maps of the area and befriended local fishermen, who took them out on the lake and innocently pointed out the exact location of the sheds in which the airships were housed. Having established this position on his maps, he persuaded the fishermen to take him and Brock across the lake, under cover of darkness, to see the factory at close quarters. They then put him ashore alone at a quiet place just north of Friedrichshafen and arranged to pick him up there the following night.

Although PB was discreet with his surveillance, his size and general presence did not make it easy for him to disappear into the landscape and it was not long before the staff at the factory became suspicious and troops were alerted. Realising what was afoot, he took refuge in an empty house nearby,

Receiving instruction from Robert Barnwell at Brooklands in 1913

After gaining his RAeC certificate. Dot sitting on the running board of 'The Birdcage'.

Supermarine Aviation Works, Woolston, 1914

(opposite) With
PB.1 at the
Olympia Aero
Show

PB (nearest camera) leads
PB.1 down to the water for
flotation tests, 1914

PB.9, the 'Seven Day Bus'.

PB at the wheel with Hubert Scott-Paine and Carol Vasilesco behind.

with the intention of lying low until dark. At dusk, just as he was about to leave for his rendezvous with Brock and the fishermen, he saw a large car draw up outside and from it climb three German officers. As they made their way to the house, leaving the driver at the wheel, PB anxiously scanned the room for something with which to defend himself and his eye lighted upon a heavy ornamental lion on the mantelshelf. Grasping it in one of his huge hands, he lowered himself from the window just as the Germans entered the house. He then stealthily approached the waiting car from behind, knocked out its driver with his makeshift weapon,[1] bundled the unconscious man out into the road and, dodging the bullets of the officers, drove off into the night to where his boat and an anxious Brock were waiting. Armed with his maps and the valuable information that had now been gleaned, he and Brock then set off for home on another of PB's hair-raising drives through Switzerland and France, which at times had poor Brock wondering whether he would ever see his family again.

Meanwhile, back in England, five pilots had been individually instructed to stand by for special duties, the nature of which would be revealed at a later date. Squadron Commander P. Shepherd, the senior officer of the five, was told only that he would be leading a raid on an unspecified target. Squadron Commander E. Featherstone Briggs, an engineer as well as a pilot, was given the task of arranging for five newly built Avro 504 biplanes, each capable of carrying four bombs, to be crated in sections with spares. He was also made responsible for finding a few trusted men who would be capable of quickly and efficiently re-assembling the aircraft. It was the job of Flight Commander John T. Babington to select six of the best 80 hp Gnome engines he could find, together with the smallest number of fitters necessary for their installation. Flight Lieutenant Sidney V. Sippe and Flight Sub-Lieutenant R.P. Cannon were merely told to provide (as were the others) their own blankets and sleeping bags.

Soon after his return from France, PB went to the Admiralty to collect sufficient money to complete his plans and such documents as would ensure free passage through France for his party, which now numbered five pilots and eleven air mechanics. The selected men were then told to report to Southampton on 10th November to board the cargo boat *Manchester Importer*. The biplanes by this time were packed in wooden crates, on the outside of which had been painted in red, large letters of the Russian alphabet, of no particular significance but designed, according to PB, to throw any spies off the scent.

These were loaded into the hold of the ship and the members of the secret mission met aboard the vessel. By then Shepherd had been give a brief outline of what was in store for them all but was told to keep this knowledge to himself and that final instructions and money would arrive from the Admiralty before the boat left. When sailing was imminent and there was still no sign of

1. He kept the ornamental lion all his life, prominently displayed on his own study mantelpiece, and often regaled his family with the story of how he came by it.

the expected messenger, he began to get worried. However, just as the gangway was about to be drawn up, a large white sports car appeared round the corner of a warehouse and screeched to a halt alongside the vessel. From it stepped PB, wearing his monocle and a somewhat unorthodox version of a Royal Navy officer's uniform—a jauntily-angled, white-covered cap (out of season in November), a jacket on which the gold buttons were placed at untraditional angles and a silk shirt of his own design with a diamond pin at its collar instead of a necktie.

He ran up the gangway carrying a small bag and a bundle of papers which he handed to Shepherd. Then, with a wave of his hand to the other officers, he conspiratorially whispered to Shepherd that he would see him 'on the other side', ran back down to the quay, jumped into his car and was away before those on the *Manchester Importer* could draw breath. It was certainly a memorable introduction for the group to the man who had been chosen to plan the whole operation in which they would be engaged.

When the ship was at sea, Shepherd glanced at the papers and opened the bag, which he discovered contained 500 gold sovereigns and a bundle of French banknotes. The party knew by this time that they were bound for Le Havre but only Shepherd had been told the final destination. As promised, when the boat arrived 'on the other side' PB was waiting for them, having taken his sports car and himself over on the cross-Channel packet. He was now dressed in a more traditional uniform, no doubt for the benefit of the French authorities, with whom he had made arrangements for a special train to be shunted alongside the dock where the *Manchester Importer* would tie up. Under cover of darkness, he then set about supervising the transfer of the crates with their conspicuous Russian markings.

It was unfortunate that the electric power plant broke down during the unloading but, unperturbed, PB soon had everyone in their shirt-sleeves, heaving the weighty crates manually on to the waiting train. Even the senior officers in the party, with ranks considerably higher than his own (a humble Volunteer Reserve sub-lieutenant) were apparently recruited for the task. By midnight all were aboard, including PB and his white sports car.

The train then steamed off across France, making only one stop on its way in a quiet stretch of the countryside. Here the car and its driver, now in civilian clothes, were put down. Within minutes both had disappeared into the darkness. What PB did between that time and his arrival at a disused factory siding near Belfort to meet the train is not known but it is more than likely that he was anxious to make the necessary arrangements with the Mayor of Belfort who was privy to the intrigue.

From the siding the crates had again to be manhandled, first onto trucks and then, after a short journey by road, into one of the large hangars at the French airship base. Here PB produced his maps and the information he had managed to glean about the Zeppelin sheds at Friedrichshafen and divulged his plans for the raid. He impressed on the men that they were not, under any circumstances, to leave the hangar, cold and draughty though it might be, until they had been given permission to do so. Here they would work, eat and sleep until the final preparations for this very secret operation had been made. He alone would be their link with the outside world.

The crates were unpacked and the service mechanics began assembling the Avros, trying out the specially constructed bomb release gear and filling the fuel and oil tanks. Four twenty-pound high explosive bombs were prepared for loading onto each of the five aircraft. By 15th November, less than forty-eight hours after the party had arrived at the base, the work was complete and it was now the pilots' turn. They had been allowed out of the hangar for a short while to inspect the airfield and had been dismayed to find that the ground was rough and contained a number of large loose stones. Nevertheless, they found one area which seemed reasonable and Shepherd decided to try it out. It was unfortunate that by this time he had succumbed to the intense cold of the hangar and was already a sick man, which may have been the reason why he failed to see the large boulder in the path of his machine when he attempted to take off. This caused one wheel to collapse and the undercarriage to buckle, which left only four of the Avros serviceable.

The weather then deteriorated and Shepherd became so ill that PB transferred him to a hotel in Belfort. He was still not well enough to fly when, on 21st November, PB and the other pilots decided that conditions had improved sufficiently for the raid to be attempted, so Sub-Lieutenant Cannon took Shepherd's place. PB then briefed the pilots as to the layout of the factories and with his maps went over the course he suggested they should take.

The route to their target would, he told them, be an indirect one, for they would have to skirt the northern border of Switzerland to avoid infringing that country's neutrality. This would entail flying over the mountains of the Black Forest rather than heading south between the two arms of Lake Constance. Timing of the departure was crucial. If they left too early, the Zeppelin sheds might be obscured in cloud whereas if they were too late it would mean returning to the base at dusk when landing could be hazardous.

The pilots already had problems enough. There was no guarantee that the engines, which were by no means new, would stand up to flying such a distance, let alone allow for any extra mileage should the airmen become lost. This was more than a possibility as, for security reasons, the French had insisted that no maps were to be carried in the machines. Keeping warm was another important factor to be considered for no special clothing had been issued and the pilots were flying in open cockpits. Most chose to wear warm underwear, long woollen scarves wrapped round their necks and chests, thick greatcoats, flying caps lined with wool or fur and goggles to protect their eyes from the fierce winds. Their ordinary naval issue boots, however, were hardly suitable for the icy temperatures around their feet—even if the boots had been soaked in brandy, which was reckoned to prevent frostbite.

The plan was for the pilots to leave at five-minute intervals and Briggs, Sippe and Babington managed to achieve this successfully, starting soon after nine-thirty on that bright November morning. Unfortunately, Cannon, who was the last in line, broke his machine's tailskid just as he was about to become airborne and much to his annoyance was forced to remain behind. With PB he watched the last of the three aircraft disappear from view, after which PB took his leave and slipped away to a small hotel just across the border in Switzerland, to await a telephone call with information about the raid from a contact he had made near Friedrichshafen.

Although they had started off within a few minutes of each other, Briggs soon left the other two pilots behind and then they, too, lost contact in cloud as they approached Lake Constance. Briggs managed to fly straight to the target and drop his bombs but his arrival immediately alerted the base, its guns went into action, his fuel tank was holed and he was forced to land. As he did so, he found himself surrounded by a group of angry civilians who set about him with such gusto that he had to be rescued by troops and taken to a nearby hospital.

As he approached the target, Sippe saw several hundred men close to the main hangar and released his first bomb to distract the gunners before dropping two more on the factory and hangar itself. He tried to release the fourth but the mechanism failed and as he was by then under heavy fire, he decided to fly down the lake and return to Belfort.

Babington was last to arrive at the scene. By this time shells were bursting all round him. He just caught a glimpse of Sippe on his way back down the lake and saw, through a haze of smoke from a burning building, that the large hangar was still intact, so decided to aim his bombs at that. As he dived he noticed a second shed and what looked like an aeroplane with people gathered around it, but stuck to his original plan of unloading his bombs on the large hangar. This was just as well as the machine he had seen below was Briggs's Avro and his fellow pilot was already having enough problems fending off the angry mob.

Having discharged his bombs, he felt sure that he had damaged the hangar and as one particular machine-gun platform was giving him trouble he made a stab at silencing it. He dived down to place himself in such a position that, if they continued firing, the Germans would be aiming directly at their own shed. As he had hoped, they quickly held their fire and he was able to deliver a long burst at the platform before turning at last for home.

As he flew along the lake the mist swirled below and navigation became more difficult. Worse still, he began to run out of fuel and was forced to land in a field, not sure if he was in Germany, Switzerland or France. As he did so, a man approached him brandishing a pitchfork, followed by a youth who looked equally menacing until Babington managed to make them understand that he was English. Fortunately, he was in France and when his identity was established, he was taken to a telephone to report his whereabouts. He was then given food while he waited for a car to take him back to Belfort.

PB's contact had reported that the raid had been highly successful and on the day after the two pilots' return, the French showed their appreciation by awarding Sippe and Babington the Légion d'Honneur at a parade of their troops at Belfort. With the mission now completed, the machines were once again crated up and made ready for shipment and the personnel began the homeward journey.

As PB had borrowed a second car for use during the operation, he recruited Sippe and Babington to drive it back to Paris for him while he drove his own. They watched him set off—as usual, much too fast for the icy conditions—but caught him up barely sixty miles out of Belfort, with his sports car wrapped round a tree. Fortunately he was not injured and managed to travel home with the two pilots, after depositing the borrowed car in Paris.

Despite some criticism from Swiss diplomatic circles who claimed that the aircraft had, after all, flown over their territory, most officials were full of praise for the success of the raid and Churchill was reported as saying that it had been 'a remarkable feat of aerial initiative'.

Although, according to the official German records, no Zeppelins were actually destroyed, the bombs that fell on the airship sheds demolished a newly completed hydrogen-producing plant, causing an explosion and fire which threw the whole base into confusion, and this resulted in more anti-aircraft protection being deployed as a precaution against further raids.

All three pilots were later awarded the Distinguished Service Order but there is no record of PB having received any decoration for his important part in the operation's success, although some historians now refer to it as having been one of the 'most audacious and brilliantly planned attacks' to be carried out against the Zeppelin menace.

The raid proved to have been even more successful than was originally thought, for two of the eleven bombs dropped had fallen on the airship sheds, seriously damaging a Zeppelin in one and destroying the gas works in another. An explosion followed the latter, which had caused yet more damage and the whole plant had been thrown into confusion. Anti-bomb nets were put up and more anti-aircraft guns were diverted to the base as an added precaution against further raids.

CHAPTER EIGHT

After making his report to the Admiralty, PB took time off to see Dot at Steep Hill and Scott-Paine at the factory. There was still very little work coming in at Woolston and Scott-Paine was spending most of his time helping out at the Sopwith shed. At the beginning of November the company solicitor had to inform the Registrar of Public Companies that it was 'impossible to get on at all, consequent upon the war and the inability to obtain funds to pay any fees whatever' and a new agreement was entered into on the 18th. According to this, during PB's absence in France, Delves Broughton had undertaken to pay any debts incurred by his friend. He also showed willingness to put more money into the concern but the whole situation at the Woolston works was still far from satisfactory and Scott-Paine urged PB to give him more control over its management. On 5th December he wrote in his diary: 'Made arrangements with PB to take over complete charge of the factory. I find it over £800 in debt, no credit anywhere and only six men in the place, a very big handful to get on with'.

The balance sheet at that time showed that from 1st May to 5th December 1914, the Company's total losses had been £848 8s 8½d—despite the sale of a motor-launch, the old Farman machine and the works lorry. The assets amounted to more than £11,000 and included four aircraft: the PB.7, the PB.9, an old Radley England Waterplane and a mysterious PB.13, which was apparently a variant of the PB.9. With the exception of the PB.7, all the machines were complete with engines and with these in such short supply, Scott-Paine judged that they, at least, would prove an asset to the struggling company.

He had been trying for some time to persuade PB to obtain more work for the factory and in the early months of 1915, thanks to Murray Sueter and others, contracts began to materialise to build aircraft from other company's designs, under licence, and to repair damaged machines. Sopwith, Avro and the Royal Aircraft Factory at Farnborough all began to make use of Woolston in this way and the factory slowly returned to life. More workers were engaged and as time went by it even became possible to develop more machines with the PB prefix.

When PB handed over responsibility for the running of the factory to Scott-Paine, he retained only his shares—which by then were greatly reduced in number—and his name on the letter-head of the company. At the beginning of January 1915 he transferred from the RNVR to the Royal Naval Air Service and became an acting flight lieutenant attached to the Air Department at the Admiralty. Even so, during most of that year his commission seems to have allowed him sufficient freedom to spend a great deal of time at Woolston, working on his aeroplane designs and inventions, most of which he duly registered at the Patent Office. In March he submitted outline designs for a 'rotary bomb-dropping apparatus', a strange 'motor vehicle' and an 'experimental aircraft'- probably the PB.23E. In October and December other aircraft patents were registered, together with his design for the continuous playing of a gramophone record. This contraption had two arms fixed together at an angle so that as one finished playing the record, the other started a repeat performance without further attention—providing, of course, the clockwork motor had been wound up sufficiently.

The PB.23E was a single-seat pusher biplane scout, powered by an 80 hp Le Rhone engine. PB called this machine his 'push-proj', because he thought the nacelle resembled a projectile, or shell. For covering the nacelle, he had the then revolutionary idea of using light alloy sheet metal instead of the usual fabric and plywood and when the aircraft was first test flown at Hendon in September its gleaming nacelle caused some of the onlookers to nickname it the 'sparklet'. However, after this test, because of some instability in flight, modifications had to be made and an improved version, the PB.25, was completed the following year.

The wings of this machine were swept back, instead of straight, as in the PB.23E, the nacelle was fabric-covered, the engine was changed to a 100 hp Gnome and, among other modifications, the Lewis gun was moved up from the nose of the nacelle to a position easier for operation by the pilot, who was also provided with a streamlined headrest. Twenty of these modified machines, known officially from then on as the 'Pemberton Billing Scout', were ordered by the Admiralty but were never considered sound enough for active service so the RNAS went on to use them for experimental and training purposes.

Joseph Crabtree Taylor, who was to be associated with the aircraft industry for most of his life, went to Woolston in 1915 to take charge of aeroplane testing. In his memoirs he described PB as 'a most dynamic personality with a great flair for inventing things' and told of how the staff at Woolston were always working on one or other of his pet ideas:

> Many of his inventions were sound, but years ahead of his time, and for that reason were usually turned down. One of his ideas was to build a small waterproof hangar on top of a submarine to carry a seaplane with folded wings. The scheme he had in mind was for the seaplane to be placed in position in the hangar at the submarine base. The submarine would then travel under water to the scene of operations and surface, after which the wings could be opened out and the seaplane prepared for action in a few minutes.

According to Taylor, PB's idea was put into practice some years later but he received no credit for its conception. This strange flying boat was probably the PB.27, known also as the S.S.1 or 'submarine Scout', and was another version of PB's slip-wing flying boat. It had thirty-two foot span wings mounted on top of a fifteen-foot long boat hull containing the engine with a single pusher propeller. There was also a direct shaft drive to a water propeller and the wings, booms and tail were built into a single unit for easy jettisoning in an emergency. As it turned out, this submarine-stowed flying boat and its successor, the PB.31, never graduated beyond the project stage. In the later design the boat had an independent power plant and an engine mounted in the fuselage, which also carried the biplane's tail plane, rudder and fin.

When Taylor arrived at the factory its employees were busily engaged in producing twelve Short S.38 pusher biplanes, working on the modifications to the PB.25 and constructing the first of the massive and imaginative Nighthawk Quadruplanes designed to combat the Zeppelin raids—the PB.29E.

The first German air attacks on Britain were by float planes on Dover and the London docks in December 1914. Damage from these was negligible but in April of the following year, Zeppelins began bombing raids which increased the mood of despondency among the British people, already depressed at that time by the heavy Army casualties and the loss of life and shipping caused by the U-boats.

After seeing the results of these raids, PB persuaded the Admiralty to let him pursue an idea he had for a slow-flying night patrol aeroplane that would counter any further attacks by what he termed 'those bladders of death and destruction'. He knew that Zeppelins approached their targets quietly and under cover of darkness and invariably escaped before fighters could reach their altitudes. To counter this he envisaged an aircraft that would have a maximum speed of 80 mph and a minimum of 35 mph. Such a machine would, he thought, need to be powered by two engines fitted with silencers and be equipped with dual control. It would also have to be capable of climbing to 10,000 feet in twenty minutes, and be able to loiter at low speed for at least twelve hours. A searchlight would be provided for picking out the target and a machine-gun to 'shoot the Zeppelins out of the sky'.

So convinced was he that this new aircraft would succeed, that he built the PB.29E within seven weeks of the design being drawn, entirely at his own expense and for a total cost of £6,000. The result was an unusual quadruplane powered by two 90 hp Austro-Daimler engines mounted as pushers on the second wing, to which the fuselage was also attached. This contained two seats for the pilots and supported the triple fins and biplane tail unit. A small searchlight was mounted in the nose. Provision was also made for another crew member, together with his Lewis gun on a moveable platform, in the middle of the third and top wing of this strange machine.

PB took the PB.29E for flying tests at Waltham Cross and in February 1916 it also underwent trials at Chingford in Essex, but here it crashed and was wrecked. Even so, the Admiralty appeared to have been impressed by its possibilities and took an interest in its successor, the PB.31E, which Scott-Paine later went on to produce on his own with many

Three Avro 504s at Belfort prior to raid on Friedrichshafen

Staff at Woolston. Scott-Paine in centre (standing), 1915

PB.31E, the 'Night Hawk' twin-engined quadruplane

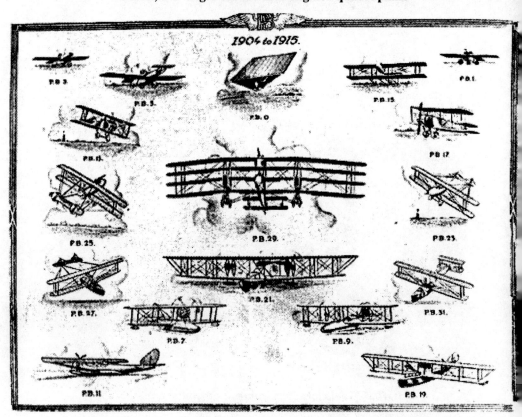

Drawing from *Air War: How to Wage It* depicting his aircraft designs

Electioneering in PB.9 (the 'Seven Day Bus') at Mile End, 1916

(above) The young MP

(left) Electioneering in East Herts, 1916

Punch cartoon: The Hustler from East Herts. 'Mr Pemberton Billing introduces himself to Mr Tennant and Mr Balfour'

refinements.[1] This second quadruplane was powered by two 100 hp Anzani engines and the cockpit was totally enclosed in a glazed cabin amidships. All the interior wooden parts were fabric-covered to minimise injury from splinters in the event of a crash. The incorporation of a sleeping berth was originally planned for off-duty crew but this idea was not pursued, though a spare seat was provided beside the pilot. There were also two further gun positions containing two Lewis guns and a one-and-a-half pounder Davis non-recoil gun. The searchlight was carried on the nose of the fuselage and was controlled by the front gunner moving a lever on the starboard side of the cockpit.

The official performance figures for the PB.31E did not live up to expectations. The speed was quoted as only 60 mph at 6,000 feet and the time taken to climb to 10,000 feet was estimated to be at least sixty minutes. As an airship could rise more rapidly, having once jettisoned its load of ballast, there would have been little chance of the quadruplane catching up with it—unless, of course, it was already in the vicinity. Although two were ordered, only one was ever completed and flown and even this was scrapped at Eastchurch in July 1917. But it is interesting to note that certain features of this cumbersome machine were taken up many years later and used in a modified form in other service aircraft.

Long before the PB31E was completed, however, PB had severed his links with the factory. As for the other inventions on which he had been working in 1915, few came to fruition. His rotary bomb-dropping apparatus, which was capable of dropping incendiary flares or bombs in a stick of one every twenty feet, was believed to have been manufactured later by the HMV Company and there was even some talk of it being fitted to the quadruplane, but there is no evidence that this was ever achieved.

Joseph Taylor also wrote of working on some of PB's curious cars during this period and on one in particular that, not surprisingly, brought PB into frequent conflict with the police: 'It was a complete freak, it had a streamlined aluminium body, without doors, windscreen or windows, fitted onto an Austro-Daimler chassis, and he entered the monster through a hatchway in the roof and steered by periscope...There was also a Bugatti sports car, with three-inch diameter copper exhaust pipes. We spent hours cutting bits off the ends of the pipes until we had the right note to satisfy him'.[2]

Most of PB's cars had been doctored by him in one way or another, either to give them the additional power needed for the very high speeds he favoured or just to put his own distinctive stamp on them.

1. One of the members of the design team for the PB.31E was a newcomer to Woolston, Reginald J. Mitchell, who was later to produce racing seaplanes for Supermarine and the famous Spitfire of World War Two.
2. This was, in fact, a Napier, which PB had bought in 1913. During his ownership it underwent several body changes.

There is no official record of why PB left the RNAS when he did, but, allowing for his usual exaggerations, the story he told of the events leading up to his decision seems convincing. When the Zeppelin attacks on England were at their height, he was given indefinite leave from the Service to develop his PB.29E and he and Scott-Paine began work on this in November 1915. By Christmas Eve the machine was all ready to be crated up and sent away for trials, save for what PB termed 'certain small instruments' needed for testing its engines. After several frustrating telephone calls to the Government department responsible, he was finally promised that the instrument she needed would be despatched immediately and would reach Woolston between nine and ten that evening. When this failed to happen, he telephoned yet again and angrily complained that he had kept his faithful workers hanging on at the factory in the hope that work on the quadruplane could be completed that night. The official listened to PB's furious tirade and then told him, in a calm, slightly patronising manner, to keep his hair on and wait until after the holiday. At this, PB flung down the receiver and his Service cap after it to show his disapproval of bureaucratic red tape and his sheer frustration that 'even in the middle of a bloody war against a powerful and relentless enemy, official departments were *easing up* for Christmas'. As most of his employees knew only too well, PB himself would rarely have let the matter of a public holiday stand in the way of completing any project.

It was this experience, he maintained, that finally prompted him to leave the Service and try for election to the House of Commons so that he could, as he put it, 'raise hell' over such examples of lassitude, which he believed stemmed directly from the political heads of the country. He wrote to the Admiralty that very night applying for his resignation and on 28th December received a reply from Murray Sueter. He acknowledged PB's letter and took the opportunity of passing on to him 'in confidence' that: 'Mr Churchill and Lord Fisher were very pleased with the way you organised the Lake Constance raid, and have instructed me to note your name for advancement. If any question of your promotion arises, or any honour is suggested for your war services, I will do my best to press your claims on the authorities'. Sueter's letter was followed on 5th January by the Admiralty's official acceptance of PB's resignation and the proposal, in recognition of his service, that he should be 'promoted to the rank of Squadron Commander with seniority from January 1st, 1916'.

CHAPTER NINE

The idea of entering Parliament had crossed PB's mind many times. He genuinely believed that with all the experience and knowledge he had acquired during his thirty-five bustling years, he had something of worth to offer the country and that the moment had now come for him to make a stand on the issues that were particularly dear to him. He was certainly not alone in criticising the way affairs were being managed by Asquith's Coalition Government at that time, for there was considerable discontent in many quarters.

Since his Fambridge days, as his early articles in *Aerocraft* clearly indicate, he had stressed the need for Britain to have an effective air policy. By the end of 1915 he had become even more convinced than ever that the organisation of the flying sections of both the Army (Royal Flying Corps) and the Royal Navy (Royal Naval Air Service) left a great deal to be desired. While pilots of both Services were endeavouring to fight enemy aircraft that were generally far superior to their own, interdepartmental wranglings were being conducted in Whitehall over which of the Services should have the responsibility for Britain's air defences. What was needed, he felt, was a co-ordinated plan or overall direction from outside the two Services which could also encompass all areas of aeroplane production—in other words, a *third* service devoted to air matters only. His opinions were backed strongly by several of his aeronautical friends—particularly Charles Grey, the editor of *Aeroplane* magazine—and all hoped he would seek election to put forward these views in Parliament.

Within days of coming to his decision, he moved from his London pied-a-terre at Essex Court to a larger apartment in the Middle Temple, 4, Elm Court—judging it more suitable for the politician he hoped soon to become. He engaged a secretary and typist and waited hopefully for a seat to become vacant.

He knew little of politics or electoral procedures but he had many friends anxious to help. One such acquaintance telephoned him on 9th January, soon after he had installed himself and Dot at Elm Court, with the news that there was a vacancy at Mile End, in the East End of London. This arose due to the elevation to the peerage of the Hon. Harry Lawson, its former Conservative and Unionist member. Another friend urged him to seek the advice of a man who had the reputation of being an expert in political affairs. Unfortunately PB quickly discovered, after appointing him as his agent, that the man was not as knowledgeable as he had been led to believe. Several other experiences followed which made him realise, with a shock—for he had always been fiercely patriotic and firmly believed such people to be above suspicion—that some in political life were as susceptible to corruption as those he had encountered in the business world.

This was particularly the case when his newly acquired agent introduced him to a politician whom PB never named but referred to afterwards as 'very well-known and experienced.' This man offered to get him into the House of Commons within the month, on receipt of £3,000 payable in advance and returnable should this not be achieved. Much to the politician's surprise, PB firmly turned down the proposition and later described the episode: 'he couldn't grasp my aims and ideas any more than I could approve of his, so it was rather in the nature of two men shouting to each other in different and unintelligible languages across a sea of misunderstanding.'

By this time he had also become disillusioned with his agent and, against this man's advice, presented himself to the Unionist Party Central Office, thinking that if he put forward his reasons for wishing to enter Parliament he might find the backing he needed.

After discussions with the Chairman, Arthur Steel-Maitland, he was told that the Unionist Party would be prepared to accept him as one of their official candidates but he would be expected to give 'certain undertakings' should he be elected. This he refused to do—which came as no surprise to those who knew him well, for few could visualise him ever being prepared to toe any party line. Consequently, at the nomination meeting at Mile End in late January, the local committee chose the other nominee, Warwick Brookes, despite some eloquent, if perhaps ill-advised, pleading by PB:

> Look here, we're at war, and we've got to win the war. We shan't do it if things go on as they are now. So far as Conservative and Liberal policies are concerned, wash me out. I want to go to the House of Commons to get a strong Air Policy, and to attack the men whose muddles and indecisions are responsible for the position we shall soon be in unless strong action is taken... You are here Conservatives and Liberals together—then why not return an Independent who is neither? Judge us as men!

From that moment on, as an Independent, he began a rigorous election campaign against Warwick Brookes, using as one of his slogans: 'Billing and Business v. Brookes and Bungling'. His first speech was conducted from his Napier car which, by mistake, he had actually parked *outside* his constituency, near the street market at the top of Mile End Road, but he still managed to gather quite a crowd. He attracted a good deal more attention a few days later, for he hit on the idea of making his speeches from the cockpit of his old PB.9, which he had ordered to be towed up from Woolston.

With his previous experience on the stage, he found few problems with the delivery of his electioneering speeches and knew just how to project his forceful personality upon his prospective constituents—whether speaking to them in the streets from his PB.9 or at larger meetings in the local Palladium. Crowds followed him everywhere and his words were greeted with an enthusiasm seldom bestowed on a newcomer at such gatherings. The *Daily Mail* of 18th January 1916 described the 'Flying Candidate' of Mile End in glowing and revealing terms:

> although new to politics, he could give many an old practitioner a lesson in the artifices of electioneering. In only a few days he is as familiar to Mile End as the People's Palace itself...He is tall and powerful, drives a high-power car with an exhaust that to say the least is audible and addresses electors in a great megaphone voice that could be heard above the engine, if he set his aeroplane going. He is the personification of the battling energy of an aeroplane in a gale and although he talks of nothing else than the Air Service, his vigour and intense conviction are very effective.

It was indeed extraordinary that throughout the election campaign he fought on this one issue—an effective air policy—and made no effort at any time to appeal to those constituents who may have been more interested in other matters. In fact, one astute reporter commented, he would 'spring inevitably clear of them as a soaring aviator rises clear of street traffic problems'.

By far his largest gathering was on 23rd January at the Mile End Palladium when Horatio Bottomley, editor of *John Bull*, Ben Tillett, secretary of the General Workers' Union and Sir Henry Dalziel, proprietor of *Reynolds News* all spoke on PB's behalf to a crowd so enormous that a fresh audience had to be ushered in each hour. It was later alleged that both Bottomley and Tillett gleaned a certain amount of financial benefit for themselves from the support they gave him at this time and that Bottomley in particular used PB's surprisingly trusting attitude to reap even more gratuities for himself from the campaign. If this was the case, it would not have been the only occasion when PB's judgement had been at fault and he was manipulated by others for their own purposes—despite Dot's warnings. By all accounts she made no secret of her dislike of Bottomley, but then she was always the better judge of character and more able to stand back and assess a situation objectively, while her volatile husband invariably acted on impulse.

Aware of the interest he was creating, it was not long before newspapers favouring the Government candidate started publishing articles aimed at discrediting PB. There were veiled suggestions that he had left the RNAS under a cloud, which he immediately scotched by publishing the official letter from the Admiralty accepting his resignation.

On the very eve of the election, a letter appeared in most of the national newspapers, purporting to have been written by Arthur Balfour (then First Lord of the Admiralty) to Warwick Brookes. This commented on a speech made by PB during his campaign, which appeared to suggest that the Government discriminated between the East and West Ends of London when Zeppelin attacks took place. Balfour had allegedly written:

If Mr Billing is correctly reported...he is endeavouring to persuade persons living in the East of London that their interests are neglected because they are poor; and that only because the wealthier parts of the town were attacked was trouble taken to meet Zeppelin raids. The statement is untrue; but its untruth is the least part of its criminality. A man who endeavours to make political capital by suggesting that the military arrangements of the Government are due to class selfishness and not to a single-hearted desire for the general good, is playing a most unpatriotic part.

PB was given an opportunity to reply on the same day and his letter was given prominence in journals owned by the Northcliffe group, who had been very supportive throughout his campaign. It is clear, however, that it had been dashed off without care or thought for he assumed, not for the first time, a great deal too much, too soon:

As a fighting man I can only interpret the occasion and singular violence of Mr Balfour's letter to Mr Brookes as a sign that the Government realises it has lost Mile End...While Balfour is accusing me of encouraging the enemy, in a vain effort to save Mile End for the Coalition, bombs are actually being dropped on Kent...In reference to these statements of mine, which have apparently so occupied the mind of Mr Warwick Brookes that he referred them to Mr Balfour, I can only say of them 'What I have said I have said'. Perhaps the happiest answer for Mr Balfour to Mr Brookes—a drowning man clutching at a straw to save himself—could have been tersely phrased in a sentence which Mr Balfour has made his own and historic, 'I am a child in these matters'.

Unfortunately, PB had underestimated the loyalty of constituents to a political party. On election day, 25th January, despite providing car rides to and from the polling stations for the voters and the general feeling of goodwill he and Dot had encountered, it was Warwick Brookes who topped the poll with 1,991 votes against PB's 1,615. However, running the Government candidate so close at this, his first venture into politics, was a laudable achievement.

In the *Sunday Pictorial* of 30th January, Bottomley wrote of 'The Moral of Mile End' and said that PB's votes meant more than a liking for 'Billing, Beer and Bottomley; they meant business' and that there was no 'cooing' in the other party dovecotes as a result—'only Billing'. It was indeed true that in certain Parliamentary circles such strong opposition to a Government candidate added credence to the view that there was widespread discontent in the country over the manner in which the war was being handled by the Coalition Government under Asquith, particularly with regard to aeronautical matters.

PB was not as depressed as Dot had expected him to be after his defeat, for his disappointment had been partly assuaged by the reaction of his supporters after the result had been announced. They had burst into the hall, closed around him and borne him off, shoulder high, to his car. Here several torches were turned on his face and the crowd waited expectantly for him to speak. He vividly described this strange experience later: 'I spoke to them, though what I said I don't know. I had never in my life before been so moved, so thrilled. It was a most extraordinary sensation to stand there, in the dazzling light, gazing over the peopled darkness, where I could not see one face, but I felt the great heart of the crowd beating.'

His state of euphoria lasted for a few days and during this time he made up his mind that if another seat became vacant he would fight it on his own, now that he knew the ropes. Mile End had opened his eyes to the methods used by what he termed 'the well-dressed crowd of swindlers and scoundrels, cut-purses and 'make-a-bits' he had encountered during his campaign. Years later he wrote that the administration of the country then appeared to him 'as a sorry and sordid play, in which politicians are the actors, the Pressmen are the dramatists, vested interests pack the House—and the public pay the price'.

Reaction set in a few days later but Dot, who was well used to the black moods of depression that assailed her husband after weeks of abortive activity, encouraged him to pursue an idea he had for collecting together some of his recently published articles and incorporating them into a book. He found a publisher and within a month or so *Air War: How to Wage It* was on sale. He dedicated it to: 'the memory of those gallant men who gave their lives at the call of duty and by their courageous airmanship proved the wonderful possibility of the great service for whose world ascendancy I plead'.

The book was an attempt, he wrote, to deal with the main problems and how they could best be met. It would 'point the way to the creation of a great air service worthy of our best traditions and grand enough to meet the demands of our Imperial power'. It was to realise this dream that after anxious thought he had surrendered his commission in the RNAS believing that, as a civilian, with his voice and pen he could at this moment of crisis best serve his country.

In addition to his articles in the *Daily Mail, The Referee, Reynolds News* and others, he included extracts from some of his *Aerocraft* magazines. His ideas, first mooted at Fambridge, for an Imperial Air Service were put forward, together with a scheme for defending the country against aerial attack, which appears to show an astonishing foresight when compared with the similarity of methods actually employed in national defence more than twenty years later.[1] The book also contained a fold-out plate of sketches showing what he claimed to be his aircraft designs to date. He had always used odd numbers to differentiate these (with the exception of the PB.2), sticking to his old superstition that they brought him luck. But for reasons known only to himself, in this book he decided to change all the original aircraft numbers so as to include his early gliders and monoplanes from 1904-15. Consequently his old PB.1 from then on became PB.7 and so on. To add further to the confusion of

1. See Appendix II: 'A Man and a Plan'.

later historians, some aircraft were not listed in the book at all and one that was—the PB.31(SS1)—had, in fact, never been built.

At the back of *Air War: How to Wage It* was a note to the effect that all its profits—together with any fees he had received from his newspaper articles and the sale of his recorded gramophone speeches in connection with his campaign for an Imperial Air Service—would be paid into a special account. This would be earmarked for 'propaganda works' pending the appointment of a committee for the fund's administration. But it was two months before he had the opportunity to pursue this particular idea further for by the time the book came out in late February 1916, he was already engaged in another contest for a Parliamentary seat.

After the announcement of the result at Mile End, PB had pledged that he would 'fight the next by-election in any constituency within reasonable distance of London on the policy of Great Britain's supremacy in the air'. He little thought at the time that such an opportunity would present itself within the month, but on 18th February he heard that Sir John Rolleston intended to resign as Unionist Member for East Hertfordshire and immediately alerted the press of his intention to contest the vacancy. As a result, the next day's newspapers carried the official notification of Sir John's resignation, with the news that PB would be seeking election at East Hertfordshire as an 'Independent Air Candidate' and that he intended to hold a meeting that same afternoon at Bull Plain, a large open area in the middle of Hertford, to introduce himself to his prospective constituents.

The speed with which all this had been arranged impressed the people of East Hertfordshire. Encouraged by the arrival of an advance party of London journalists bent on covering the meeting, several hundred people turned out on what proved to be a cold, rainy Saturday afternoon, to listen to this exciting new candidate. However, their initial enthusiasm began to wane when he failed to appear at the appointed time of four o'clock. Two of his supporting party stepped in to outline PB's background and reasons for wanting to enter Parliament and tried to reassure the crowd that his arrival was imminent but after nearly an hour's wait, some people became restless and began to drift away. Their departure was halted, however, by the throbbing sound of a high-powered engine and, amid cheers, PB made a spectacular arrival, steering his torpedo-shaped car through to the makeshift platform. He had been delayed at the London wedding of his old friend and co-director at Woolston, Delves Broughton, and had driven the thirty or so miles at break-neck speed in heavy rain. The old charm soon worked its magic however, and the applause was deafening when he wound up his short address with: 'I assure you that although you won't have a politician to represent you in Parliament, you will have a man who will stand by you, work for you and above all work for his and your country'.

The meeting was well covered by both the national and local press and two days later *The Times* carried a leading article on 'The framing and enforcement of a broad constructive policy with regard to the country's air service'. This did much to further PB's electioneering campaign, for it listed all the proposals he had been advocating himself.

On 26th February, the *Hertfordshire Mercury* commented on PB's attractive personality and the fact that he was already the main topic of conversation in morning and evening trains to and from the City. Despite being 'handicapped by the lack of party machinery' he had become a very popular figure in the constituency. Five days before the election, on 4th March, it reported that he and Captain Henderson, the National Government candidate, had both been working at high pressure. The third contestant, W.H. Rolfe, the Independent Agricultural Candidate, was apparently considered to be something of a joke and not to be taken seriously.

PB was certainly putting everything he could into his campaign. In just under a fortnight he had chatted with hundreds of electors, addressed 116 meetings and travelled almost 1,500 miles around the constituency in his distinctive car with 'Send up your own airman' emblazoned on its side. Without doubt he brought colour into the lives of the people of East Hertfordshire in that exceptionally cold, bleak February and early March, when many were living in fear of further Zeppelin raids and news from the war fronts was generally gloomy.

At one meeting in Ware he made a dramatic entrance in a leather motoring coat smothered with snow. This caused the waiting audience to spring to its feet and cheer him lustily in appreciation of the way he had battled through the blizzard to reach them. On another occasion in Hertford he evoked much laughter and applause with the comment: 'When I ran away to sea at thirteen, my parents' friends said they were afraid I would come to a bad end and I am wondering if this means the House of Commons! If so, perhaps I can do something there to help put them straight'.

As at Mile End, the children followed him everywhere and his popularity was strengthened when he handed out favours of red ribbons with model aeroplanes imprinted on them. His election leaflet was, in the words of the *Weekly Dispatch*, 'the shortest on record...calculated to impress the electors with the shrewdness and originality of its author'. It consisted of a single sheet of headed notepaper on which was written: 'The accompanying illustrations express with far greater eloquence than any words of mine, the urgent and crying need to have an airman in the House of Commons who understands his job. Never let it be forgotten that the ballot is secret and you can vote according to your judgement and your conscience without fear of any man.' The illustrations to which he referred were lurid pictures by a Dutch artist showing the destruction of a city by Zeppelins. His plea to the electors to vote according to their own judgement was obviously written with an eye on the powerful party machine which by this time was geared heavily against him.

Before his arrival on the scene, it was generally assumed that there would be no contest and that the Unionist nominee, Captain Brodie Henderson, would automatically take the seat. He was a Justice of the Peace for Hertfordshire, had lived there for the past seventeen years and, with his wife, had always taken a keen interest in local activities. He also came from a family with strong Parliamentary connections and seemed the ideal candidate for this mainly agricultural community. Yet it was PB who appeared to be catching the people's imagination and many of Henderson's meetings were loudly heckled by supporters of the 'Flying Man' as he was dubbed in the constituency. It was at this stage that the 'campaign of calumny' as PB described it, began. According to his account, women were brought down from London and went from house to house to insinuate and assert 'all sorts of vile rumours concerning myself and my wife...that I was an undischarged bankrupt, that I had been flung out of the Navy for many grave misdemeanours, and that I was a spy in the pay of Germany'. Scurrilous handbills on the same lines were also issued but he dealt with these by collecting and redistributing them with the added footnote: 'Mr Pemberton Billing thinks too much prominence cannot be given to this type of electioneering.'

Soon after this episode, a friend in the Air Department of the Admiralty (possibly Murray Sueter himself) told him that he had seen a letter from the East Hertfordshire Unionist Party organiser, Sir John Boraston, to the First Lord of the Admiralty, Arthur Balfour which read: 'I am sorry to trouble you so much about Billing, but he has undoubtedly captured the imagination of the public. The seat is in danger, and unless we can discredit him I fear he will be returned for East Herts'.

It appeared that the Air Department had been asked to search among its files for any information likely to prejudice PB's election chances and his friend thought he should be aware of this. It is to his credit that PB did not use the Boraston letter during his election campaign or stoop to such tactics himself and it was with a clear conscience that his only retaliation was to print hundreds of leaflets, just prior to polling day, urging electors to 'Vote for a Clean Fighter'.

Meanwhile, the national press was keeping a close eye on events at East Hertfordshire. The *Daily Mail* and others under the Northcliffe umbrella firmly supported PB (though he strongly denied suggestions that he was being financed by Northcliffe), while the *Daily News* and the *Daily Chronicle* favoured Henderson. Spies from the opposition shadowed PB and took careful note of all that he said, in the hope that he would make one of his notoriously wild statements which could be taken up and used against him. One very persistent spy followed him everywhere but sometimes found it impossible in his small car to keep up with PB's powerful machine and would arrive too late from one meeting to cover the next fully. Amused by such close attention and no doubt with the intention of embarrassing the opposition, on one occasion PB offered the man a lift to the next meeting and the surprised spy accepted. This gave PB the opportunity to proclaim later, tongue in cheek, that by so doing the man had not only saved important expenditure at a time when there was great need for economy in Government departments, but had also ensured that the Coalition would not now miss a single one of his words.

Polling day, 9th March , turned out fine. Despite all that had gone before, Henderson's supporters seemed quietly confident that, as at Mile End, voters would not desert their traditional adherence to the Unionist party. Those who followed PB appeared even more sure of a victory—even offering long odds that he would be elected by a large majority. He and Dot drove twice around the whole constituency, calling at every polling station along the way and at Bishop's Stortford were disturbed to discover that on the previous night some misguided supporters had smeared red paint and mud over the opposition's committee room, polling station and even private houses, scattering his leaflets everywhere as they did so. This action, he felt, was bound to spoil the image he had been trying to promote of being a 'clean fighter' and might even lose him votes—something which it was later confirmed did actually happen. But at the final count he still managed to top the poll with 4,590 votes to Henderson's 3,559.

All agreed that it had been a hectic campaign and at its close PB was beginning to feel the strain. After the result, with Dot at his side, he acknowledged the cheers of the crowd, proposed a vote of thanks to the returning officer and gratefully retired to a nearby hotel to rest but his constituents discovered where he was and clamoured for him to come out and say a few words. Brief as these were, they evoked more applause and the crowd's sympathy, when he asked if they would be good enough to spare what voice he had left 'to tell them in the House of Commons what has to be done'. It was, however, four days before he was due to enter the House and most of these he spent in bed, recovering from the pace and pressures of the previous weeks.

CHAPTER TEN

T he impact of PB's victory over the party machine was felt throughout the country. All the national newspapers gave space to the results of the by-election and commented upon what they understood to be its implications. Even the staunchly pro-Government *Daily Chronicle* admitted that his success was 'a very remarkable event on which the newly-elected M.P. is entitled to plume himself' and the general feeling was that his achievement was an indication of the public's dissatisfaction with the way the nation's affairs were being handled, particularly with regard to air matters. Many felt that once he entered the House this vital young man would soon bring about changes. His many congratulatory messages echoed this same theme, which was ably and succinctly expressed by one telegram from a well-wisher: 'Delighted the B.P. (British Public) now have PB as M.P'.

After all that had gone before, it is hardly surprising that when he presented himself at the House of Commons for the first time, on 14th March 1916, there was great speculation as to how he would conduct himself. *Punch*'s cartoonist, H.F. Townsend, depicted his arrival at Westminster in a cloud of dust, bowler-hatted and seated in a winged car, sounding his horn at Balfour (First Lord of the Admiralty) and H.F. Tennant (Under-Secretary of State for War) who were shown leaping away in fear of being run down by this impetuous 'Hustler from East Herts'. There was also a description in *Punch*'s 'Essence of Parliament' column by W.A. Locker, describing how ministers passing through Palace Yard on their way to the House had shuddered as they caught sight of the parked torpedo-shaped car. The writer went on to comment that if PB had jumped straight from the steering wheel into the Chamber with his 'eloquence still at white heat' and had managed to get his fulminating message off his chest, strange things might have happened.

It must have been very difficult for PB to have been forced to listen to what he considered interminable ministerial replies to boring questions while he awaited his first summons. He wrote later that on entering the House he had felt almost the same sensations that he had experienced when he first set eyes on the gaming rooms at Monte Carlo. Everything about it seemed so unreal.

He listened with some admiration to the 'subtle way Ministers gave their evasive replies to members' questions' and was amused by the 'apparent somnolence of some of the occupants of the Treasury bench', before his reverie was interrupted by the Speaker's sonorous voice summoning new members to take their seats and he rose to his feet. As he did not belong to any party, he did not have the usual official escort but was accompanied instead by Sir Henry Dalziel, his friend and proprietor of *Reynolds News*, together with a Unionist member, Ronald McNeill. They proceeded to the table in the customary way, three steps at a time, with bows between each. PB signed the book, shook the

Speaker's hand and then slipped out behind the Chair, ran back through the lobby and re-entered the Chamber to take, for the first time, the corner seat that was soon to become notoriously familiar to all his fellow members.

After listening patiently to Tennant giving what seemed to be an endless report on Army estimates, he was on the point of nodding off with the sheer fatigue of the past few weeks when he heard mention of anti-aircraft defences. The Under-Secretary for War was claiming that these had already been completed for London and similar protection would soon be afforded to the rest of the country. The supply of aeroplanes was also ahead of the supply of engines and pilots, despite as many qualified pilots being produced each month, as the total number the country had managed to mobilise at the start of hostilities. At this, PB saw his chance and—much to everyone's astonishment, for it was most unusual for such a very new member to take the floor so soon— he caught the Speaker's eye and within seconds was on his feet making his maiden speech.[1]

For the first six months of the war, he told the House, the air service was 'rich in leadership and poor in material' but during the last six months it had been 'richer in material but infinitely poorer in leadership'. Encouraged by the laughter and cheers that followed this statement, he went on to reiterate all the major points of his election speeches, including the need for an 'Imperial Air Service worthy of our Imperial power' and a plea for more air offensives against the Zeppelin bases. He ended by urging that the bombs which were being stored and due for delivery to many places in Germany should be 'delivered forthwith and without further delay'.

His words were well received and the general impression was that he had made a very creditable debut. The *Daily Mirror* reported later that it was the opinion of several MPs that if he concentrated on the air and 'avoided any crank cliques' he would almost certainly be 'in authority' long before the war was over. Winston Churchill, writing to his wife from France on 25th March, also commented that the speech had struck him as very good and that 'it must disturb the complacency of the Govt.—if anything could.' Clementine Churchill agreed but did not consider that the new MP had sufficient political strength behind him and, in replying, wrote that some people seemed to think PB had an axe to grind, being 'an unsuccessful aeroplane builder' and that, in her opinion, he was 'a rather flashy young man'. Others who shared her views had expected a more flamboyant first speech and were surprised at how nervous he had appeared to be, mopping his brow several times and more ill at ease than on any occasion during his large electioneering meetings. *Punch* summed up his performance by commenting that although the speech had been good, it had not been 'entirely equal to the advance *billing*'.

The following weekend PB went to Hertfordshire to meet his constituents for the first time since his election and bolstered by their

1. See Appendix I.

enthusiasm returned to London with fresh vigour, determined to shake the Government out of its apparent apathy over what he considered to be the urgency of the air situation.

On 22nd March, only eight days after his maiden speech, he startled the House by getting on his feet once more and subjecting members to a lengthy and inflammatory tirade against the Government's handling of aeronautical matters. He criticised those chosen to serve under Lord Derby on the recently inaugurated Joint Services Committee to investigate aircraft construction; the number of expensively trained pilots who were 'quill driving instead of machine driving' in the Air Department of the Admiralty and—warming to his subject—went on to make a strong indictment of the machines being used by the Royal Flying Corps. These, he claimed, were referred to by the pilots as Fokker fodder:

> Every one of our pilots knows that, when he steps into one, if he gets back it will be more by luck and by his skill than by any mechanical assistance he will get from the people who provide him with the machines. I do not want to touch a dramatic note this afternoon, but if I did, I would suggest that quite a number of our gallant officers in the Royal Flying Corps have been rather murdered than killed.

His words were greeted with the shock he intended and when Tennant got up to reply, he chided PB for using the word 'murder' which he said was untrue. But PB again sprang from his seat claiming that if his statement was challenged he could produce evidence that would shock the House. Members immediately cried, 'Do it now!', to which he replied that he would do so at an 'early occasion'.

This time the press reports were not as kind as on the occasion of his maiden speech. The writer of *Punch*'s 'Essence of Parliament' summed up the general feeling:

> Mr Pemberton Billing essayed another and longer flight to-day, but had a good deal of engine trouble...Members became more and more impatient as the orator became more and more dogmatic; and when he rhetorically demanded the name of 'one man to whom we could turn to solve the problem' they derisively chorused, 'Billing!'

But PB was determined to prove his point. He immediately contacted all those friends who had access to official records or were in any way concerned with aircraft, to help him compile a list of flying 'casualties'- aeroplanes and pilots—and to keep him informed of anything else that might be useful in putting his case before the House. Most agreed to do so and during the days that followed naval officers, civil servants, journalists and pilots were to be seen walking boldly into the Temple, making as if to pass Elm Court and then, after a quick look around to make certain they were not being followed, darting quickly up the stairs to PB's apartment. He had several rooms with interconnecting doors leading onto the outer hall and two or three people could often be at Elm Court at the same time without even being aware of the others' presence. PB, of course, revelled in such subterfuge and Dot appeared to enjoy it as much as her husband, often helping to extricate his informants from potentially tricky situations which, on occasions, almost took on the character of a French farce.

On 27th March, five days after his 'murder' speech in the House, he was the principal speaker at a large London meeting concerned with air-raid protection in that city and used the opportunity to reply to his critics. He began by saying that he had gone to the House to tell the truth 'because that is the only place in England where the Defence of the Realm Act does not handcuff your hand or seal up your lips' and no power on earth was going to prevent him from saying what he knew to be true in the interests of his country. He then gave his well-known views on defence and aircraft generally and finished his speech on what later proved to be an extraordinarily prophetic note. After forecasting how towns and cities could be laid waste overnight by increasingly powerful bomber forces, he pointed out that the aeroplane could nevertheless become a 'winged messenger of peace', for: 'Before many years have gone by, perhaps one blow such as I suggest will be struck and when a terrible and bloody war is brought home to them in *hours* instead of years, the people of the world will rise up and say, "This must not be"'. He then foresaw a 'council of nations' meeting together so that this could be brought about.

Afterwards, he told reporters that he had been invited to address similar mass meetings all over England and Scotland but that his next engagement would be at the House of Commons for, armed now with the evidence he had promised to produce, he was ready to lay some disturbing facts before its members.

There were distinct shuffles of impatience all round the Chamber when he rose from his corner seat the following day but a hush soon fell when he began to read out the posthumous letter of a young pilot to his father, complaining of the condition of both the machines he had been flying and the aerodrome from which he had taken off. The young man's father had sent it to PB, saying that this was not the only time his son had written of the problems he and his fellow aviators had been encountering and that, in his opinion, if pilots were not killed in action it only seemed a matter of time before they would meet with an accident.

Slowly and dramatically, PB then went on to read a long list of fatal accidents attributed to faulty machines and at the close it was apparent that he had achieved his desired effect. The *Daily Telegraph* reported next day that his speech 'clearly demanded an answer and the Government showed great discretion in promising an immediate inquiry.'

However, the promise alone of a judicial inquiry was not enough for PB.

Until a date for this had actually been fixed, he was determined to turn every Tuesday's question time into an 'Air Debate' which resulted in him becoming known to his fellow members as not only the 'Member for Air' but 'Hot Air'. *Punch*'s Parliamentary correspondent claimed that he would hardly be surprised if the next time he walked down Whitehall, he found sandwichmen out with boards inscribed:

> Westminster Aerodrome
> Flying every Tuesday
> Billing breaks all records...

In his first three weeks PB had 'displayed unprecedented dexterity in catching the Speaker's eye and filled more columns of *Hansard* than many members had managed during long Parliamentary careers'. On 12th April, a week later, the same correspondent reported that:

> At the close of his by now customary catalogue of defects in the air service he offered personally to organise raids on the enemy aircraft Headquarters and believed he could bag as many Zeppelins in a day as the Government could in a year by their present methods of misplaced guns and confidence.
> Tennant will confer with Pemberton Billing as to how to make best use of his services. It seems the House for some time will have to do without its weekly lecture...Under the shadow of his impending bereavement, Mr Tennant is bearing up as well as can be expected.

Outside Parliament, PB was equally busy. At the beginning of April he took over some old offices in the Market Square in Hertford for use as the headquarters of his recently founded 'Imperial Air Convention', having already published forms in local and national newspapers inviting signatures pledging support for his campaign. Thousands responded and those without the published forms sent postcards instead. Nearly 5,000 attended an inaugural meeting for covenanters at the Albert Hall in early May and he was called on to speak at further gatherings throughout the country for by that time there were few people in Britain who were not aware of PB and the cause for which he was fighting.

When he made an appearance in court on 6th April, for driving his car at the 'excessive speed' of 40 mph in Chiswick the previous January, even the magistrate, on fining him £5, could not resist quipping: 'Remember you are not in space when in Chiswick High Road, but on land'.

Two months later he was in court again, this time for driving at over 20 mph in Hampstead. He was actually 'speeding' at 43 mph—the highest ever proved in that court, according to the magistrate—and this time the penalty was £8. These were the first two occasions on which he had been caught breaking the speed limit, but they were certainly not to be the last, for it was not in PB's nature to tackle anything at a leisurely pace, particularly when he was behind a wheel.

Although he usually enjoyed the publicity that followed most of his activities, less welcome was the series of biting personal attacks made on him by the *Daily Chronicle* in the middle of April. The first, on the 17th, was headed:

The Genius of the Air
Amazing career of Mr Pemberton Billing M.P.
'The-Little-Hawk-Which-Is-Always-Hunting-Trouble'

The article began:

> The member for East Hertfordshire has been hailed as a new driving force in politics and the 'King of the Air'. While waiting for the organisation of a great air department which would overshadow the Navy, with a Cabinet Minister at its head, he has created an unofficial Ministry on his own account.
>
> He has taken the air under his wing, tours the country, and has a staff at work getting information for him. He shocks the House of Commons by his audacity and language—a new kind of Parliamentary Billingsgate—and he drags information out of Ministers for his own satisfaction and, incidentally, for the information of the enemy.

There then followed a short resumé of his life, which the newspaper had obtained from an article PB had recently written in a South African magazine, in which he had revealed that the Zulus had a special name for him—'Twumatish'—which meant 'the-little-hawk-which-is-always-hunting-trouble'. In the days that followed the *Daily Chronicle* set out to prove that he was still living up to this name and that many of his claims relating to his knowledge of aircraft and air matters were unfounded. 'His talents as an inventor are unquestioned', the newspaper reported, 'but if not restrained [he] would design machines more original than practical... Mr Pemberton Billing's reputation as an air-strategist is based chiefly on things which he has said, not on things which he has done'.

The third article in the series was written by F.W. Lanchester, an engineer with aeronautical experience, who made no secret of his dislike of PB and his tactics. This dated back to the time he had endeavoured to address a meeting on behalf of the Government candidate during the East Hertfordshire by-election and had been howled down by PB's supporters for daring to criticise some of their hero's wilder statements. In the *Daily Chronicle* article, Lanchester had an opportunity to publish a detailed refutation of some of PB's extravagant claims which he said had all been noted during his electioneering speeches by a 'competent reporter'.

Headed 'Mr Billing as Inventor', the article was divided into columns headed 'The Invention' and 'The Fact'. It discounted PB's claims for his quadruplane, his statement that he had served 'eighteen months of the war on two fronts' and his supposed conversations with Steel-Maitland prior to his election. Lanchester followed this with a challenge to PB to substantiate all his statements and withdraw or acknowledge his alleged misrepresentations.

It was unfortunate that, just prior to this attack, wide coverage had also been given in the national press to the arrest of a former sub-lieutenant in the RNAS—Edgar Charles Middleton—who at that time was writing a regular column for the *Daily Mail* under the pseudonym of 'Air Pilot'. Middleton was charged, under the Defence of the Realm regulations, with trying to obtain information on aircraft and air defence from RNAS officers stationed at Dover and was purported to have said that he was there on behalf of the *Daily Mail* to 'do a spot of spying for Mr Pemberton-Billing'. As that paper had supported PB throughout his campaign, it seems more than probable that the editors knew of Middleton's intention but PB himself denied all knowledge and was disturbed to see placards issued by *The Globe* on 13th April which carried the words:

Spying for Pemberton-Billing
Airman arrested.

He immediately notified his solicitor, who began a libel action against the proprietors. This set in motion a long train of events which gave more fodder to those bent on damaging PB's popular image.

When the Lanchester article appeared in the *Daily Chronicle* on 19th April, PB felt the time had come to make a strong protest within the House of Commons, particularly as he was convinced that these attacks were politically inspired. He decided to take up the challenge contained in the article and on the day it appeared, tried to answer—in the Commons—some of the charges made against him .

He began by saying that he had come to realise that any man who dared to attempt independently to enter public life, in answer to what he believed to be 'a call of duty and a desire to do some real public service', was immediately met by the 'attack of inspired newspapers and the allegations of interested parties'. He stood for something far greater than his personal reputation but as this was essential to his work he felt he owed it to his constituents not to allow his character to be besmirched without attempting to answer his traducers.

After pointing out that he had suffered similar scurrilous attacks during the East Hertfordshire by-election, he quoted as an example the letter he had up to that time refrained from using, in which Sir John Boraston had requested Balfour to help provide information that could be used to discredit him. He also referred once more to the conversation he had had with Steel-Maitland before the Mile End election, which Steel-Maitland had consistently denied.

Answering some of the matters raised regarding the aircraft he had built and the factory at Woolston, he revealed for the first time that on entering

Parliament, in order to avoid any accusations that he was out to profit personally from his air campaign, he had sold his shares and severed all connections with his old company. Negotiations for this were still in progress but he expected these to be completed soon.[2]

The House listened intently to what he had to say and far from making him new enemies, more members joined him in pressurising the Government into setting up a Committee of Enquiry into the administration of the flying services. As a result, the first meeting of the select committee took place on 16th May, under the chairmanship of Mr Justice (Sir Clement) Bailhache, KC. Its members consisted of three eminent barristers, two engineers and a general—which provoked a witty cartoon in *Punch* showing a quartet of bewigged barristers gathered round an aircraft, all talking at once about matters which were clearly beyond their comprehension.

The Admiralty somehow managed to get the RNAS excluded from the enquiry and, according to PB, this was the result of Balfour threatening to resign as First Lord of the Admiralty should the flying wing of the Royal Navy be investigated—which seemed to be tantamount to an admission that there was indeed some cause for concern. But whatever the reason for the exclusion, it meant that the Committee's whole attention was devoted to the charges made against the Royal Flying Corps, which PB felt was an unsatisfactory situation. He was therefore in two minds whether to attend at all and was not present for the first few days of the enquiry and the press made great play of this.

The *Star* reported that 'The Pemberton-Billing gas bag has not taken long to burst ... Lord Northcliffe must find a new tool'. The *Pall Mall* commented that he was 'like a boy who, after playing with matches, had run away from the consequences'. In Parliament, both Tennant and Bonar Law remarked on his failure to appear at the Committee which had, after all, been appointed solely to investigate his charges. After this, of course, he realised he had no choice but to attend. Wishing, however, to arm himself with the latest information, he travelled over to France one weekend to visit front-line airfields and managed to persuade some French aviators to take him over the battlefield at Verdun.

Major-General Sir David Henderson, Director of Military Aviation at the War Office, was also present at the enquiry, together with a staff officer who was an eminent lawyer in civilian life. Both took part in the cross-examination of the various witnesses which included Lord Montagu, Joynson Hicks, Charles Grey and others who had supported PB's allegations of maladministration of the air services. When his turn came, PB began by producing, as he had

2. The new company, Supermarine Aviation Ltd., was registered on 20th September, 1916, with Scott-Paine as its Managing Director, and it continued to function successfully under his direction. When it passed into other hands in 1923, Scott-Paine went on to found the equally successful British Power Boat Co. Ltd., in 1927, of which he remained Chairman until his death in 1954.

previously done in the Commons, a long list of pilots he claimed had been 'murdered rather than killed'- through bad design or construction of aeroplanes and engines or by being asked to fly in unsuitable conditions. He also put forward a number of suggestions for improving equipment and for better employment of both men and machines, gleaned, no doubt, from his visit to France.

Although none of the Committee was experienced in aviation matters, according to Charles Grey its members showed an 'intelligent understanding' of the extensive subject they had to consider and approached it with open minds. PB, however, did not agree. It was, in his opinion, the usual white-washing affair, designed to let down as lightly as possible those who had been responsible for a policy which had produced such a grave state of affairs in France. Each of the instances he had quoted was explained away by saying that the pilot had been killed in the 'normal execution of his duty' or by the 'fortunes of war', neither of which he believed. When the final report was published in December, it urged that the Cabinet should create an Air Board for the express purpose of supervising the design, construction and production of aeroplanes, engines, armament and all other material for both the flying services and for output to be coordinated so that the competition between the Navy and the Army should not result in one service getting better supplies than the other.

The Air Board came into being in 1917 and the various committees set up by it eventually persuaded the Government to form a proper Air Ministry in 1918, with Lord Rothermere as its first Minister. It was PB's proud and understandable boast, that had it not been for his persistent agitation, more airmen's lives might have been lost and the formation of the Air Ministry and subsequently that of the Royal Air Force might not have come about. Certainly his scheme for an Imperial Air Service—which he published on 12th April 1916 and set out in a memorandum to Asquith at that time—bore resemblances to that eventually worked out for the formation of the Royal Air Force some years later.

But long before this all came about there was to be a change of Government, a new Prime Minister and a great deal of violent and acrimonious discussion amongst servicemen and politicians, in which PB continued to play a prominent part.

CHAPTER ELEVEN

PB spent the 1916 Parliamentary summer recess in his constituency, speaking at meetings and working out final details for a project he hoped to launch that autumn. Some months earlier he and Dot had moved into the large, Victorian Hertford House on the outskirts of the town and in May had completed the sale of their old home near Southampton. Consequently he was able to remind his constituents at meetings that summer that he had—as promised at his election—actually come to live among them. He had also carried out his other commitment to them to wake up the Government with regard to the air services. He told his eager listeners that his job in that direction was not yet over but they could always look to him for help with any other matters that concerned them. So long as he remained in Parliament he would never sacrifice his freedom of speech and action on their behalf and one day, he hinted, he would expose all the scandals he had discovered within the House since becoming a member—if only to let the British people know why the war was costing them six million pounds a day.

On 7th October, just three days before Parliament resumed sitting, he launched from Hertford his own 'independent *viewspaper*, as opposed to a *newspaper*', entitled *The Imperialist*. He had been warned by his friends that such a journal was doomed to failure, particularly when paper was short and manpower and distribution problems abounded, but the first editorial outlined his reasons for not heeding their advice:

> At a time when the destiny of our Empire is in the hands of an enfeebled and irresolute Government, the political dregs of an effete Party system; at a time when public opinion is largely formed by subsidised journalism, and a doped Party Press, surely no excuse is necessary for founding this journal, in the title of which I have endeavoured to convey its character and ambition.

It was designed, he continued, to criticise and attack men and matters 'without fear or favour' and through its pages he hoped to fight for 'an Imperial policy based on the broadest and most generous lines'.

The first issue had eight pages and included among its proposed regular features: 'The Great Game and How it is Played' (PB's own Parliamentary page); 'Things that matter' (paragraphs of pungent and pointed comment); 'Before Passing Sentence' (Lord Haldane of Cloane was the first of those chosen as candidates for prosecution); 'Women and Work: in the World, in the Home, in the Garden' and 'The Open Road' which provided several columns of sporting activities.

It was rumoured at the time that Lord Northcliffe, who had backed PB in his air service campaign and intensely disliked the Asquith Government then in power, funded the early editions of *The Imperialist*. There have also been suggestions that Lord Beaverbrook may have given financial backing at a later stage. There is, however, no evidence that either is true. From the outset, PB ran the whole enterprise himself, on a subscription basis of 8 shillings a year and without any additional income from advertising, for he claimed that only in this way would *The Imperialist* be free to speak the truth.

National pride and the generally held belief in the strength of Britain and its Empire provided at this time a much needed anchor in a troubled world, nurtured as many were by tales of Colonial adventure from such venerated writers as Kipling, a long-time favourite with PB. The fear that all this might now be slipping away through Government mismanagement of the war no doubt had some bearing on the interest *The Imperialist* created and as subscriptions began to pour in, PB felt even more confident of its success.

In the first flush of excitement over his new enterprise, he hired a large and expensive staff of writers but as time went on and costs began to mount, both staff and pages were cut. He tried to write a considerable amount of the material himself but found this left him little time to oversee the remainder. Consequently the journal soon began to attract writers who saw a means within its pages to put across their own particular, often sinister, ideas and attitudes and at first PB appeared naively unaware of their intent.

Following the excitement of launching *The Imperialist*, he returned, somewhat reluctantly, to the House of Commons after the summer recess: 'I felt uncommonly like a boy returning to school—most unwillingly' he commented in his column. Nevertheless the Commons proved a source of constant copy for him and he quickly realised the power that could be wielded by his pen—in addition to the means it provided for quoting in full his own speeches in the House.

In November, he published a scathing feature on Asquith and this brought a large, complimentary postbag to the offices of *The Imperialist*. One correspondent summed up the feelings of many others when he wrote that the leader of the Coalition Government and his Cabinet should be turned out 'neck and crop' before things got worse. PB obviously agreed and on 2nd December hinted that 'strange and sinister' things were being planned at Westminster:

The Parliamentary situation to which he referred was soon revealed when, on 7th December, after much inter-Party and Cabinet bickering, David Lloyd George finally emerged as the new Prime Minister. PB was pleased since he had written the previous week that although Lloyd George was not the realisation of the ideal *Able-Man* he was as near that realisation 'as we are likely to get in our present condition of social and political turpitude'. He had 'brains and bowels, was a glutton for work, possessed wonderful tact, indomitable determination, together with the personal charm of the Celt, which also provided him with that subtle but indispensable faculty for getting the very best out of the men he worked with and infusing them with his own enthusiasm'.

Once the appointment had become known, PB optimistically told his readers that he felt it would now be a new game in which party politics would be subordinated to national interest, although everything would depend on the new players and on their loyalty to the captain of the team.

He was extremely flattered by a highly complimentary letter from a Kensington correspondent who had suggested that the fall of the 'late and never-to-be-lamented Government' was due to criticism in the House and press, which 'dated from a certain election at Mile End and the later results at East Herts'. These, the writer claimed, had proved to those Members of Parliament who were would-be critics of the Government that, far from losing their seats, they might strengthen their hold on their constituents if they stood up for them, instead of 'lying down under the heel of the Coalition'. As for the press, the correspondent continued, though every journalist longed to write what he felt, every editor 'cringed before the Censorship and spake pleasing words to the Coalition'. Then a paper called *The Imperialist* appeared, 'full throttle and with its cut-out open—like a certain black and brazen car of which we wot—at any rate in East Herts., Southampton and London', and this paper was not suppressed: 'It was not even held up in its career by the sheltering palm of the majestic constable on point'.

So pleased was PB by the suggestion contained within the letter that his actions had been instrumental in effecting such changes that he could not resist reprinting it the following week—'in response to many requests'. He also gave a further account of his activities during the previous Parliamentary session. He had asked upwards of 200 questions on a wide range of topics apart from those connected with air matters, from 'the grievances and disabilities' of the Police Force to defective grenades and shells and why enemy banks and businesses were still allowed to operate in the country. From the weighty correspondence that followed, it was clear that his readers were suitably impressed.

The Coalition Government—mainly composed of Unionist members— was faced with a bleak outlook at the commencement of 1917. There was stalemate in France, the Navy seemed incapable of providing adequate protection for merchant ships against the German submarines and food was becoming short. The politicians were blaming the generals for the disastrous casualty figures and the generals were denouncing the politicians for their mishandling of the whole war situation. Amid such a climate of intrigue and general dissatisfaction the readership of the new publication continued to increase. Meanwhile PB himself suffered a temporary set-back with the hearing of his libel action against *The Globe*.

The case began in the King's Bench Division before Mr Justice Darling on 31st January, which happened to be PB's thirty-sixth birthday. Acting for him was a fellow Member of Parliament, Ellis Griffith, KC, while another Member, Rigby Swift, KC appeared on behalf of *The Globe*. The newspaper admitted publication of the offending placards but claimed that the wording 'spying for Pemberton Billing. Airman arrested' was not defamatory but a fair and accurate report. Ellis Griffith disagreed, saying that the placard had appeared at an unfortunate time for PB (just prior to the Air Enquiry) and that there was absolutely no truth in the suggestion contained within the article that the airman, Middleton, was in Dover to question servicemen on behalf of his client. The airman had denied all the charges and the solicitor from the Admiralty had also insisted that the man was not using the word 'spying' in the ordinary sense of the word. He had told three naval officers that he was in Dover on behalf of the *Daily Mail* 'to do a bit of spying for Mr Pemberton Billing, MP'.

From the minute he began his cross-examination, however, it appeared that Swift was not only intent upon clearing his clients of the charges against them but, as a Conservative Member of Parliament, was equally determined to humiliate and discredit one of his party's most trying adversaries. Even the Judge, who for ten years had also represented the Conservatives in Parliament, seemed to encourage the air of cynical frivolity that reigned over the proceedings but despite most of the quips from the bench being directed towards him, PB somehow managed to keep his normally fiery temper under control.

He was questioned closely by Rigby Swift about his interests in air matters and his allegations in the House that General Henderson's statements on the efficiency and training of the Air Service were untrue and was asked about the Air Enquiry itself. PB was then foolish enough to claim that the members of the Committee did not know one end of an aeroplane from the other and consequently had been 'victimised' by the Government. This gave Swift the opportunity he sought: 'How were they *victimised*,' he asked, 'besides having to listen to you for nine days?' PB ignored the laughter this evoked and replied: 'Parliamentary committees usually find in favour of the persons who appoint them'. When Swift then asked if it were by such statements he had made his reputation, PB answered that his reputation had been made by speaking the truth, which gave Mr Justice Darling the opening for a snappy rejoinder: 'Tell the truth and shame the Government'.

On the second and final day of the case, the cross-examination became even more aggressive and intense. Swift read out the derogatory articles that had appeared in the *Daily Chronicle* the previous year and questioned PB about the passages concerning his interest in the air services. Asked if he had ever built a successful aeroplane, he replied that he had and that one 'broke all records for its horse power'. 'Didn't it break itself, too?' asked the defending counsel sarcastically, adding provocatively: 'I see one of your election cries was 'Vote for Pemberton Billing and no more air raids'...*panic* in Potsdam when Pemberton Billing is elected a Member of Parliament!'

PB was by this time fighting to regain his composure: 'But I got the Government to adopt my system and there *were* no more raids, strange to relate'. Judge Darling could not resist this: 'Don't you remember how the sun shone on one occasion, Mr Swift?' Defending counsel quickly picked up the drift: 'I also remember a man as great, trying to make the tide stand still and it did not'.

Rigby Swift in his closing address to the jury said that PB had used his position in the House of Commons to 'charge those who held the highest positions in the command of the Air Service with criminal negligence, official folly and entire ignorance of their business'. PB had earlier made the mistake of confirming in the witness box that he had a photographed copy of the Boraston/Balfour letter in his possession and, when asked to produce it, had said it had since been destroyed. This gave Swift the opportunity he needed for he used PB's failure to produce the letter as a means of casting doubt on his credibility generally.

In his summing up, Mr Justice Darling said that PB had complained he had received no apology for what had been done by the defendants, but he had never given them a chance, for he had sent in his writ the very day after the alleged libel had been published. As for the letter that had been alluded to in the case, the mildest word that could apply to a man in a Government department who, according to PB, had obtained a photograph of a confidential document addressed to a Cabinet Minister and handed that photograph to someone outside who was carrying on a campaign against the Government, was 'spy'. PB had declined to mention the man's name. Why? Was it more in the interests of the man in question than in the interests of King and Country?

Thus was the whole case very neatly turned against PB and the jury returned a verdict for *The Globe*, with costs.

The press covered the case fully and the *Daily Chronicle* used the opportunity to attack its rival Northcliffe Newspapers for their previous support of PB and congratulate itself on providing, through its previous articles, 'much of the illuminating cross-examination to which Mr Billing was subjected'. The writer suggested that when PB had been 'boomed' by wild men and sensational journalists and Northcliffe had run him as a candidate, his opinion of his own importance became so inflated that it was necessary in the public interest to let his real character, capacity and standing be known. 'His case is a lesson and a warning—a lesson to him and a warning to others'.

PB was determined to fight back. At a meeting in Hertford the day after the case concluded, he announced his intention of resigning his seat and then seeking re-election in order to prove that at least his constituents retained their faith in him as their Member of Parliament. Later he began to have second thoughts, for he heard that both Liberal and Unionist candidates were already poised to contest his seat, so he decided instead to hold votes of confidence meetings throughout his constituency.

These were not as well-attended as he had hoped and many of those who came refrained from voting on whether or not he should remain as their MP. Even so, he judged that on a show of hands a fair majority wished him to stay and quickly announced this to the press, which prompted *Punch's* Parliamentary correspondent to report: 'A few days ago, after a violent collision with Mr Justice Darling, Pemberton-Billing announced his intention of resigning and submitting himself for re-election. But since then we have been given to understand that a vote of confidence proposed by P., seconded by B. and carried unanimously by the hyphen, has convinced him that resignation can wait.'

But it was not only his constituents that he had to convince. There were also the many hundreds of readers of *The Imperialist* to be reassured. On 10th February he published the first instalment of a brief autobiography with the idea of counteracting what he termed 'the case for the Persecution' and the lies that had been put out about his life. In his foreword he wrote: 'As anyone who has studied *The Imperialist* must be satisfied, I have at last a fixed purpose in life... to *attain* and *maintain* the Supremacy of our Empire in the Air, and to further our National and Imperial interests in every other direction.' Unless within the following fourteen days, he told his readers, he had received some indication of their support, he intended to cease publication of *The Imperialist*. It was not a commercially viable undertaking and if they did not believe in him or in what he wrote, there was no point in continuing what had been, and still was, a heavy drain on his resources.

The following week, in addition to the second instalment of his life story, he published an open letter: 'I am not an emotional person as a rule, but it is utterly impossible for me to express how deeply I have been touched by the many hundreds of letters that have reached me within the last few days.' Of these, not one apparently expressed the wish that he should wind up the publication and, shaky as his financial resources may have been at that time, it seems unlikely that there had ever been any real intention on his part of doing so.

Confident that he now had the support of his constituents and the readers of *The Imperialist*, he returned to the House. There may have been groans from the Government side when he continued to seize every opportunity to rise from his corner seat and put forward his views, but other members undoubtedly enjoyed his presence, for he always added colour to the proceedings.

He was certainly not a figure to be ignored, wherever he went. With his exceptionally tall lean frame, monocle and unconventional clothes—usually of his own design—he was distinctive enough, but when he was seated in his racy car, with his yachtsman's cap or bowler hat set at a jaunty angle, he never failed to draw the public to him. Despite the defamatory stories that continued to circulate about him, for many he still represented the brightest hope in what at that time was a troubled and uncertain world.

With others in the House, including Winston Churchill, he continued to press for sustained and wide-spread air raid reprisals on Germany and wrote in *The Imperialist* of 2nd June: 'The loss in life and limb would be small in comparison with the millions of men who have already been killed, the many millions more who have been maimed, blinded, crippled, broken for life in the long drawn-out horror of this war'.

A few days later he asked Bonar Law to move an early adjournment of the House to enable members to debate such a proposition but this was refused by the Speaker, who told him that he must give notice of such a proposal in the usual way. PB, however, remained standing and despite noisy interruptions from other members, attempted to carry on speaking. He was given several more warnings and eventually was named by the Speaker for not respecting his authority. One of the members from the Government benches went over to PB, hoping to persuade him to leave the Chamber quietly and at first he appeared to agree, but at the Bar he turned once more to address the House. This was too much for his companion, who then seized him firmly by the arm and escorted him out of the Chamber, amid laughter and ironic cheers.

Later in the month, after there had been a particularly bad raid on London, he tried to bring up the matter of retaliation again. According to *Punch*'s correspondent, PB 'bounced up and down like a Jack-in-the-Box' in an effort to stop the Prime Minister discussing the raid in a secret session. 'There must be a limit to this', the Speaker was reported as saying and the correspondent added: 'The member for East Herts is presumably the "limit" referred to'.

But soon he was in trouble again. This time he accused War Office officials of issuing false casualty figures following air raids, which prompted a fellow Member, Lieutenant Colonel Archer-Shee, to spring to the defence of the officials and charge PB with being 'caddish and most offensive'. PB then challenged Archer-Shee to repeat such personal remarks outside in the Lobby and the two later met in Palace Yard where angry words were exchanged and a scuffle ensued. Fortunately, the police intervened before any real harm was done and *Punch* chronicled the affair in its own inimitable manner: 'Palace Yard was the scene of the combat, which ended in Archer downing Pemberton and Billing sitting on Shee. Then the police arrived and swept up the hyphens'.

The following day a question was asked in the House about what action, if any, was to be taken over the 'disgraceful fracas' that had taken place. The Secretary of State for Home Affairs, Sir George Cave, caused great amusement by replying that the Statute of Henry VIII—under which any person found guilty of malicious striking in the King's Palace whereby blood was shed 'was to have his right hand stricken off and be condemned to prison for life'- was repealed in 1828 and any charge of assault would have to be made by the person aggrieved. 'In the circumstances it is not proposed that the police should take any proceedings'. There were doubtless several members who, by the close of 1917, wished the statute had still been in force, so weary were they becoming of PB's constant interruptions.

Outside Parliament, he had been equally busy during that year. On 29th July, following two large meetings in London, he had founded a new pressure group, the Vigilante Society, to 'promote purity in public life' and he genuinely believed that through this, and the pages of *The Imperialist*, corruption, malpractice, underhand tactics and political intrigue could all be exposed. The society also proposed that nine Vigilante Parliamentary candidates should be adopted 'to safeguard the interests of the people, as opposed to that of the politicians'. Those chosen would be expected to sign a solemn declaration that, if elected, they would not accept 'any honour, title or dignity, or any office or place of profit in the disposal of the Government'. They would neither do anything which might place them under an obligation to the Government or any other political party, nor use their positions as Members of Parliament to further their own interest. Membership, according to the constitution, would be open to all British subjects, irrespective of politics, religion or race.

The first Vigilante candidate to be nominated for election to Parliament was Alfred Baker, the Town Clerk and former Mayor of Hertford, who was put up to fight a Government candidate at a by-election at East Islington in the autumn. Baker was also the first treasurer of the Vigilante Society and had helped draft its constitution. Unfortunately, he never had an opportunity to test the pledge he had signed, for—despite the combined efforts of PB, *The Imperialist* and his fellow members of the Vigilante Society—he failed to be elected and the Government candidate won the seat by a large majority. Undaunted by the defeat, PB was quick to point out in the next issue of *The Imperialist* that this had been due to the Government candidate using as his election theme something for which he himself 'almost alone' had long fought—the promise to secure air raid reprisals against Germany.

After further enemy raids on London PB had protested in the House that the defence system was inadequate and suggested a novel warning system. Twenty or thirty small captive hydrogen balloons could, he told Members, be ready at different points to be raised to about 1,500 feet whenever a raid was likely. A long blast on the siren could give a thirty-minute warning of the enemy's approach but if a raid was even more imminent, streamers could be let free from the balloons, together with a second siren blast. As was to be expected, such a suggestion was received with derisive laughter, but his idea may well have sown the seed for the use of barrage balloons as a means of defence twenty or so years later.

By the end of 1917 he was receiving regular information from Vigilante members concerning various scandals and intrigues they had managed to unearth and some of these he brought before the House. In December he sought the reassurance of the Government that a serving officer who had signed an affidavit about 'graft, blackmail and complaints against the Ministry of Munitions' would not be posted back to France. The case, he told the House, was one of blackmail and corruption, of charging a £5 commission on every tractor coming into the country. All departments, he alleged, had known about this for fourteen days and were trying to hush it up, even the Minister of Munitions (Winston Churchill) knew of it.

The following day he pursued the matter again, saying that it had come to his notice that a trader in Queen Victoria Street was paid a commission, by way of a bribe, in order to get priority for importing these tractors from the United States. A statement had been made by the trader to the officer concerned and, having exhausted all other means of redress, the officer had asked PB to lay the situation before the House of Commons. On this occasion, much to his delight, he did receive a satisfactory reply from the Government benches. Far from sending the officer back to France, said Churchill, his leave had been extended so that he could help with any further enquiries and the whole matter would be thoroughly investigated.

As the year progressed, with no improvement in the war situation, PB was not alone among those Members of Parliament who had become disillusioned by Lloyd George and the promises he had made on assuming office. On 3rd November he wrote in *The Imperialist*: 'We may have disliked and distrusted Mr Asquith because he told us nothing. We may yet live to despise and dismiss Mr Lloyd George because he has told us much...that was not true!'

Small wonder that after this and other inflammatory and embarrassing statements by PB, both in his journal and in the House of Commons, Lloyd George should have been quoted as saying: 'This man is dangerous. He doesn't want anything.' PB, it seemed, had no intention of being diverted from uncomfortable issues by the promise of honour or office.

CHAPTER TWELVE

In the early months of 1918, PB moved the headquarters of the Vigilante Society from Hertford to St James's Place in London. On 9th February, after continued pressure from members, he changed the name of *The Imperialist* to *The Vigilante*. This was, he wrote, a concession to the members 'and *not*, let me hasten to add, to the outcry of miserable Little Englanders who purposely misread into the word "Imperialist" a policy of blood and iron'.

He had never believed that the mere lust of conquest had been the ideal of those who had founded and built the British Empire: 'That is why I believe our Empire will endure if we who have inherited it realise what responsibilities it entails upon us.' But more than the publication's title underwent a change at this period, for new contributors were introducing subtle differences within the journal itself.

In January PB engaged as his assistant editor a young American, Captain Harold Spencer, who claimed he had been invalided out of the British Army in September of the previous year after working for a time with the Secret Service in the Balkans and Adriatic. On their first meeting a few weeks earlier, he had told PB of the great injustice he had suffered resulting from his discovery of certain matters the authorities had tried to hush up. PB had been intrigued by his story and, as Spencer had seemed altogether down on his luck, had offered the American a job—little guessing that the reason for his discharge from the Army was that he was suffering from 'delusional insanity'.

A recently recruited member of the Vigilante Society, who was also a regular contributor to the magazine in early 1918 was another ex-officer, Captain Henry Hamilton Beamish, who had first brought PB's attention to the alleged case of corrupt dealings over the importation of tractors. It was he who had also been responsible for introducing Spencer to PB after encountering the American at a political meeting. Unfortunately, it was not long before Beamish's articles began taking on a virulent anti-Jewish slant and PB had to tell him in the strongest of terms that such pieces were unacceptable. When an elderly doctor, John H. Clarke, another new contributor, started using the magazine to put forward his own sinister ideas and anti-Catholic views, PB had no hesitation in telling him that he found these abhorrent as would, he felt, the majority of his readers. He had always prided himself on having a good rapport with people of every class, colour or creed and wanted *The Vigilante* to reflect this. Unfortunately he soon found himself too occupied with other matters to oversee all that went into the magazine and began leaving more and more to his plausible new assistant editor.

Anti-German feeling had gathered momentum over the past year as casualties mounted and the war continued to go badly for Britain and her allies.

PB had strenuously taken up, in Parliament and his magazine, the matter of the German and Austrian banks being allowed to maintain branches in the UK and stressed the danger of letting alien businessmen move freely about the country. When Spencer revealed some disturbing information he had supposedly discovered concerning certain German activities in Britain, PB thought the time had come to take strong action, particularly as Spencer's revelations had a bearing on another matter that had been troubling him for some time.

He had always been aware of the fact that there were several practising homosexuals and paedophiles holding positions of trust and power in military, naval and political circles and, although he had always considered himself to be broad-minded about the sexual mores of others, he felt that in wartime, with the laws as they then stood, these men presented easy targets for blackmail by enemy agents. He had often considered making this matter one of the subjects for his 'purity in public life' campaign and Spencer's revelations about a book he purported to have seen while on service now appeared to provide him with the means. Accordingly, on 26th January, he allowed an astonishing article to be published, mostly written by Spencer but under PB's name, in what was to be one of the last issues of *The Imperialist*. Headed *"The First 47,000"* it began:

> There have been given many reasons why England is prevented from putting her full strength into the War. On several occasions in the columns of *The Imperialist* I have suggested that Germany is making use of subtle but successful means to nullify our efforts. Hope of profit cannot be the only reason for our betrayal. All nations have their Harlots on the Wall but...it is in the citadel that true danger lies. Corruption and blackmail, being the work of menials, is cheaper than bribery. Moreover, fear of exposure entraps and makes slaves of men whom money could never buy. Within the past few days the most extraordinary facts have been placed before me which co-ordinate my past information.

There followed the bizarre story of how an officer on special service had discovered a book, in the possession of a certain German Prince, which had been compiled by the German Secret Service from reports by its agents:

> who have infested this country for the past twenty years...spreading debauchery of such lasciviousness as only German minds could conceive and only German bodies execute.

The book was purported to have begun with instructions regarding 'the propagation of evils which all decent men thought had perished in Sodom and Lesbia' and listed the names of 47,000 English men and women. These covered, according to the article:

> Privy Councillors, youths of the chorus, wives of Cabinet Ministers, dancing

girls, even Cabinet Ministers themselves while diplomats, poets, bankers, editors, newspaper proprietors and members of His Majesty's household followed each other with no apparent order of precedence.

Lists of public houses and bars which had been successfully 'demoralised' were given in the book and 'to secure those whose social standing would suffer from frequenting public places', comfortable flats had been acquired and furnished in an erotic manner.

The article went on to report that this 'Black Book of Sin' also revealed that agents were enlisted in the Navy with their own specific instructions. Bars were established in Portsmouth and Chatham where the stamina of British sailors could be undermined and under the guise of indecent liaison information could be obtained about the disposition of the Fleet. Even the 'loiterer in the streets' was not immune: 'Meretricious agents of the Kaiser were stationed at such points as Marble Arch and Hyde Park Corner' and details were given of the 'unnatural defloration of children who were drawn to the parks by the summer evening concerts'.

The greatest danger was to be seen in the reports of those agents who had obtained *entrée* to the world of high politics where 'wives of men in supreme position were entangled and in Lesbian ecstasy the most sacred secrets of state were betrayed', while 'the sexual peculiarities of members of the peerage' were used as a leverage to open fruitful fields for espionage. The article continued:

> There are three million men in France whose lives are in jeopardy, and whose bravery is of no avail because of the lack of moral courage in forty-seven thousand of their countrymen...numbering among their ranks, as they do, men and women in whose hands the destiny of this Empire rests.

Such a statement must have caused distress to many readers with loved ones in France, particularly as it was written within six months of the overwhelming casualties, mud and horrors of Passchendaele. But the writer appeared to ignore this in his final paragraph:

> As I see it, a carefully cultivated introduction of practices, which hint at the extermination of the race, is to be the means by which the German is to prevent us avenging those mounds of lime and mud which were once Britons...all the horrors of shells and gas and pestilence introduced by the Germans in their open warfare would have but a fraction of the effect in exterminating the manhood of Britain as the plan by which they have already destroyed the first forty-seven thousand...it is a terrible thought to contemplate that the British Empire should fall as fell the great Empire of Rome, and the victor now, as then, should be the Hun. The story of the contents of this book has opened my eyes and the matter must not rest.

PB and Spencer expected the article to produce a libel case against *The Imperialist* and copies were sent to several ministers and other Government officials in the hope that one or another might indirectly implicate themselves in a scandal by taking the journal to court but, knowing what was at stake, none dared risk such a challenge. The majority of readers, however, did take the matter seriously.

The romantic novelist, Marie Corelli, who was a founder member of the Vigilante Society and a regular correspondent to the journal, saw an announcement in the *Sunday Times*, referring to 'Two private performances for members only' of Oscar Wilde's *Salome*, due to be held at a London theatre on 7th and 14th April under the auspices of J.T. Grein's Independent Theatre Society. This immediately prompted her to send a copy to PB, with the note:

> Dear Mr Billing,
> I think it would be well to secure a list of subscribers to this new 'upholding' of the 'Wilde' cult among the 47,000.
> Yours sincerely
> Marie Corelli.
> P.S. Why 'private' performance?

Jack Grein was Dutch by birth but had been a naturalised British subject for twenty years. He was a drama critic for the *Sunday Times* and produced plays with his Independent Theatre Company which were generally considered to be daringly modern. He had founded the German Theatre in London, receiving an honour from that country for doing so, and many of the plays he performed were German translations. Although *Salome* had previously been performed on the Continent, it had been banned in Britain by the Lord Chamberlain—hence the tickets for this particular performance being by subscription only. The role of Salome in the production was to be taken by the Canadian dancer, Maud Allan, whose scantily clad appearance in another version of the Biblical story had caused a minor sensation, and there was much speculation as to whether she would be performing a similar dance of the seven veils before the members of the Independent Theatre Society.

Rumour had it that Maud Allan was lesbian and Margot Asquith's enemies said that she was, too. The fact that Maud Allan had been invited to 10, Downing Street when the Asquiths were in residence was remembered by Spencer when the Corelli letter arrived. Without consulting PB, who was ill in bed in Hertford at the time, he began fitting together what he saw as a veritable jigsaw puzzle of intrigue.

Here was a man, he figured, with obvious German sympathies, putting on a dubious play in the nation's capital by a well-known homosexual, with a lesbian in the chief part, who had friends in high places. Having sought the advice of a doctor friend as to a suitable anatomical term to imply lesbian tendencies, on 16th February he published, on the front page of *The Vigilante* (as the journal was by then named), the following paragraph:

The Cult of the Clitoris

To be a member of Maud Allen's [sic] private performance in Oscar Wilde's 'Salome' one has to apply to a Miss Valetta of 9 Duke Street, Adelphi, W.C. If Scotland Yard were to seize the list of these members I have no doubt they would secure the names of several thousand of the first 47,000.

When Dot saw the paragraph and the implication was explained to her she was horrified and told her husband that this time his journal had gone too far. Many of his friends agreed and pointed out that, as it bordered on the obscene, it could lead to criminal proceedings being taken against him for issuing, as its proprietor, an indecent publication and the penalties were heavy in terms of fines and imprisonment. PB immediately stopped Spencer from enlarging on the story the following week, but by then it was too late.

In early March the solicitors of Grein and Maud Allan started criminal proceedings against PB for the obscene libel implied in the title 'The Cult of the Clitoris' and he was served with a summons. Afterwards, however, they were shown a copy of *The Imperialist* for 26th January, which explained the reference to the 47,000, and an additional summons was served on him for defamatory libel. He made two appearances before a crowded Bow Street Police Court at the beginning of April, at which he conducted his own spirited and lengthy defence. In the process he managed to trap Grein into admitting his German connections and even to describing as 'poetic' some of the more salacious passages of *Salome*, which PB chose to read out to the Court. On the evidence of the prosecution, however, the Magistrate decided to commit PB for trial at the Old Bailey.

When asked if he wished to make any statement before committal, he claimed that there was no evidence of any libel. The paragraph referred to simply stated that Grein and Maud Allan were engaged in presenting a performance which was calculated to appeal to moral perverts and those practising unnatural vices. In the performance Salome was depicted as fourteen years old. The exhibition of an overpowering passion of a child of tender years for the prophet John the Baptist, culminating (as Oscar Wilde intended it should) in the representation of a physical orgasm, was calculated to attract moral perverts who, whilst they might not be prepared to go to such extremes, would nevertheless seek satisfaction in watching it. He held that any public man who refrained through lack of moral courage from criticising and attacking such matters had failed in his duty.

He appeared in court not only as a Member of Parliament but as President of the Vigilante Society, founded to promote purity in public life.

Neither he nor his Society posed as guardians of public morals but those who practised the vices to which reference had been made left themselves open to blackmail and this had national and international significance. He had not alleged that either Miss Allan or Mr Grein were members of the cult but they had chosen a moment when the country's very existence was at stake to produce the most depraved of the many depraved works of a man who had already suffered an extreme penalty at the hands of the law for practising this unnatural cult.

He finished his long discourse by saying that he welcomed the opportunity he now had of putting his case before a jury at the Old Bailey and hinted at other evidence which he intended to submit there. After such a titillating performance, the atmosphere at Bow Street was electric. Both press and public agreed that, if this was a foretaste of what was to come at the Central Criminal Court, nothing would keep them away.

PB made his first appearance at the Old Bailey on 24th April and immediately asked for an adjournment in order to enter a Plea of Justification, to substantiate what had been written and prove that the offending piece was published for the benefit of the public. The Judge agreed to his request on condition that he undertook to make no further comment on the legal proceedings, either in Parliament or in his journal, and the trial was postponed until 29th May.

It has been suggested[1] that the real reason for PB's wish for a postponement was that he had just been invited to join the generals at the War Office in a plot to thwart Lloyd George's plans for secret peace talks with Germany at the Hague and to oust the Prime Minister and his Coalition War Cabinet from office.

The generals had continually blamed the Government for the disastrous manner in which the war was being conducted and in particular for the situation then existing in France where, despite frequent warnings, the shortage of British troops and supplies had given the Germans the opportunity to advance successfully in their long-planned spring offensive. One of Lloyd George's sternest critics, Lieutenant Colonel Charles à court Repington, the military correspondent of the *Morning Post*, had many powerful friends and influential contacts in neutral Holland and it was doubtless through them that he first heard of the moves afoot to hold peace discussions, under the guise of German plans for an exchange of prisoners of war. He also knew that the War Office and Admiralty were opposed to any such exchange, for they believed the Germans would immediately return their repatriated soldiers and sailors to action. Nor would the military or naval officials be in favour of an ignoble peace for, with the war situation as it then was, any talks aimed at ending hostilities would clearly be to Germany's advantage.

1. According to Michael Kettle's book of the trial, *Salome's Last Veil: the Libel Case of the Century* (Granada Publishing, 1977)

The generals were more for hanging on in anticipation of the promised American military support and figured that the downfall of Lloyd George would enable them to take over the War Cabinet and bring the conflict to a successful end, without interference from what they considered to be his amateur strategy. It was to help achieve this, according to Michael Kettle, that on 23rd April Repington is purported to have approached PB at his London apartment with the suggestion that he ally himself to the generals' cause and help frustrate the peace moves, by using the Old Bailey as a platform to discredit certain politicians, provoke more anti-German feeling in the country and mount fresh attacks on supposedly subversive alien activities. Repington would have known by this time that at least one prominent Anglo-German family living in England was directly involved with the Hague discussions. In return, PB is believed to have been promised the full support of the *Morning Post*, for Repington's editor H.A. Gwynne had already crossed swords on several occasions with Lloyd George over his policies and would not be sorry to see his departure from Downing Street.

Whatever the truth behind these theories, highly feasible as they undoubtedly seem to be, it is certainly true that PB was aware of what was going on at the Hague and disapproved of the way the talks were being handled. He probably knew also of the moves being made behind the scenes in Government and party circles, aimed at ridding the House for ever of the fiery member for East Hertfordshire, who continued to make a nuisance of himself and ask too many awkward questions. Early in May a letter addressed to PB arrived at the office of *The Vigilante*:

Grosvenor Court Hotel
Davies Street
London, W.1.
6th May, 1918

Dear Mr Billing,

Please forgive the gross impertinence of an entire stranger in writing to you. But although I'll admit until a few weeks ago I'd really never heard your name (I've not long returned to England), you've touched upon a subject very near to my heart—by that I mean you are endeavouring to carry out (and I'm sure you will succeed) a work my godfather spent his life trying to complete. He tried very hard to save England from becoming a 'glorified Berlin' where its morals were concerned.

Many times he was quite rudely informed he was a 'fool'- and of course the war was not on then; had it been so and had there been so much evidence at hand he would probably have been successful, but unfortunately he died before this present crisis. But *you* are alive and *you* can carry on, and any help I can give you I'll most willingly offer. It may be a strange subject for a woman to choose, but I just feel I want to carry on the work he commenced.

I am so *glad* you inserted that paragraph in *The Vigilante*. Of course you were sued for libel, because when you wrote it you apparently 'hit home', and I consider always that a libel action is merely a cloak of pretended innocence for the apparently guilty. Also I will say that I do not consider you were nearly severe enough when you said the 'first 47,000'—I should have written the 'first 470,000'. There are places around here not a hundred yards from my hotel where the disgusting devices adopted by the late Oscar Wilde are hourly carried on, and considering the main people concerned in these places, or to put it plainer, the principle habitués, are men high up in naval and military circles, then one wonders how many of our state secrets and army positions are exposed under these conditions. I say most vehemently that if these conditions were to cease our armies would be in much better positions.

One cannot write everything on paper, it would take too long, but if you'd care to take luncheon with me any day this week or next, I may be able to tell you many things that may interest and help you.

May I wish you all success.

Yours very sincerely,

(Signed) Eileen Villiers-Stuart

Eileen Villiers-Stuart was a young socialite in her late twenties. For five years, until his death in action in 1917, she had been the mistress of the Hon. Neil Primrose—Lord Rosebery's son and former Chief Whip to Asquith. During this time, in March 1913, she had married a bus driver from Putney, Percival Douglas Bray, but the pair separated by mutual consent after only a few weeks. This seems to indicate that it had been an arranged marriage to cover some embarrassing situation, perhaps the birth of a child of whom Neil Primrose was the father. Hearing that Bray had been killed in France in 1914 and with Primrose by then abroad, she had married a Captain Percival Villiers-Stuart of the Cheshire Regiment in July 1917. When he was sent overseas, she left his home in Ireland and returned to her previous high-flying life in London.

She claimed later, in a sworn statement on 27th June 1918, that she had written the letter to PB on instructions from 'certain Political Associations in London' whose sole idea had been to trap PB in a compromising situation, which would not only damage his character but put an end to his political career. The plan was for her to meet him and persuade him to visit a male brothel in Duke Street off Grosvenor Square where he would then be secretly photographed. However, on meeting him for lunch a few days afterwards, she had been 'so impressed with his sincerity and the purity of his motives' that she had decided to throw over her employer and give PB all the information she could for use in his defence.

Although she strongly denied it later, she was apparently so enraptured by him at this first meeting that she very quickly succumbed to his physical charms and did, in fact, become his mistress for a while. There also appears to be some family evidence to show that PB had another similar, though transitory, liaison just prior to the trial. A young Christian Science fanatic, whose name was never revealed, came to his apartment with the express purpose of having a child by him.[2] It has also been suggested that she had been delegated by her movement to do so, in order that PB would have an heir to carry on his campaign to save the country—and the world—from some of its evils. How she managed to get him into bed on those terms, particularly as she was said to have been 'very plain', is difficult to imagine and one can only suppose he found the idea behind her proposition too flattering to resist.

After entering his Plea of Justification on 21st May—claiming that he was not guilty and that the alleged defamatory statements in the indictments were true—all seemed set for PB's appearance at the Old Bailey eight days later. In the intervening period, it was agreed in Cabinet that the British delegates would meet their German counterparts at the Hague, for the supposed discussions on an exchange of prisoners, Lloyd George having earlier in the month managed to overcome a strong vote of censure in Parliament concerning his general handling of the war. However, only a few days before PB's trial was due to begin, the Germans launched an offensive in France and were making strong headway towards Paris.

For the British public, to whom the war seemed never-ending, this latest news was almost too much to take and it must have been a relief for many to read the full press coverage of the high jinks at the Old Bailey, during the six days of what *The Times* later referred to as 'A Scandalous Trial'.

2. She did, in fact, have a son whom she showed to PB after the trial, but he had no interest in continuing the relationship. Years later, mother and son visited the small school run by the husband of PB's sister, Mary. She recognised the woman's name—though she did not tell her so—and was relieved when her brother's rather sickly offspring was not, after all, accepted at the school.

CHAPTER THIRTEEN

As in his previous libel case against *The Globe* which he had so ignominiously lost, PB found on his arrival at the Old Bailey on 29th May that the Coalition party machine appeared to be once more arrayed against him. Even the rota of judges had been altered so that his old adversary Darling, now Acting Lord Chief Justice, could take the case. Leading the Prosecution for the Crown was a Conservative Member of Parliament, Ellis Hume-Williams, KC, whose instructions from the Cabinet members of his party appear to have been the same as those given to Darling, namely to prevent at all costs PB prejudicing talks at the Hague by revelations about Germans or aliens in Britain and to scotch any attempt to name those in high places who might be among the 47,000 in the alleged 'Black Book of Sin'.

PB insisted on once again conducting his own defence and was surprised to learn that the three charges would be tried separately, beginning with those concerning Maud Allan, for he was hoping to save repetition of evidence by including Grein's case at the same time. He was also hoping to use the Dutchman's German and alien connections as a means of giving credence to his statements that there was cause for concern over allowing such people to move freely about the country. As it was, the first charge read out that day was that PB had maliciously published a false and defamatory libel in *The Vigilante*, implying that Maud Allan was a lewd, unchaste and immoral woman, who was about to give private performances of an obscene and indecent nature 'so designed as to foster and encourage unnatural practices among women' and that she associated herself with persons addicted to such unnatural practices. To this, he pleaded 'Not Guilty' and offered his Plea of Justification.

He then surprised the court by making a formal objection to Darling, claiming that the Judge had frequently brought an atmosphere of levity into the cases he had tried. He was about to refer to his own case against *The Globe* as an example, when Darling sharply interrupted: 'The fact that you take an unreasonable view of me cannot be any reason why I should not try your case, because by the same process you might exhaust every judge on the Bench.'

PB again protested that all he wanted was a fair trial but his plea was ignored by Darling who ordered the case to proceed. Had the Judge known what was in store for him, he might well have decided differently. As PB had chosen to defend himself, he could not be sent down for contempt of court without the case being suspended and as it progressed, it became increasingly obvious that Darling was quite incapable of controlling the extraordinary events taking place in his courtroom—let alone curbing some of PB's more outrageous behaviour, audaciously directed towards the press and an enthralled and crowded public gallery.

Two further charges were then read out: that he had maliciously published a false and defamatory libel against Jack Grein and an obscene libel against Maud Allan. To the former he again pleaded justification but to the latter, for which he knew there could be no justification, he entered a plea of 'Not Guilty'.

In opening for the prosecution, Hume-Williams said that the libel against Maud Allan was of 'such a gross kind...so outrageous in its form' that proceedings had been taken under criminal law instead of by the institution of a civil action. He then outlined her successful career as a dancer and gave a brief description of *Salome*—'written by that extraordinary, perverted genius, the late Oscar Wilde'. Although, he continued, the idea of Salome kissing the dead lips of the severed head of John the Baptist—which in life had refused her kiss—may be unpleasant to some, there was not one word in the play which would suggest 'even to a prurient mind' anything but the passion of a woman for a man and the tragedy which so often resulted. Nor was there anything in it to suggest the horrible vices referred to in the libel. He then touched briefly on the implication behind the offending title 'The Cult of the Clitoris' and on the article that followed concerning 'the 47,000', after which Maud Allan took the stand and PB began his cross-examination.

He started by saying he intended to prove 'certain perverted tendencies' were inherited. Then, much to Maud Allan's understandable distress, he produced a book and asked if a photograph appearing in it was that of her brother. The man depicted had, it appeared, been executed in San Francisco some years earlier for murdering two young girls in a church belfry and outraging them after death. Although visibly shaken by this unexpected revelation of such a painful family matter, she admitted it was indeed her brother but courageously stood up to PB's further questioning and the implication that her performance in Wilde's play—parts of which he read out to the court—was in any way indicative of inherited sadism.

On the following day PB announced that he intended to prove further that *Salome* was an impure and immoral play, calculated to harm public morality, and would be calling on medical evidence as to its true meaning and intention, as conceived by Wilde. He also intended to prove the existence of the 'Cult' referred to in the *Vigilante* article and to call the writer of both that and the piece about the '47,000', together with several other witnesses. But it was Eileen Villiers-Stuart who was first to be summoned. By this time, according to the statement she made later, Eileen's former employers had threatened her with her life unless she returned to them but she was determined to go ahead, whatever the cost.

PB started by questioning her about the existence and contents of the Black Book, despite objections from the Judge and Prosecuting Counsel that it must be produced before it could be used as evidence. He countered this by saying he could prove that the book did exist, even though he did not know its present whereabouts. Eileen claimed that she had been shown it in the summer of 1915 by Neil Primrose over tea with their friend, Major Evelyn Rothschild, in the Hut Hotel at Ripley in Surrey. Primrose had first heard of it through Captain Spencer in May of that year and had somehow managed to get hold of it. She had turned its pages and had it explained to her by the two young officers. They had then driven back to London, where they had left her in order to return to their duties, taking the book with them. Both men had since been killed in Palestine.

PB's next question, 'In action? In the ordinary way?' was so heavy with insinuation it was sharply overruled by the Judge. So instead he asked if she could remember any of the names mentioned in the book. At this, Darling quickly intervened with a further reminder that the book would have to be produced before its contents could be used in evidence but PB chose to ignore this. Was, he asked Eileen, the paragraph on 'The First 47,000' justified by what she had seen in the book? Again the Judge protested, but PB's next question was treading on even more dangerous ground: had Eileen's life ever been threatened as a consequence of what she knew? She replied that it had. Here the Prosecuting Counsel sprang up to object, saying that such a question had nothing whatsoever to do with the case. Darling agreed, sternly reminding PB that he had already been allowed a great deal of latitude and that, if he insisted on conducting his own case, he must do so according to the rules of evidence. If he did not know how, he should have employed someone who did.

This comment infuriated PB, for he felt the Judge was, once again, deliberately setting out to antagonise him. White with anger, he pointed his finger at Darling and all but shouted at Eileen:

'Is Mr Justice Darling's name in the book?'

'It is,' she shrieked back.

Then she turned to the Judge and, still at the top of her voice, told him that the book *could* and *would* be produced and that, while he sat there, men were being *killed*.

Above the hubbub that followed, she and PB continued their shouted exchanges:

'Is Mrs. Asquith's name in the book?'

'It is.'

'Is Mr Asquith's name in the book?'

'It is.'

'Is Lord Haldane's[1] name in the book?'

'It is.'

This caused Darling to intervene once more and he asked Eileen to leave the box. 'You dare not hear me,' she retorted—and stayed where she was. The

1. Asquith's Lord Chancellor from 1912-15, who was dismissed because of his alleged German sympathies.

Judge told PB he was determined to protect people who were not present in court and forbade him to continue this particular line of questioning.

PB was obviously still angry but he paused for a second before questioning Eileen about the letter she had written to him on 6th May which—he hastened to tell the court—had a definite bearing on the case. The Judge immediately asked for the letter to be produced if it were to be used as evidence but refused to let PB leave the court when he asked if he might fetch it from a safe nearby. PB therefore asked Eileen an alternative question: did she know about houses in London 'conducted for the purpose of practising criminal and unnatural vices?' When she said she did, he asked if any were conducted for 'political reasons' and she mentioned the house of a Lally Highfield at 11A, Duke Street, near Manchester Square. This brought about another heated exchange with Darling, who threatened to end the case if PB did not conduct himself properly. Eileen then cheekily interposed with the comment that if PB were convicted she would carry on in his place and for this was promptly ordered to leave the court.

Spencer was next to be called. He claimed that in 1913 he had been a member of the International Commission to Albania and became ADC to the German Prince William of Wied at his palace in the Albanian capital of Durazzo. He left the country in September 1914 but before then had seen some of the Prince's private papers. The book containing the 47,000 names was among those documents belonging to German Intelligence. The Prince had shown it to him and they had discussed it at some length. He had made notes from it and these were in store with his luggage. He had later reported his discovery of the book to the Commander-in-Chief of the Adriatic Fleet who, he believed, had passed the information to Admiralty Intelligence. On his return to England he had also laid the information before the Foreign Office and Military Intelligence but, he told the court, 'there was great political pressure brought to bear and I was warned that if my reports were published the whole fabric of Government would be undermined.' Until he met PB he had come to the conclusion that the Germans had such a grip on affairs, nothing could be done.

He then revealed how he had discovered a 'clique', while serving as a political officer in Italy in the autumn of 1917. This clique was engaged, he claimed, in trying to restore Asquith to power and make a peace on German terms. From this revelation he went on to divulge the names of other well-known people he claimed were involved, including that of Mrs George Keppel, the mistress of the late King Edward VII, who travelled to Holland as one of the messengers between those concerned in the conspiracy in both England and Germany.

The whole courtroom was agog as he then told of how he had discovered that the German Secret Service was working without hindrance in Rome and that his reports were not being forwarded by the British Embassy there because the British Ambassador was being blackmailed by the Germans. When he had tried to convey these findings back to England through a commander aboard a British battleship, he had been advised to return to his old GHQ at Salonika. However, on arrival he was immediately ordered to serve in the trenches. When he refused, he was bundled into an ambulance, taken under armed guard to a small hut on a hilltop and locked up. Here, he was eventually seen by some medical officers who said he was suffering from hallucinations and was placed in an asylum, from which he subsequently escaped and returned to England. A medical board of three doctors had then examined him and pronounced him fit, but after he had completed a short training course with the Royal Flying Corps, the War Office had decided, after all, to invalide him out of the service.

This was all far removed from the business in hand but the public gallery lapped it up. The whole story was rather reminiscent of *The Stealthy Terror*, a popular novel of the time by John Ferguson, which told of how the Foreign Office put away, as subject to 'hallucinations', certain Secret Service men who had learned too much. But the Judge still let Spencer ramble on.

When it was the turn of Hume-Williams to cross-examine him, Spencer's stories became wilder than ever. He said that, on returning from Albania, he had actually met the Prosecuting Counsel at a dinner party and during a private conversation had told him that British Secret Service agents who knew too much were being marooned on lonely islands on the orders of British Government officials acting for the German Secret Service. At this, the astonished Hume-Williams strongly denied ever having met Spencer before.

The next day three doctors followed Spencer into the witness box on PB's behalf, to give their views on what they considered to be the depraved sexual implications in *Salome* and the effect its performance might have on certain unstable people. Dr Arthur Serrell Cooke was a medical practitioner who had dabbled in psychiatry, particularly sexually-orientated disorders. Under PB's astute questioning, he managed to convey that both Jack Grein and Maud Allan showed signs of certain perversions; that sadism was a congenital, hereditary disease and that the play *Salome* was full of implications which healthy-minded people would reject with disgust but which could delight those who were perverted.

Sir Alfred Fripp, the King's personal surgeon, said that he had come to the court to give evidence from a sense of duty. Although he had not actually read the play, he could see that certain passages, to which his attention had been drawn, could 'pervert the onlooker'. There was, he agreed with PB, moral and sexual perversion in all grades of society in England, 'even in the ruling and governing classes'. PB's next question was even more loaded: 'Do you know any members of our governing classes who *are* moral perverts?'

'How does that arise?' interrupted the Judge.

'It arises,' replied PB, 'on my Plea of Justification with regard to the first 47,000, which number in their ranks Privy Councillors, youths of the chorus, wives of Cabinet Ministers, dancing girls, even Cabinet Ministers themselves.'

Here Hume-Williams protested that this was totally irrelevant to the case but PB had made his point.

The third doctor, Leonard Williams, had a Harley Street address and moved in fashionable society circles. He agreed with the previous witnesses that *Salome* was a sadistic play and that it was detrimental to the public welfare, disgusting and calculated to harm public morals.

PB thought the jury had been impressed by the eminent medical men's evidence and arrived at the Old Bailey on the following morning, the fourth day of his trial, with some confidence. Mrs Keppel and several of her friends were in court when he arrived. She had come, her barrister informed the Judge, to deny emphatically Spencer's allegations. She had not been in Holland since war broke out, neither had she seen any German agent, nor had she acted as an emissary between England and German agents abroad. The Judge refused, however, to allow her to make this statement personally, saying that only evidence which had a bearing on matters relevant to the trial itself could be accepted. Nor would he allow either the prosecution or PB to bring any War Office files into court to prove statements about Spencer's sanity, unless the medical officers concerned could also be produced. PB therefore proceeded to call one of his star witnesses, Lord Alfred Douglas, who had translated *Salome* from Wilde's original French into English.

Since Wilde's death, Lord Alfred's attitude towards his former intimate had changed and his love for Wilde had been replaced by a bitter hatred. In reply to skilful questioning by PB, he told the court of the 'diabolical influence' Wilde exerted on everyone he met, describing him as 'the greatest force for evil in Europe during the last 350 years'. The play *Salome* was intended to be an 'exhibition of perverted sexual passion excited in a young girl' containing 'sodomitic passages cloaked in flowery language'. Wilde, he said, had written the play after studying the work of Krafft-Ebing. In his evidence, Dr Serrell Cooke had also referred to the findings of this Viennese professor, who had been the first to investigate the sexual aspects of cruelty and given "sadism" its name. Serrell Cooke had even suggested that Wilde must have had the professor's book, *Psychopathia Sexualis*, in front of him all the time he was writing the play.

Lord Alfred's cross-examination led to some angry exchanges with the Prosecuting Counsel and the Judge, when old letters between him and Wilde were read out by Hume-Williams. The letters, Lord Alfred claimed, had been stolen and he made it clear that he would not be cross-examined in such a way as to help out 'the gang of scoundrels' that the Counsel was representing.

PB then questioned him about one particular letter written to *Truth* magazine after Wilde's trial, twenty-five years earlier. In this, Lord Alfred had claimed that the acts which resulted in Wilde's incarceration were practised by 'men in the best society, members of the smartest clubs, Members of Parliament, Peers, etc' and that at Oxford he had 'known hundreds...not to mention a sprinkling of Dons'. Lord Alfred agreed that what he had written then was a fact and that it was 'a great deal truer now'. He also realised that, because of the possibility of those concerned being blackmailed, there was some political significance attached to such behaviour.

The drama critic of the *Morning Post*, G.E. Morrison, who had already written a strong condemnation of *Salome*, was next on the stand and reiterated the comments he had already made in his review, that the play was a 'bizarre melodrama of disease'.

He was followed by a Jesuit priest, Father Bernard Vaughan, who also denounced the play as being a 'constructive treason against the majesty and sanctity of God'. Much to the court's astonishment and the delight of the public gallery, on leaving the box the priest turned to PB and, raising his hand in a gesture of blessing, said: 'May God prosper your cause. You are surely doing His work, my son'. Even PB was temporarily taken aback and could only murmur, 'Thank you, Father' before tackling his next witness.

Dr John H. Clarke was the Vigilante Society committee member whose strange, anti-Catholic articles had been challenged by PB when they first appeared in his magazine. He agreed that the publicising of Oscar Wilde's writings at such a time was 'the work of no friend of England'. Another medical practitioner, Dr Arthur Everard, appeared next and agreed with his colleague that *Salome* was 'a most abominable and blasphemous production'. A similar view was taken by the final witness that day, Bernard Weller, the assistant editor of *The Stage*. By this time it was midday and PB pleaded that he had a violent headache and was too ill to continue. It being a Saturday, the Judge was only too happy to agree to an adjournment over the weekend.

When the case resumed the following Monday, before an even more crowded courtroom, Darling revealed that he had been the recipient of many abusive letters containing accusations against those involved, together with other communications seeking to influence his judgement. One particular postcard he had received contained a libellous attack on a witness and he intended to send this to the Public Prosecutor. At this, PB immediately sprang up to say that he had suffered in the same way and that Eileen Villiers-Stuart had also been sent an anonymous message that she would be shot from the public gallery should she again appear in the witness box. After Hume-Williams added that Maud Allan, too, had received several obscene communications there was a frisson of excitement throughout the court. The trial's fifth day certainly promised to be as eventful as the others.

When PB announced that he had decided to call Jack Grein to the stand as one of his witnesses, Darling reminded him that legally he could not now cross-examine Grein, nor discredit his evidence. Undeterred, PB tried instead to embarrass Grein with probing questions concerning a Government subsidy to present English plays for performance in neutral countries and his meetings with Robert Donald[2] at the Ministry of Information about those selected for performance in Holland and Scandinavia. In fact, as PB knew full well, the subsidy had been hurriedly withdrawn by Beaverbrook, the Minister— presumably for fear of any repercussions—after reference was made to it at Bow Street. Prosecuting Counsel quickly objected to the matter being brought up again and Darling agreed it was irrelevant to the case. PB therefore asked for his opinion on the nature of Wilde's play and, after some discussion, Grein said that he looked on *Salome* as essentially 'a work by an English pen in the spirit of Eastern art' and that personally he had never found any of the material offensive.

It was Eileen, however, who once more caused a sensation on her return to the witness box. She revealed that in May 1916 she had tried to pass on her knowledge of the Black Book to none other than the Leading Counsel for the Prosecution, Hume-Williams. He had told her, she said, that there were 'too many people involved for anyone to make a personal sacrifice by exposing it'. There were, she claimed, two other people present at the time, her husband and a Mrs Wynne (a very intimate friend, it later transpired, of Hume-Williams). At this point the Judge suggested that Hume-Williams might like to pass the rest of the cross-examination over to his junior, Travers Humphries. But Eileen had another shock in store for the court. She went on to make the astonishing statement that both Neil Primrose and Evelyn Rothschild had actually been 'murdered' because they knew of the book and its contents[3] and followed this by saying that she had also seen Grein's name in the book as one of the German agents in England.

She then claimed that she had been told by Primrose, shortly before he went to Palestine in the late summer of 1917, that the book was back in Berlin in the possession of a former Prussian guardsman. (This was a hint at an acquaintance with Count William Bentinck, whose castle in Holland was to be the venue for the forthcoming discussions, supposedly about an exchange of prisoners.)

After she had been further cross-examined by Junior Prosecuting Counsel, Darling asked Eileen some searching questions about her marital status. She confirmed that she had married for the second time in July 1917, her first husband, Percival Douglas Bray, having been killed in France in the first month of the war. She had met Neil Primrose in 1912 or 1913 and understood that he had married in 1915. She and PB were puzzled by the Judge's interest and neither guessed that the postcard Darling had passed to the Public Prosecutor was the reason, or that Eileen would soon be only too aware of its contents.

The Judge then closed the cases for both the Prosecution and the Defence

2. Robert Donald was also editor of the *Daily Chronicle* and an old adversary of PB.
3. This was later strongly denied by their commanding officer, who claimed they had died while leading their men with great gallantry under Turkish fire.

and proceeded to rule on exactly which of the published words had constituted the libel against Maud Allan. In his opinion, these were 'The Cult of the Clitoris' and the first sentence of the paragraph which stated that the performance of *Salome* was to be privately shown. Taken together these implied that it was an indecent play to be performed only in secret. The libel did not cover the article on the 'The First 47,000'.

'Am I to understand,' asked a bemused PB, 'that I am not able to make any reference to the evidence which has been brought forward in connection with that book in my address to the jury?'

'I have said what I have said,' Darling replied. 'I have told you and I hope you understand it, that it is absolutely unnecessary for you to prove the truth of your plea with regard to those matters.'

So PB now had to justify the truth of what had been written in the paragraph heading and in the first sentence of the piece in *The Vigilante* and prove that both had appeared for the public benefit. He paused for a second and then, turning to the jury with his most appealing smile, began his final address:

> We have come at last nearly to the end of the trial which, I am sure, has been a strain on all of us... I have undertaken and accepted responsibility for a libel—because it *is* a libel on somebody—I have accepted responsibility for something I did not write and of which I knew nothing until eight or nine hours after it was published and issued, because I deemed it in the public interest to do so.

If the accusations were untrue then the appalling rumours with which the country was becoming surfeited should be denied in a public place and what better place than a criminal court of justice? If they were true, then 'the light of day should be let in'.

He made further references to the:

> mysterious influence which seems to have dogged our footsteps through the whole conduct of the campaign... which, after three and a half years of war, keeps German banks still open in this country, leaves Germans uninterned ... and for two and a half years has paralysed the Air Service and prevented us raiding Germany.

PB was obviously not going to waste such an opportunity to air his other favourite themes.

'What is the position in France to-day?' he asked. 'It is worse than in August 1914'. Using all his acting skills to advantage, his voice heavy with emotion, he proclaimed: 'The best of the blood in this country is already spilled; and do you think I am going to keep quiet in my position as a public man while nine men die in a minute to make a sodomite's holiday?'

This was strong stuff and totally contrary to the Judge's ruling but he was allowed to sail on, without interruption. He told of how he had first published *The Imperialist* and *The Vigilante*, at an annual loss of about £5,000, in order to attack vice and corruption in high places and he did not lose £5,000 a year 'just for the privilege of libelling people'.

Despite all that had been implied before, he then denied that he had ever suggested that Maud Allan was a lesbian, only that she pandered to others who practised such unnatural vices. The real issue, he asserted, was not whether he had libelled Maud Allan but whether *Salome* was a decent or indecent play and whether it was in the public interest that it should be produced. 'Compare the paragraph with the play itself. Is there anything in that paragraph one half so indecent, one half so revolting, as any one passage...from that play?'

When he went on to attack the Prosecuting Counsel for the way Lord Alfred Douglas had been treated in the witness box and accused the Judge of bullying, Darling intervened to reprimand him sharply and threatened to expel him from court if he did not behave himself.

His last fervent plea to the jury brought a great burst of cheering from the public gallery:

> I ask you to send me away from this place with the confidence that a verdict of twelve of my countrymen will give me to carry on the very heavy task which, in the interests of my country, I have seen fit to commence.

He had scarcely given the proof necessary to justify the libel on Maud Allan, but felt reasonably sure that he had gained the jury's sympathy, yet he was only too aware that the following morning it would be the Prosecuting Counsel's turn and he knew how easily attitudes could be changed by skilful rhetoric.

On the sixth and final day of the trial Hume-Williams began his summing up by reminding the jury that it was not the play that was being tried but the personal attack on the character of Maud Allan. If PB believed that there were so many men and women corrupted by sodomy and lesbianism and under the domination of the Germans, he should be allowed to conduct his campaign in his own way but not 'march to success upon the ruins of a woman's reputation.'

It was not unlikely, 'considering what we know of German ways and German thoroughness', that a list did exist of people in prominent positions in England, or that Spencer saw it, but 'out of that truth the whole of this imaginative superstructure has grown'.

At this point, fearing the Prosecuting Counsel's summing up was going too well, PB began interrupting at every opportunity. The Judge once again rebuked him for his behaviour but, skilled barrister that Hume-Williams was, he soon turned the interruptions to his own advantage:

> Gentlemen, I want you to understand this, and Mr Pemberton Billing may interrupt me every other word and every moment, I intend to say it and to lay it before you. This is not an accidental libel...It is a deliberate attack upon the fair fame of an innocent person and everything proves it.

He then gave a very telling summary of PB's tactics, saying that he did not think it would be proper to conclude without reference to the way in which PB had chosen to conduct his case or the objects he had in view.

> Perhaps it is not a bad idea instead of having an Advocate...to come into Court yourself, particularly if you are a Defendant, if you have got certain gifts of speech, if you have been, as Mr Pemberton Billing is careful to tell you he has been, an actor for four years. You will probably be able to impress the jury... that you have got a great grievance, and the first thing you do to make it effective...is to insult the Judge. Then get the jury to believe that you are not being fairly treated. Juries are always sympathetic... The next thing to do, of course, is to outrage every single rule for the proper conduct of the case. Sneer at the rules of evidence. Say as often as you can to the jury, 'Oh, I know nothing of the law, I know nothing of the rules of evidence... The plan adopted in this case is to introduce as many names as possible of people who are not represented and have nothing to do with the case, and throw at them as much mud and dirt as you can possibly get into your hands and go on doing it.

It was all so close to the truth of what had been happening over the last few days that PB's only means of defence was once again to divert the jury's attention by asking why the prosecution had not called those people mentioned by his witnesses. With great satisfaction Hume-Williams was able to throw this back at him as being 'yet another instance of dishonest interruption'. PB knew perfectly well that, although he had given their names, these people could not be called to give evidence because they had nothing to do with the trial. He had intimidated everyone connected with the case and created an atmosphere, with his friends in the gallery and his followers outside, that was solely calculated to intimidate the jury.

Even worse than his attacks on public individuals, insults to the Judge and dirt thrown at public men, was the piece of evidence he had put to Maud Allan about her brother being a murderer and his later stated intention of proving that sadistic tendencies ran in the family:

> Whatever the result of this trial may be, this fact, which happened years ago, and which she and her family would gladly forget...was thrown in her face by a man who says he is a reformer...Of all the shocking attacks this case has witnessed, that is the most unmanly, the most un-English and the worst.

When Hume-Williams concluded his summing up by saying that he entrusted the jury with the reputation of 'this innocent woman'. PB began to show signs of strain (as, indeed, did poor Maud Allan, who by this time was sitting quietly weeping in the body of the court) but even this did not prevent him from trying to interrupt the Judge's final address.

Darling ignored these attempts and calmly carried on, reminding the twelve perplexed men that it was their duty to decide if Maud Allan *had* been libelled by the heading to the paragraph concerned. Did it tend to hold her up to dislike or defame her character? Was it calculated to produce a breach of the peace? Was it true in substance and fact? After almost an hour and a half, during which PB sat in the dock white-faced and tight-lipped, convinced that all was lost, the jury returned and pronounced him 'Not Guilty'.

The Judge was totally unable to control what happened next. His lips were seen to be moving but his words could not be heard, as the entire public gallery rose to its feet, cheering, waving and stamping with delight. PB continued to sit in the dock, dazed and unsmiling, not sure if he had heard aright. When at last the clamour died down and order was restored after the removal of the more rowdy and unruly elements, the Prosecuting Counsel said that as there was no evidence to offer on the other indictments concerning Grein and the obscenity charges, PB was therefore not guilty of these either.

Darling then made his own statement on the play itself which, he said, should never have been produced in public or in private and went on to refer in particular to the scanty costume Maud Allan was said to have worn as Salome. He commented on other such 'representations by actresses clad in almost nothing at all' and said that if those in authority had not the power to prevent these performances, he hoped that women would soon make it their business to see that much more purity was introduced into such productions. As Darling rose to leave the court, a now confident PB also got to his feet and to everyone's astonishment, had the temerity to ask if he might be awarded damages, an audacious suggestion which Darling chose to ignore.

PB's supporters clustered round to offer their congratulations and Dot, who had watched the whole of the proceedings in fearful fascination from the public gallery, was close to tears of relief. They left the court together with PB's arm protectively around her and with an elated Eileen trotting beside them. On the steps of the Old Bailey they were greeted by a crowd of more than a thousand well-wishers and police had to clear a path for them to reach their car. With a last wave, PB then drove off to a quiet celebration with friends at the offices of *The Vigilante* in St James's Place. His enemies meanwhile, frustrated in their attempts to bring about his downfall, were already plotting other ways of discrediting him and wreaking their revenge on Eileen for her betrayal.

CHAPTER FOURTEEN

Press reports on the result of the trial were mixed. Most considered that Darling had handled the case badly but some sympathised with him for having to cope with the tactics employed by PB. Others, such as the *Daily Mail*, praised his stand on the matter of aliens and for bringing more 'purity into public life' by exposing those in high places with a 'too easy tolerance of evil'. *The Times* devoted most of its main editorial to a summary of what it considered to be a 'deplorable libel action' and was, on the whole, critical of PB and what had been allowed to take place in court. Its final paragraph, however, commented that even if the state of affairs, which PB and his friends had sought to represent as existing in the country, had been grossly exaggerated and limited to an 'infinitesimal section' in every class:

> The tolerance of evil is a fertile breeding ground of suspicion. No public man or woman can afford unnecessary contact with questionable companions...If one of the consequences of the Billing case is to give new value to the ancient virtues, to make public men and women realise that their responsibilities are not ended with their public functions, to remind them that countless eyes are watching their doings and their associates, then there may be some compensation after all for the work of a scandalous week.

PB was pleased by this statement for he felt it gave credence to what he had been trying to point out, both in *The Vigilante* and at the Old Bailey, and undoubtedly his revelations had caused some upheaval in London society circles.

During the trial, there were those who had been genuinely fearful that their names might be the next to be quoted as being in the Black Book. This is evident from the letters between Duff and Diana Cooper[1] during this period. Diana wrote of how Olga Loewenthal, a well-known singing teacher with suspected lesbian inclinations, was 'in a bad anxiety about the Billing case'. According to Diana, Olga had 'only a small chance of being overlooked' at the Old Bailey, as she came under 'alien, vice and house of ill-repute!' In an amusing letter back from France, Duff Cooper wrote that while the trial was in progress, no-one there spoke or thought of anything else and that the general feeling was that anybody who was anybody was in the book and that it was 'very second-rate to be in the 53,000 and not in the first 47'. When the case came to an end, Duff Cooper expressed his dismay at the result and at the 'twelve idiotic jurymen and utterly inept judge', adding: 'but I suppose one should be grateful to Billing. He has kept the whole army amused for several days and provided a topic of conversation to officers who can never find one for themselves.'

1. A Durable Fire, Letters of Duff and Diana Cooper, 1913-50, edited by Artemis Cooper (Collins, 1983)

Poor Margot Asquith, whose name had actually been mentioned as appearing in the book, apparently became quite paranoid while the trial was on and imagined that her every movement was being observed.[2] She was obviously not alone in this for PB was quoted as saying later that he had heard of many others with, perhaps, more cause for concern, who temporarily ceased their dubious activities for fear of being discovered.

But did the Black Book really exist? As Hume-Williams pointed out at the trial, it is quite possible that the Germans did possess some sort of record of men and women in public life, with notes as to the ways pressure could be exerted upon them. Whether either of PB's main witnesses actually saw such a record is, however, questionable.

Eileen admitted, in a sworn statement made before police officers some weeks later, that Spencer had told her before the trial that he had never in fact seen the book and had only learned of its existence from Neil Primrose. Even so, on PB's instructions, he intended to go into the witness box and swear that he had, so as to corroborate her story. According to her statement, she had protested at this but PB said it had to be done or *she* would not be believed. The three of them had then worked out, on the eve of the trial, what each would say.

The chances are, however, that she was not telling the truth either. Her claim to have seen the book could only have been supported by the two young Army officers who had supposedly gone through it with her and they were both dead by the time of the trial. In any case, the families of Evelyn Rothschild and Neil Primrose both stated afterwards that the two were not together in England at the time Eileen alleged she had been shown the book at the hotel in Ripley. From her behaviour, as exemplified later, she was never the most truthful of ladies. So who can one believe?

Perhaps PB's version of the book's origin, which he confided to his family many years afterwards, is closest to the truth. He said that he had known all along that there never was such a volume and that the whole affair had been triggered off by his and Spencer's desire to frighten off those in prominent positions whose sexual tastes could have led to them being blackmailed by German agents. Spencer had written the first piece about the book for *The Imperialist* but PB had been responsible for the actual number of names quoted in it. He told his family that this had been arrived at by using his telephone number at Hertford—47—with a few extra noughts added 'to give the necessary impact to the story'.[3]

But was he just trying to save face by telling his family only a half-truth, concealing the fact that initially he had been completely taken in by Spencer's story about seeing such a book while in the service of Prince William of Wied in Albania? The Prince later officially denied that the American had ever been on his staff and claimed that he had no knowledge of either Spencer or of any

2. Margot: A Life of the Countess of Oxford and Asquith, Daphne Bennett (Gollancz, 1984)
3. This was indeed his telephone number at the time.

THE VOICE OF THE VIGILANTES

ENGLAND
SCOTLAND
IRELAND
WALES

THE **IMPERIALIST** ▣

ANZAC
CANADA
AFRICA
INDIA

CONDUCTED BY N·PEMBERTON-BILLING · M·P

THE ONLY NEWSPAPER THAT DOES NOT ACCEPT ADVERTISEMENTS AND THEREFORE IS FREE TO SPEAK THE TRUTH.

Portrait from the cover of his life story, *Imperialist Press,* 1917

THE VIGILANTE, JULY 20, 1918

PUBLISHED IN THE INTEREST OF PURITY IN PUBLIC LIFE

ENGLAND
SCOTLAND
IRELAND
WALES

THE **VIGILANTE** ▣

ANZAC
CANADA
AFRICA
INDIA

FOUNDED 1916 BY N·PEMBERTON-BILLING · M·P

THE ONLY NEWSPAPER THAT DOES NOT ACCEPT ADVERTISEMENTS AND THEREFORE IS FREE TO SPEAK THE TRUTH

P.B. LIBEL CHARGE

Mrs Eleanor Villiers-Stuart, first witness for the defence

Mr. Justice Darling, who is presiding at the trial of Mr. Pemberton-Billing.

Lord Alfred Douglas, who is to be called as one of the witnesses for the defence

There were some dramatic scenes at the trial of Mr. Noel Pemberton-Billing, M.P., yesterday, when witnesses for the defence were called. – (*Daily Mirror* photographs.)

Leaving the Old Bailey after the trial

Dot, 1918

'Black Book' until he had read reports of the trial in neutral newspapers. Spencer could well have heard, during his Service days, of the existence of some kind of list and with his twisted, deluded mind have fabricated the rest.

PB wrote later in 'The Truth of the Trial', published in *The Vigilante,* that when he met Eileen for the first time: 'without the slightest suspicion in my mind I confided to her the truth behind the pending trial.' Within a few days of this interview she passed on to him 'matters of the utmost gravity in connection with the 47,000'. Almost on the eve of the trial he introduced Eileen to Spencer: 'For the purpose of substantiating in my own mind, by cross-examining each in the other's presence, the somewhat amazing information ... which I decided I was not only justified in making public but that it was my duty to do so'. Neither she nor Spencer wavered over this 'evidence' in court—which could have been the result of careful rehearsing beforehand. But whatever the truth of the matter, PB always maintained that the highly dramatic story of the Black Book helped to achieve what he had set out to do.

The very day the trial came to an end, PB was back in Parliament, ready to resume his battle to curb the activities of those enemy aliens who were still being allowed to go free and to stem the corruption that he was convinced was crippling the war effort. Less than a week later he addressed an enthusiastic gathering of a thousand or more at the Queen's Hall in London, concerning these issues, and an even larger gathering at the Royal Albert Hall on 15th June. This meeting was held on a particularly fine, sunny afternoon when one would have thought the attractions of the park opposite would have had more appeal, yet nearly ten thousand men and women from every level of society attended. After a concert of songs and organ music, PB—the only speaker— quietly appeared on the platform to a tumultuous ovation. The audience listened to what he had to say with rapt attention, punctuated by frequent outbursts of cheering. As at the Queen's Hall meeting, detectives and uniformed police mixed with the crowd in expectation of trouble but, as his friend Charles Grey recorded in his diary: 'although PB was obviously worn out by the strain of the trial, he was very peaceful and patriotic and gave a sound, moderate speech.'

After the events at the Old Bailey, it must have come as quite a surprise to those in the audience expecting a stormy oration to discover a man who talked instead with quiet dignity and apparent sincerity. He had no difficulty in gaining support for the newly sponsored Vigilante candidate, Henry Beamish, for an impending by-election at Clapham, nor for the resolution that had been worked out by the Society's committee, of which Beamish was now Treasurer and one of the leading figures. The resolution, which was passed unanimously, called on the Government to take immediate steps to denaturalise and intern forthwith all enemy-born subjects and to take powers under the Defence of the Realm Act to provide that all aliens should, for the duration of the war, 'exhibit on the lapel of their coats the emblem of their nationality'.

PB had been outvoted by his committee about Beamish's idea of aliens wearing identification badges, for he felt this might lead to many innocent people suffering at the hands of those who took their anti-German feelings to extremes. His main concern had always been to root out those with enemy connections still holding influential positions in Britain and force the closure of German and Austrian banks. Dot was even more uneasy about this latest resolution since her own family had German origins—a fact PB appeared to have forgotten. She had stood by him throughout the trial and had even tried to ignore his philanderings with Eileen, whom she had neither liked nor trusted from the beginning, but she could not let him go on ignoring the dangers she could see arising from his naive association with some of the Society's more obsessed members.

The reports of the Albert Hall meeting and the resolution which Beamish intended to use as his platform at Clapham antagonised the members of the War Cabinet even further, intent as they still were on preventing further damage to the talks at the Hague, which were at that time going through a difficult passage. Soon after PB had walked from the Old Bailey a free man, moves had been made by the politicians to try and undermine the evidence given by his major witnesses, figuring that if it could be proved that either Eileen or Spencer had perjured themselves, PB's current popularity with the general public would be instantly diminished. In correspondence with Bonar Law on the matter, the Attorney General had indicated that unless one witness confessed and denounced the others, there was little chance such perjury could be proved. However, by this time an attempt was already being made to achieve this.

Three days after the Albert Hall meeting, on the instructions of the Director of Public Prosecutions, Eileen was arrested on a charge of bigamy and appeared at Marylebone Police Court the following day. Apparently, on reading of the trial at the Old Bailey, the mother of Percival Bray had notified the police that her son—Eileen's legal husband—was alive and he had subsequently been traced to France. When he heard what had happened, PB immediately arranged bail for Eileen through a member of his Vigilante Society's Finance Committee, James Collings. At the same time he suggested she make a statement before a commissioner for oaths, to put on record all that had gone before; how she came to write to him in the first place and then changed sides; the threat that, unless she returned to her political employers and secured the downfall of PB her life would be in danger, and her firm belief that this latest move was the result of her change of allegiance.

This she did on the 27th June, claiming that she was being prosecuted for bigamy not by her first husband whom she believed to be dead, nor by her second, but by the Public Prosecutor. The prosecution in her opinion was a vindictive one, launched solely 'because of the assistance I gave to Mr

Pemberton Billing upon his trial and the evidence I gave at the Old Bailey'. She believed that her political employers had entered upon a crusade against PB and the Vigilante Society and everyone who assisted him at his trial.

It had been suggested to her that divorce proceedings would be taken against her citing PB as co-respondent. 'This is a wicked suggestion for anyone to make,' she stated righteously. All her relations with him had been 'most honourable' and both he and every other member of the Vigilante Society had always treated her with respect. It was infamous for any person to suggest that there had been any immoral relations between her and PB, 'or any other officer or member of the Vigilante Society'. If she had written 'to any person or persons' anything which could be construed as implying that her connection with PB or the Vigilantes had been 'anything less than honourable', no such suggestion had been intended. This again indicated Eileen's unreliability, for only a few days earlier, Basil Thomson, the Assistant Commissioner of Police, had notified the Prime Minister[4] that Pemberton Billing, the author of a 'purity campaign', had been living during his trial 'in illicit relations with one of his chief witnesses'. The source of this intriguing piece of information had, apparently, been none other than Eileen herself.

Having her swear the incriminating indictment concerning her former employers, turned out to be a shrewd move on PB's part, for by this time he was beginning to suspect that Dot might be right and that Eileen was not, after all, to be trusted. Like all his other extra-marital adventures, his affair with her had been very transitory, a mere passing infatuation for a physically attractive woman, but Eileen would have preferred a more permanent arrangement. Perhaps, by agreeing to make the statement, she had hoped to entice him back but she must soon have realised that their brief affair was over and that for him Dot had always been the only woman whose love he valued. Consequently, Eileen's next action was as much that of a woman scorned as of an adventuress striving to save her own skin.

On 15th July she made another extraordinary statement, this time before two police officers. In this she accused both PB and Spencer of perjury at the Old Bailey and PB of having visited certain munitions factories to get employees to sign an undertaking to strike if called upon to do so. Those who knew PB well would view the latter part of her statement with great suspicion, for he was always vehemently opposed to any form of strike, particularly in wartime. There was certainly not a shred of truth in what she alleged, for the only document requiring signatures then being circulated was the Vigilante Society's petition demanding the internment of aliens and the closure of enemy banks. Even so, her signed statement was sent the next day by Thomson, the Assistant Commissioner of Police, to Bonar Law's secretary, J.C.C. Davidson, accompanied by a letter marked 'Confidential', it read:

4. According to the diaries of Maurice Hankey, secretary to the War Cabinet, who was present on that occasion.

I think it may interest Mr Bonar Law to see the enclosed statement by Mrs. Villiers-Stuart. Her bigamy case is coming up for trial next Saturday and it will be a blessing if she repeats this kind of statement in the dock. I dare not hope for so much. In the meantime the divorce proceedings are rather hanging fire. I am seeing the solicitors about this to-morrow.

From this and Davidson's reply it seems clear that Eileen, in return for her information discrediting PB and Spencer, had been promised a quick divorce to save her from standing trial for bigamy. She explained this 'indefinite postponement' of her trial to PB and his colleagues by saying that it was part of the political plot to keep her in a state of uncertainty. It was also a ploy to discredit the Vigilante Society by holding her trial 'at some appropriate critical or psychological moment'. PB immediately decided to publish this explanation in *The Vigilante* of 20th July, together with the statement she had made to him on 27th June and the following week published her first significant letter to him of 6th May suggesting a meeting. All this had the effect of completely invalidating what Eileen had told the police and as her statement could not now be used, PB and Spencer were freed from any risk of perjury charges and she was committed, after all, to appear at the Old Bailey on 14th September charged with bigamy.

It was revealed at her trial that she had never received any conclusive evidence of Bray's death—only hearsay from another soldier—although she had tried, unsuccessfully, to establish from the War Office whether or not he was still alive. She had claimed to be a widow on her marriage to Villiers-Stuart and had told him and his family that her first husband had been a South African millionaire who had left her a large fortune. It was this and many other similar fabrications that proved her undoing. Despite PB (very generously, under the circumstances) engaging the well-known barrister Sir Edward Marshall Hall, KC to defend her, she was caught out so many times by the shrewd prosecuting counsel that in the end no-one believed anything she said— least of all the judge—and she was sentenced to nine months imprisonment. The whole case proved once again to PB that Dot had been right and Eileen was not to be trusted. Her other fears concerning *The Vigilante* and those he had gathered around him in the Society had by now also been justified, for much had happened during the three months preceding Eileen's trial.

After his meeting at the Albert Hall, PB had stepped up his anti-alien campaign in Parliament and continued to ask questions about the number of suspect people working in Government departments or those who had changed their names but were, he believed, of enemy origin. His Vigilante candidate, Beamish, was defeated at Clapham on 21st June by only six hundred votes which showed, he wrote in his magazine, that, despite 'the mean and dirty tricks employed by the opposing Coalition candidate', support for the Vigilante Party was growing. Just prior to the election, Spencer sent a telegram on behalf of Beamish to the Prime Minister referring to the internment of all enemy-born subjects in the country but the telegram was never received and when PB asked the Assistant Postmaster General in the House of Commons on 24th June if he would take the matter up, his request was refused.

On that same day he caused further embarrassment in certain political circles by putting another of his now famous supplementary questions in the House, concerning the closure of German banks: 'Is not the inability of the Government to deal with this question due to the German banks financing certain British political parties?' He knew he was treading on dangerous ground for there could well have been some truth in what he said, but was resolved to pursue his campaign to the end.

Throughout the next week he made several unavailing attempts to get the Government to agree to a date for discussion of the whole alien question and the closure of enemy banks and on 1st July tried yet again. This time he determined not to leave the Chamber until he had received a satisfactory answer. A fellow Member of Parliament,[5] writing anonymously in *The Vigilante*, described what happened next: 'Don't let us try to explain it away, let us rather look behind the 'scene' for its significance. Mr Pemberton Billing, MP, the most loved man in the country to-day by those who love their country, the most hated by the gangs and cliques battening on the War, has been suspended from service in the House of Commons. He disobeyed the ruling of the Chair amid the jeers and gibes of men who have better reason to fear him than the public know.'

PB had asked leave of the Speaker to move an adjournment to discuss a 'definite matter of urgent public importance'—the subject of aliens—which, he reminded the Speaker, he had asked for on the previous Thursday without success. The Speaker replied that since then there had been a blocking notice to prevent it.[6] PB asked what this was and whether it was in the interest of the enemy or the country that such a notice should be put down. There followed further heated exchanges between them, after which the Speaker ordered the Clerk to read the Orders of the Day, which signalled the close of Question Time. At this, PB rose once more to say that he had not seen any blocking motion and when the Speaker told him that he should 'look in the Order Book', asked: 'Are we to understand that all it is necessary to do, to prevent free speech in the House on so urgent and important a question as the internment of enemy aliens, is for one of their Government friends to put down a blocking motion?'

On the Speaker replying that he had no intention of discussing the procedure of the House, PB again sprang to his feet and, ignoring the cries of 'sit down, sit down' from other members, angrily retorted that he refused to do

5. *The Vigilante* described the writer only as 'one of the best-known journalists in England to-day'.
6. According to Parliamentary records, this was because a more substantive motion had since been tabled on the same subject.

so when there were 'a lot of damned Germans running about the country'. This prompted the Speaker to order him to leave the Chamber but PB stubbornly remained where he was. There were more heated exchanges, during which the Speaker threatened him with suspension if he did not obey and issued the warning that such suspension could last for some time. Bonar Law, as Leader of the House, moved that this should be done but PB remained in his seat, saying: 'I'll not leave. I'm doing what I conceive to be my duty.' The Speaker then directed the Sergeant-at-Arms to remove him, but after a brief word the officer reported that the recalcitrant Member still refused to go. The House was then temporarily suspended and four hefty attendants were called. They wrenched PB from his hold on the back of the bench, seized him by the legs and shoulders and carried him bodily from the Chamber, struggling and shouting as he went, 'Intern the aliens.'

The writer of the *Vigilante* article closed his account with:

> Realise this: that at any moment we may be in the perils of a premature peace. It is quite possible that some day we shall hear of secret 'pourparlers' and it may be of the gravest importance that the House of Commons should discuss the situation by means of such a motion for adjournment as Mr Pemberton Billing sought to introduce...As I watched PB carried from his place and flung into the lobby amid unmanly cheers...I could not help hoping that the 'scene' might have a permanent effect on the House of Commons. If it means that Members will yet insist upon an amendment of the rules of procedure which will render blocking motions null and void, then PB will have worked a Parliamentary reform which the combined power of all parties has been unable to effect...
>
> The man who put down the insulting and stopping motion is Mr R.D. Holt, a ship owner. And the irony of it! For Tuesday's paper, which gave that discreditable information, reported the torpedoing of another hospital ship *as the outcome of the information of a spy.*

The sinking of this ship put an end to any further compromise peace talks and Lloyd George's Cabinet quickly swung round to what PB and his colleagues had been advocating all along. On the very next day, not only did Bonar Law publicly condemn the sinking as another example of 'German brutality' but Lloyd George also told the press that he had selected six Members of Parliament to investigate the whole alien question. This committee very quickly advised the immediate implementation of all the measures for which PB had been pressing prior to his suspension. *The Times* was obviously in full agreement and referred to the German banks in London as having been 'notorious in the past as the most effective of all the weapons of German penetration'.

All this was clearly not yet enough for PB who believed in sustaining the fight until the measures had actually been taken. On the evening following his removal from the House, he attended a play, *The Hidden Hand*, at the Strand Theatre and as the curtain fell, to the astonishment of the audience, he addressed them from his box about what he considered to be the play's bearing on the alien situation.

The next day he nominated Spencer as the third Vigilante Parliamentary candidate for a by-election at East Finsbury and another telegram was sent to Lloyd George, offering to withdraw the candidature if the Vigilante's recommendations on the alien question were adopted. He also pledged that the Society would not pursue a petition to the King on the same lines as the resolution passed at the Albert Hall. Lloyd George gave no direct answer to the telegram but chose that same day to announce in Parliament that a 'ruthless comb-out of enemy aliens' had begun and that German banks would no longer be allowed to operate.

CHAPTER FIFTEEN

July 1918 proved a traumatic month in many ways for PB. On the 5th, all three members of the Vigilante finance committee—Beamish, Clarke and Collings—sent him a letter of resignation, claiming that he had been spending large sums of the Society's money without their sanction. They claimed that despite their warnings in June that he should not incur any expenditure over £10 without their approval, he had disregarded their instructions and consequently they had decided they could not allow their names to be associated with the Society 'as at present controlled'.

PB immediately replied saying that he was most anxious that nothing should be done which could in any way reflect on the good name of the Society. He therefore suggested that every member should be made aware of the committee's letter of resignation and the reasons which had first occasioned friction between himself, Clarke and Beamish—namely that Clarke was 'endeavouring to turn the Society into an anti-Catholic movement', while Beamish was anti-Jew. The reasons should also be given, he felt, for the final breach: 'the unfortunate and regrettable incidents in connection with the financial arrangements for the Clapham by-election' for which, he was quick to point out, he was not entirely responsible.

It was agreed that an extraordinary general meeting of the Society should be held at the Queen's Hall at the end of the month to discuss the whole matter. In the meantime he was furious to discover that his old enemy the *Daily Chronicle* and other newspapers had got hold of the story and were inferring that he had been administering public funds in a dishonest manner. To make matters worse, a disturbing article appeared in the *Daily Chronicle* of 8th July, following upon information received from Government Secret Service sources, as a letter sent a week earlier to Davidson, Bonar Law's secretary, indicates. The writer commented on the recently formed Government advisory committee on the alien question and added: 'It is a curious coincidence that the real director of the Prime Minister's Advisory Committee, the Chief Vigilante—Mr Pemberton Billing—should himself be married to a lady of Prussian origin. No suggestion is made against the lady's patriotism, but what would have been said of some other member of the Government had he been equally happily married to such an estimable lady of irreproachable character and patriotism— but also of Prussian origin?' The report then gave details of Dot's father's German background and went on: 'It is said that Herr Schweitzer became naturalised and all his eight children were born in England.' There was nothing to show, the writer continued, that he was not a loyal, law-abiding citizen of his adopted country but if the Vigilantes' committee was exposing such cases, why not take this one up?

Whether at PB's instigation or through her deep sense of loyalty to him and his causes is not known but Dot immediately wrote to Sir George Cave at the Home Office, claiming (quite erroneously) that her father was of Swiss origin, his family having come to England three generations previously. Two of her three brothers had volunteered to serve in the war and one had been killed in November 1914. She then made a surprising and exceedingly rash statement in which she claimed that she would welcome a careful investigation and: 'If it is found that there is a drop of enemy blood in my veins, I demand that I be interned at once, as an example, and so that there be no excuse for the Government to shelter any longer their enemy-born supporters and relations.'

PB's accompanying letter was scarcely guaranteed to improve his chances of a speedy return to the House either, for his closing paragraph read: 'if it had not been for her [Dot's] loyal devotion and encouragement I should not have been able to have carried out my campaign against enemy agents in our Privy Council, Government and House of Commons...to avert the consequences of which your guilty companions are fighting with their backs to the wall.'

A few days later, Spencer came up with another of his stories. This time he said that he had heard of a plan to arrest PB under the Defence of the Realm Act for making statements prejudicial to the Government and that this would be followed by raids on the Billings' home at Hertford and the Vigilantes' office in St James's Place to look for incriminating documents. Warming to his subject, he also claimed to have heard that, since PB's arrest might be accompanied by patriotic demonstrations throughout England, it was proposed to certify him as insane and detain him 'as a person suffering from hallucinations'.

Curious though it may seem, even at this stage PB actually believed Spencer's far-fetched stories and, although Dot and their friend Charles Grey were by this time very sceptical and tried to warn him, he refused to listen. He was too busy giving Spencer his full support in the East Finsbury campaign, dashing around the constituency in his bright yellow car and attracting the usual excited crowd of curious onlookers

According to *The Times*, on the eve of the poll PB, Spencer and nearly a thousand supporters besieged a meeting of the other Independent candidate, A. S. Belsher. Fighting broke out, Belsher's car was wrecked and stones were hurled through the windows of the hall where he and his colleagues were sheltering. When police reinforcements were called, they immediately ordered PB to stop using his car as a temporary electioneering platform for when he spoke out against aliens and military shirkers, it encouraged the rowdier element among his audience to turn on those they considered to be in this category. At length the ringleaders were arrested and order was restored.

PB's version of the affair in *The Vigilante* was that sixty 'roughs—the very scum of the docks, burly ruffians of the lowest type' were brought into the constituency to 'assail and terrorise' Spencer's supporters. They charged into the first ex-soldiers they encountered but crowds rushed to the rescue and the bullies had to take refuge in the hall. Meanwhile, PB claimed, the ex-servicemen tied a rope to his car and towed it out of harm's way. The bullies then cautiously reappeared from the hall, only to be chased to the shelter of Moorgate Station by two to three thousand women, 'wives and widows of servicemen' according to PB. Whatever the real truth of the incident, the derogatory reports in the press must have lost some support for Spencer as the Coalition candidate romped home with double the number of votes expected.

On 18th July, after further research, the *Daily Chronicle* published more revelations about Dot's antecedents, claiming that her grandfather had been Postmaster General in Danzig and that, although her mother was a Montagu, she had actually been born in Germany and that Dot's father had not, after all, been naturalised. 'Will Mrs Billing be interned?' their headline asked, followed by the sub-heading: 'Mr Billing's Prussian Association.' The whole affair was naturally very upsetting for Dot who, after her previous letter of denial, was now powerless to contradict the matter further. She knew that there were also members of the Vigilante Society who were dismayed at the discovery that their President's wife had origins which qualified her as one of the 'aliens' they had been seeking to intern. But, brave woman that she was, it did not prevent her from joining her husband at the Queen's Hall on 27th to face 400 members of the Society for the Extraordinary General Meeting, called to discuss the resignation of the three members of the Vigilante's finance committee.

Beamish, acting as spokesman for the other two, began by saying that, prior to their taking over, PB had largely financed the concern himself and was lavish in his expenditure. When the finance committee was elected it was the members' duty to see that the money was carefully spent. Against their wishes, PB had refused to let a collection be taken at the Albert Hall meeting, at which there were nearly 10,000 present, because he considered it against the constitution of the Society. It was because of this that the committee had finally decided to resign, as such a collection would have brought in upwards of a very necessary £1,000. He and PB lived on different spheres. He lived on earth while PB 'lived perhaps in heaven'.

In his reply PB said that when he joined a fight, until it was over it was his whole world and winning was the only thing that mattered. The Vigilante Society—'practically the only political organisation to be reckoned with', according to the *Daily News*—was one man with a definite aim and a few faithful followers. What was lacking in money and numbers was made up in determination. Such a fight could not be fought with committees—these were nothing but 'talk, talk, talk'. He had therefore disregarded the finance committee's rules concerning collections.

The essential thing was unity within the Society and when a rumour is started that 'a man who has given £75 out of every £100 from his own bank' is maladministering funds, just because he refuses to take a collection on terms which are against the constitution of the Society, it made him feel very bitter.

He next spoke of his disagreements with Beamish and Clarke over their policies, saying that he felt that questions of religion should not interfere with the Society. He liked to think that 'if people lived a decent life in this world, they would no doubt stand a good chance in the next—whatever their religion might be.'

By this time the audience was almost wholly on his side, but Beamish still refused to return as Treasurer, saying that although he admired PB intensely, he realised that he needed the 'finances of a Rothschild' to carry on the work he was doing. PB, however, had won the day. The future of the Society was left in his hands, to reform in any way he thought fit but the strain of the past few weeks was beginning to tell.

The Vigilante of 3rd August, which gave a verbatim report of the Extraordinary General Meeting of the Society, noted that the magazine would be temporarily suspended during the Parliamentary recess as PB was 'under doctor's orders to take a complete, if brief, rest from his labours'. He had lost nearly three stone in weight since he had first entered Parliament two-and-a-half years earlier and was looking gaunt and ill. He had always been prone to violent headaches at times of stress and feeling there had been far too many of these in recent months, Dot persuaded him to see their doctor, who immediately advised a complete change of scene.

At her suggestion, she and PB spent a blissful few weeks sailing from Burnham-on-Crouch and overhauling and refitting his small motor-yacht *Freedom*. She knew from past experience that being on or near water had a calming effect on her husband and she, too, always enjoyed the carefree days afloat. It had been a distressing year for her as well and she needed the change as much as he did. PB's naivety with regard to others and excessive enthusiasm for his current cause was never easy to live with at the best of times and the past few months had been particularly difficult.

By the time they returned to their home at Hertford in early October the war news was good, the Germans were retreating on all fronts and there was much talk of a General Election in the offing. Although by the normal rules of the House he should have been allowed to return to his seat at the resumption of the session after the summer break, PB was still suspended from Parliament. He had written to the Speaker on the matter but had received a frosty reply, the gist being that only when he had apologised for his unseemly behaviour would he be allowed back into the House. This he had no intention of doing. Instead he set out on a comprehensive pre-election tour of his constituency to explain the situation to his electors.

He began his tour on 18th October at Ware and to his astonishment was there presented with a writ issued on behalf of Percival Bray, citing him as Eileen's co-respondent in the impending divorce case. Eileen had apparently been served with a similar writ at Holloway prison a few days earlier. Trying, as he always did, to unman any possible criticism, he publicly announced what had happened from the platform of the hall and immediately gained the sympathy of his audience by saying that this was just another move by his enemies to crush him once and for all as Member for East Herts. He then appealed to his listeners to help save him from being blackmailed by 'this group of crooks'.

In the midst of his election tour, it was clear that the war was at last coming to an end and when, on 11th November, the Armistice was signed, PB and Dot joined their friends in the euphoric celebrations that followed. He was not allowed much respite, however, for on 14th November, it was announced that the General Election would be taking place in a month's time and he became involved in an even more hectic round of meetings—sometimes as many as nine a day. Even the *Hertfordshire Mercury* was impressed, commenting that he seemed 'quite equal to half a dozen political agents' and that his skills as an orator made him 'a star of the first magnitude'. His ability to manage elections, the newspaper commented, could not be equalled by either the Coalition candidate, Barnard, or the newly appointed Labour representative, Cyril Harding. Much to the delight of all the local lads, for it was an unusual innovation in those days, he attached a loudspeaker to his bright red sports car and played his recorded electioneering song, to the tune of 'Tramp, tramp, tramp, the Boys are Marching', from a gramophone perched on one of the seats:

> Vote, vote, vote for Pemberton Billing,
> Knock old Barnard in the eye,
> He's the man who stopped the Huns
> Dropping bombs on little ones
> He's the man who put the wind up Germany!

Judging from the letters in the local paper at this time, there were as many diametrically opposed to him representing the constituency as those in his favour. 'Why,' wrote one correspondent, 'in the face of the known and provable facts of Mr Billing's political record, can so many still maintain confidence in him?' Another disliked the methods he sometimes adopted but felt the means often justified the ends. 'He is not the first Member to be carried out of the House of Commons and he will not be the last; older politicians have gone through the same ordeal and the causes they advocated are law to-day.'

PB adopted no particular platform for his electioneering, except in the general terms of rehabilitation in a peacetime Britain. He soon became aware during his travels that the people of Hertfordshire shared one major problem with the rest of the country: there was a desperate shortage of houses for the returning servicemen and by late November was already investigating ways to overcome this pressing need.

Polling day, 14th December, dawned wet and miserable but PB's distinctive red favours, which had been widely distributed, were very much in evidence. Although counting was not to take place until the 28th December and the result was not expected until two days later, the *Hertfordshire Mercury* of 21st December hazarded a guess as to who the successful candidate might be: 'If noise and boys count for anything, Mr Billing will romp in.' In the event, PB justified his supporters' belief in him for he was returned with his majority doubled—due largely to the new women voters whom he had made a special point of impressing throughout his campaign. He was well pleased with what had been achieved, particularly since the defeat he inflicted on the Coalition candidate was almost a unique achievement in that particular General Election.

On the announcement of the result in the New Year of 1919, there were scenes of such enthusiasm that PB was, for once, rendered speechless with emotion. After the usual formalities were over, he and Dot drove back to Hertford House where he had arranged a reception for several hundred of his supporters. A large tent was erected on the lawn to take the overflow from the house and the men, women and children seemed unconcerned by the cold January weather, enjoying the light refreshments provided, accompanied by music on the gramophone and a few tunes played by PB on his amazing 'Orebestrelle' organ. (He had bought this a few months earlier and, although not a competent musician, found playing it—often for hours at a time—a wonderful means of relaxation.)

During the following few days, he drove to the other areas of his constituency and was particularly touched by a small gilt-covered notebook presented to him by one group of supporters. On it they had engraved:

> Presented to Noel Pemberton Billing Esq., MP by his friends in Hertford and District General Election 1918—Majority 2470.
> Honour to him, self-complete if lone,
> Carves to the grave one pathway all his own
> And heeding nought that man may think or say
> Asks but his soul, if doubtful of the way!

The poetry may have left something to be desired but he knew the sentiments behind it were genuine. The warmth of the gesture and that of the Hertfordshire people determined him more than ever to direct the whole of his attention from then on towards their welfare. With both *The Vigilante* and its Society by this time in the process of being wound up, he felt certain he would be more able to accomplish this.

The few copies of *The Vigilante* that had appeared since that of 3rd August contained only blank pages, for reasons that were never explained. On 8th February 1919, however, a four page 'Review and Valediction' compiled by the Vigilantes' former secretary, Euphemia Tait, proclaimed that both the journal and the Society had been brought to an end. The piece began with a biblical quotation:

Behold the sower went forth to sow; and when he sowed, some seeds fell by the wayside... As an organisation the Vigilantes no longer exists. As individuals, those who are Vigilantes in spirit and in truth maintain their purpose, hold tenaciously to their ideals, and will continue so to do while life lasts...

When the attempt was made to organise the Vigilantes it never occurred to the founder, Mr Pemberton Billing, that the Society might itself become tainted with the very evils it was formed to fight, infected by the very disease it was out to cure. Many seemed to regard the society as a mere 'talking centre' where they could voice personal grievances or utterly irrelevant ideas...

The President had tried, the article continued, to fight on alone when 'those to whom he would have entrusted the task failed him'. Following upon the Extraordinary General Meeting he had decided that for the time being 'the work must be carried on by individuals, the faithful few who are Vigilantes indeed.' Reference was then made to the citing of PB in Eileen's divorce case which was later 'ignominiously withdrawn'- presumably because it failed to effect its primary purpose, the defeat of Mr Pemberton Billing in the recent election.

The rest of this final issue was devoted to how *The Vigilante* and the Society were to be wound up and included the audited balance sheet, which showed that PB paid the outstanding deficit of £4,780 from his own pocket.

It is clear that Spencer,[1] Beamish, Clarke, and others whom PB had trusted, had genuinely caused him a great deal of distress and soul-searching in recent months. After the meeting in July, all three went their separate ways and although PB had promised, during his medically-enforced summer break, to draw up some new form of constitution for the Society, he was too disillusioned by all that had happened to do so. In his final 'President's Message' he wrote that he had been forced to decide whether to devote his energies to keeping the domestic details of the Society 'in one harmonious whole', or whether he should devote his time to actively fighting for its ideals in the House of Commons, on public platforms or in newspaper columns. During their quiet time together on the *Freedom*, he and Dot had discussed the whole affair and it was probably through her that he eventually came to his decision.

Arthur Telford Mason, who wrote several short books in fable form 'concerning men and the things that men did do at the time when there was war' was, perhaps without realising it, closer to assessing PB at this period than

---

1. In 1921 Spencer was involved in yet another libel case for giving 'totally false information' in a magazine he was then editing. He was convicted and sent to prison for six months. On his release he was again in trouble, being charged with 'disgusting behaviour', his mental condition having by this time deteriorated considerably. There is no evidence that he ever saw PB again after the break up of the Vigilantes, and PB never spoke of him afterwards.

most when he wrote at the close of 1919 in *The Third Book of Artemas*:

> Now Byl Lyng was an ardent youth that did gallop his *tongue* without a bridle; and he was cast out of the House of the Rulers because of his naughtiness.
>
> And there were many that despised him utterly, accounting him *only* as a puff of wind. But there were many also that were in other mind; and, when the time came, they sent him back again unto his seat among the rulers.
>
> Now it came to pass that a *certain* person spake unto him concerning a *certain* person that did know a *certain* person that had seen a *certain* book. And, behold, within the book there were names to the number of forty and seven thousand and all sinners.
>
> And when Byl Lyng heard about it, *what* it was, then waxed he very hot. And he went up before the judge and he expounded *the matter* fully. And his enthusiasm did rule the place of justice, and he became *very* wild.
>
> And when he had delivered himself of all *those things* that he intended for to say, the people were amazed. And they said, the one unto the other; Verily, there is *some* guy that pulleth the leg of this young man; for the book which he quoteth, is it not the same that telleth Who is Who?
>
> And when Byl Lyng heard that the people, they did scoff at him, his spirit sank very low. And he betook himself off unto a quiet place, and he chewed mud. And when he came forth again, he was as one new born, for he spake concerning a house, being of his own invention *and* very saving of fuel.
>
> But concerning the forty and seven thousand persons, *and* all sinners, of them he spake no word.

PB had, indeed, 'come forth' with one of his highly original ideas—this time for solving the country's housing crisis. After consultations with architects, engineers and many of his women constituents he had, within a few weeks, designed a cheap, easy to maintain, eight-roomed house which could be quickly erected by using the then revolutionary idea of factory-made units delivered directly to the site in sections. An integral part of the design was the large square central stove which could serve as a fire-place for four rooms at once, heat the water, dry the clothes and cook the food. In summer it could become a slow-combustion stove, with its heat cut off from any or all the rooms by protective screens. It was a novel idea, and as 'Artemas' had commented, 'very saving of fuel'.

CHAPTER SIXTEEN

Soon after his re-election PB called a meeting of his constituents at Hertford to talk about what he termed 'Reconstruction' and how he hoped to assist the new Government tackle the housing situation and provide what Lloyd George termed 'homes fit for heroes to live in'. He told the packed hall that he proposed to erect, as a model for others to take up if they wished, five houses of different designs. One would be constructed in patent concrete slabs with a tiled roof and the others in a new composite material which 'seems to possess extraordinary possibilities'. The foundations for the first of these would be laid within a few days in a meadow close to Hertford House, his home at Bengeo, and building would be completed within six weeks at half the cost of the recently published Government scheme. He also announced his intention of standing for the next vacant seat on the County Council as he felt it needed 'vitalising'- which prompted the local paper to comment on the 'fear and trembling' among Council members at the thought that PB might disturb their equanimity and 'brush the cobwebs from their old-world placidity'. They need not have worried for when a seat did become vacant at the end of March, much to his disappointment, he failed to get elected.

The general reaction of the Hertfordshire people to his proposals for solving their housing crisis was that if anyone could help bring this about PB could, for his boundless energy and enthusiasm were by now well known. By the end of January the national press was alerted to the construction going on at Bengeo and the resultant publicity led to an avalanche of letters asking for more details of his designs.

In an article for the *Sunday Express* of 2nd February he asserted that he was neither a builder nor an architect, he was just anxious to use what constructive ability he possessed to eliminate the drudgery so often the lot of the average working man's wife. He firmly believed that the provision of comfortable homes meant the creation of happy families and the ultimate stability of the State, whereas the perpetuation of the hovel meant 'the creation of Bolshevism'. Slum houses, he felt, should be condemned and suitable sites should be bought instead on the outskirts of towns where people could live in a healthier and more congenial atmosphere.

He told the Town Council in late February that he visualised the Hertford of the future as a thriving commercial and business centre, with all its slums cleared away. In their place would be built establishments of work that would be 'architectural adornments to the town'. Homes would be built outside in a healthy 'garden' environment amidst trees and countryside. His own houses at Bengeo, he told Council members, were all designed on this principle and were being laid out in a leafy crescent where most of the original trees and hedges were being retained.

The *Daily Express* had by this time decided to hold a Model Homes Exhibition in London in the early summer and PB proposed to show models of his houses there, together with his innovative central stove actually in operation. Tests on this in the spring had proved successful and he claimed that he had danced on it with delight, so pleased was he with the results: 'It threw a cheerful fire into four different rooms at the same time, kept an oven hot for baking, heated dinner plates above it, boiled the kettle, provided hot water for the domestic supply—including the bathroom—and heated radiators for four bedrooms, all on half-a-dozen handfuls of coal'.

On 30th March, in an article for the *Sunday Express* entitled 'The Genie of the House', he also mentioned the nation-wide interest the tests had aroused and added that he was about to experiment with both a gas jet and a paraffin burner to see if they were feasible alternatives to solid fuel for summertime use. However, not all the experts were as enthusiastic when the stove was shown at the exhibition in the Central Hall, Westminster in May.

The whole of the basement was devoted to PB's housing plans and in particular his stove, which *Building News* described as: 'a complicated and ingenious affair, very likely to get out of order after a little ordinary use. The workaday housewife probably would soon bring it to grief and the radiators, of which there are seven, would speedily begrime the walls to which they are attached.'

The Builder, although agreeing that plenty of heat could be poured out into the room by such an arrangement and that the further development of the stove would be watched with interest, also noted that no attempt had been made to 'mitigate the effect of the black, mean-looking patches in the angles of the rooms'. But a point the magazine did make in favour of the housing plan itself was that 'cottages of this type could be superimposed on each other like a stack of library shelves.'

Progress on the houses at Bengeo was slower than PB had anticipated, due initially to the weather. A reporter from the *Daily Express* who visited the site some weeks after the work commenced noted that, although the buildings were scaffold high, they were embedded in snow and ice. When conditions finally improved PB had another, far more disturbing, setback. He was told by the Hertford Town Council that work on the houses must cease immediately as their construction transgressed the building bye-laws, to which PB replied that if that was the case the antiquated bye-laws would have to be altered. But it was not until later in the year, when he managed to satisfy the Council by producing slightly modified plans drawn up by an architect, that work was allowed to continue.

He was even more frustrated when the Public Health Committee caused another hold-up in September, by ruling that the houses could not be occupied until other requirements had been satisfied. This presented him with a personal problem for in August he had decided to pull down Hertford House, with the idea of including a new home for Dot and himself within his scheme. Fortunately, they still had the London apartment to fall back on but it was not until the following year that all the difficulties were overcome and they were able to occupy the new 'Hertford House' in what became known locally as 'the Garden Village at Bengeo'.

Although throughout most of 1919 and 1920 he was busy with one or another aspect of his housing schemes, he did not neglect his normal Parliamentary duties. With his mind directed more towards peaceful projects, which he approached in a calmer, less aggressive manner than hitherto, more Members of the House were inclined to listen to him. Even so, he was well aware that there were certain others who still found his presence an embarrassment and an irritant and would not hesitate to discredit him, given half a chance.

Out of Parliament he was praised, in the spring of 1919, for his frank and fearless speeches concerning what he termed the 'strike fever' then hitting the country. He told an audience of working men at Hertford that he himself had once gone on strike in South Africa because 'cheap coolie labour was being exploited at half-a-crown a day when white men were demanding 27s 6d', but would sooner 'cut off his right hand than add to his country's troubles at such a time as this'. The men listened with rapt attention to what he had to say and, surprisingly, did not attempt to leave or even heckle him during his speech, although many clearly disliked what they heard. This was also the case a month later when he spoke on similar lines to another gathering of belligerent men, telling them that their unsettled situation had been brought about by 'an active minority, unrepresented in the House of Commons, devoting their misdirected eloquence to inciting the industrial classes to strike'.

After the recent events in Russia and with the conditions then prevailing in England, he was not alone in fearing that there were many 'would-be Bolshevists' in the country prepared to incite trouble among the lower-paid workers living in poor conditions. He was genuinely sympathetic towards the working class—though he deplored that particular term, he told his constituents, believing that the perpetuation of class divisions such as these was one of the 'most regrettable' aspects of life in England at that time. On the other hand, he was not in favour of increasing the dole money to the unemployed, for he felt that this could so easily become a 'bribe to idleness' and the money could be better used in setting up ways of providing them with proper paid employment.

When there was a serious threat of a police strike in May 1919, he addressed a mass meeting of the National Union of Police Officers in Trafalgar Square, saying he understood their grievances but pleading with them to think seriously before committing any rash action. A month later he received a letter from Loughton Police Station, signed by several officers, authorising him to convey a message to Lloyd George on their behalf, informing him that if he would agree to a committee of inquiry into police conditions, any action would be postponed until the Peace Treaty talks that he was then engaged in had been completed in Paris. Unfortunately, the Prime Minister rejected this proposal and despite PB's further pleadings, refused to see a delegation of the Union in Paris. Two months later the Police Force was on strike—a hitherto inconceivable situation for the British people and one which PB was convinced could have been avoided had Lloyd George been prepared to listen to their grievances.

Several grand victory balls had been held in Hertfordshire during 1919 to celebrate the end of the war, but dancing had never interested PB, so he usually sent along a prize and made an excuse for not attending. He was nevertheless determined that the 12,000 children within his constituency should have their own special celebration and announced in July that he intended to send all those over seven years of age, together with their teachers, to the seaside for a day in September—a treat most had never before experienced. His plan was to organise a special train to take them to Clacton or somewhere similar and provide meals for them all en route. His impulsive announcement threw the railway authorities into quite a state for much as they would have liked to carry out his well-intentioned idea, 12,000 children plus several hundred teachers was rather more than they felt able to handle in one day. Catering for such a large number was equally impossible to contemplate. He therefore came up with an alternative: he would hold three giant open-air parties—at Bishops Stortford on 15th September, Hertford on the 17th and Cheshunt two days later.

These parties were to be remembered with pleasure for many years to come. PB and Dot had just returned from their summer break during the Parliamentary recess, having spent a few happy weeks sailing from Burnham-on-Crouch. Looking tanned and wearing white flannels and yachting cap, PB made quite an impression on his young guests, many of whom followed him around wherever he went.

At all three parties, lunch and tea were provided and there were numerous sideshows, a conjurer, ventriloquist, juggling clown and Punch and Judy show. The *Hertfordshire Mercury* reported that the arrangements were 'admirable in every respect'. Except at Cheshunt, where leaden morning skies brought heavy rain, the weather was kind and there was plenty to eat and drink. PB appeared to be everywhere at once—'happy as a sandboy', according to the newspaper—as he helped to cut sandwiches, pour lemonade, organise races and ensure that the entertainers were at their posts at the correct time. Music was provided by a small orchestra to which some of the older children enjoyed trying out the latest dance steps. At the Hertford party alone, half a ton of cake, 1,000 loaves of bread, 210 pounds of jam, numerous jars of potted meat and other goodies were all consumed during the day. 'some rather smoky tea' was made over a bonfire at Cheshunt, according to the memory of one child, while another recalled that the lemonade was transported to the ground at Bishops Stortford in the town's water cart, normally used for laying the dust on the roads.

PB bore the entire cost of all three celebrations himself and his generous gesture did not go unrecognised. At Cheshunt, a local craftsman showed his appreciation by presenting him with a wrought-iron fire screen, the design of which incorporated PB's initials surrounded by roses—to make up for the fact that his political life 'had not always been strewn with roses'.

The cost of the parties and the increasing expenditure involved in his building project were offset to some extent by a successful speculation which came to fruition at this time. He had managed to buy a German submarine for £5,500 and to sell it as a victory souvenir for £12,000 to his fellow MP, Horatio Bottomley. This later went on tour around the country as a publicity stunt for Bottomley's paper, *John Bull*, after undergoing considerable renovation. How PB came by such a vessel in the first place remains a mystery but he still had many friends connected with boat-dealing from his buccaneering days and it was doubtless obtained through one of these.

Soon after the children's parties Dot became seriously ill, though the nature of her illness was never fully explained at the time. From all accounts her lungs and heart seemed to be badly affected and the symptoms lasted for many months. As their new home had still not been completed, Dot spent a long convalescence with her friend Beatrice Grey at Sidmouth in Devon, where it was felt the milder climate would be better for her. As PB never liked being parted from her for long, this meant many speedy journeys to the West Country to visit her in his newly acquired six-cylinder Renault Black Prince. He and Charles Grey joined their wives in Sidmouth for Christmas and in the evenings PB entertained them by showing silent films on his recently-acquired Kinematograph. This prompted him to connect the projector with the gramophone to produce 'talking pictures', and a few weeks afterwards he built the prototype model of what he later called his 'combined phonograph and picture-displaying apparatus'.

The rest of that Christmas was spent either playing his gramophone or tinkering with his Renault car. He was never one to treat any car gently and for weeks had been driving the Black Prince too hard. A year or so later he tried to sell it to a fellow MP but the would-be purchaser discovered it no longer possessed all the attributes PB had claimed for it, so he sent it back and demanded a refund of his deposit. When PB refused, saying the transaction had already been made, the MP understandably took him to court and won his case. Unfortunately for PB this latest appearance in court happened to coincide with a particularly difficult patch in both his private and public life.

By the spring of 1920 PB and Dot had moved into their new Hertford House and the other houses at Bengeo had nearly all been built. Encouraged by their success, in April he decided to form a company—Pemberton Billing

Economic Homes—with a view to producing more on the same principle, using the stoves and prefabricated wall units he had designed. Hoping to find markets for these all over the world, he had already patented the stove in Australia and was in the process of doing the same in America. A factory was built at Ware, a few miles from Hertford, and carpenters, bricklayers and other craftsmen who had previously been working in munitions factories were engaged. The first orders started to come in and by the early summer all looked set for a profitable enterprise. There was some trade union infighting at his factory in June—only too common in the country at that time—but PB handled the situation firmly and this earned him the respect of his workers, most of whom appeared to be glad of such well-paid and congenial employment when there was much industrial and political unrest elsewhere. Within a few months, however, this situation had changed.

Towards the end of the summer, in order to provide work for returning servicemen, he decided to take fifty or so unskilled but secondary-educated men (mostly ex-officers or NCOs) into his factory with the intention of training them to become supervisors or salesmen for the company. However, this did not please the craftsmen, who resented the ex-servicemen being brought in to work with them in such a capacity, even though they were to be paid only a minimal wage. Aided and abetted by certain revolutionary elements outside, which seemed set on aggravating the situation, one by one the craftsmen began to leave until eventually it became impossible to find enough skilled men to replace them or for production to continue. As a result, in January 1921 PB was forced to close the whole factory and the company went into liquidation.

Apart from the factory and the partly-completed houses at Bengeo, the company's only assets were the world patents for his central stove and, as the most valuable of these were in Canada and the USA, to help realise some capital to pay his shareholders, he decided to visit Toronto and New York in early February to negotiate their sale. Unfortunately, after two months in America he returned to England empty-handed.

He was bitterly disappointed at the outcome of the whole venture for he had put a great deal of effort into what he believed was a worthwhile cause. He had visualised his factory as being a model for others run by the Government—using, perhaps, old munitions factories—to build similar units for quick house construction. These, he thought, could then be sold to builders on credit and paid back in instalments and he was convinced some 200,000 homes could be built very quickly this way, using 'Ford-like' mass-production methods, without the taxpayer contributing a penny.

He had persistently tried to interest the Government in his ideas but to no avail. As early as June 1919 he had written an open letter to Dr Christopher Addison, President of the Local Government Board, generously offering all the British patent rights on his stove to the nation in an effort to help bring down costs should they decide to use his scheme. When he heard that Addison—the man appointed by Lloyd George to provide accommodation for the returning servicemen—had just been eased out of office for his incompetent handling of the whole housing situation and his extravagant waste of public money, PB was more frustrated than ever. Due to Addison's mismanagement, by the spring of 1921 the price of houses had risen to nearly three times what PB had envisaged as being necessary for building by his methods and were far too expensive for most people to afford.

Even before he left for America, PB had warned the Commons what was happening, but without effect. He began to feel increasingly powerless to achieve anything as an Independent MP yet did not feel able to align himself with any of the political parties. Unemployment had more than doubled during his absence abroad and industrial and political disputes abounded. Meanwhile Lloyd George was, in his opinion, using devious methods to remain in office. On 27th May 1921, feeling thoroughly disillusioned by the whole Parliamentary scene, he wrote to the Speaker of the House of Commons:

Dear Mr Speaker,
Since the last General Election, when Mr Lloyd George was returned to power with an overwhelming majority by a deluded electorate, he has ingeniously and consistently employed that majority to vary the ancient procedure of your Honourable House for the purpose of sterilising the independent critics of his bureaucratic and dishonest administration.

As I do not consider that it is compatible either with the dignity or honour of a public man of independent views to remain in an Assembly so unwholesome and unfair as the present Prime Minister has rendered the once free and independent House of Commons—at the instigation of a camarilla of International financiers with whom he has so closely identified His Majesty's Government—I should be honoured if you would inform me what steps it is necessary for me to take to be released forthwith from the necessity of continuing to attend as Parliamentary representative for East Hertfordshire.

I remain, Yours faithfully,
Pemberton Billing"

When the announcement was made public the immediate reaction of his constituents was one of dismay, as expressed by an editorial in the *Hertfordshire Mercury*: 'We may have differed at times in regard to his political colours and methods but have consistently recorded his sincerity and high patriotic ideals... The Garden Village will remain for many years to come as an example of his energies and practical desire to help the community.' PB's 'fire of energy and vitality' had been drawn on, according to the report, to an unlimited extent over past months and needed replenishing. Dot's recent illness was also put forward as a possible reason for PB coming to his decision. It was indeed clear to all who knew her that Dot was looking frailer than ever, despite PB having arranged for her to have a few months' holiday with friends in the South of France.

The national press reported his retirement in mixed terms. Whereas some regretted the disappearance from the House of 'one of its most interesting, forceful and picturesque personalities' the *Saturday Review* drew attention to yet another aspect: 'He is a clever engineer but decidedly restless. He seems to us rather like the typical American who does not think he is getting on unless he is getting out after a while into some other place or job.'

To a certain extent this may have been true, for PB had not changed over the years. Once a project had lost its initial attraction—because he had achieved what he had set out to do or had discovered something more exciting—the old interest was invariably jettisoned in favour of its successor. On the other hand, had his abilities been recognised in Parliamentary matters, it is interesting to speculate whether he might, after all, have decided to remain for a few more years and subsequently proved himself an asset not only to East Hertfordshire but to the country as a whole.

In the event he was soon directing his energies elsewhere, happy at the thought that he was leaving his constituency in good hands, for his old friend Rear Admiral Murray Sueter had agreed to contest the vacancy and stand as an Independent against the Unionist candidate. Much to PB's satisfaction, Sueter won the seat and continued to hold it for several years to come.

CHAPTER SEVENTEEN

There is no record of exactly when Dot and PB left the area but it is known that they sold Hertford House in the early 1920s and that it was renamed The Hythe, a name it still bears. The remaining houses on the small estate were eventually completed and sold to help settle the claims against PB's Economic Homes Company, whose affairs were finally wound up in February 1922. Dot and PB were certainly living at Twickenham on their motor-yacht *Freedom* by the autumn of 1921, having moved it to the Thames during the summer from its mooring at Burnham-on-Crouch.

From his patent applications of 1920 and early 1921, it is clear that PB's creative mind had not been entirely absorbed by his houses and Parliamentary matters. In late 1920 he had invented two golf games: 'stymie', played with a pack of sixty special cards and a map representing a nine-hole course; and 'Colonel Bogey', which involved the use of full-size clubs, a machine and a captive ball. He had intended to put these games on the market by Christmas but when his Economic Homes Company ran into problems he quickly abandoned the idea. This caused a firm of printers and lithographers to take him to court to recover the £381 10s 2d they claimed he owed for materials supplied and work he had commissioned for the two games. When the case came up before, of all people, his old adversary, Mr Justice Darling, PB strongly denied that he had given any specific orders but had only asked for proofs and an estimate, which had proved to be too expensive. Judgement went against him and there was a certain amount of adverse publicity, which was particularly unfortunate at that time for he was seeking backers for another invention which he considered had even greater potential.

In the early months of 1921, he had registered a patent for the combined phonograph and picture projection apparatus which he had been working on since the beginning of 1920, and was also experimenting with a new type of gramophone record he judged would be a necessary adjunct to the kind of talking picture he had in mind. Although he continued for some years afterwards to pursue this idea—working on the principle of a self-contained machine carrying a series of pictures on a disc with projection lamp, lens and screen, together with a turntable for records—his main attention at this time was directed towards the production of a series of special gramophone records.

The Columbia record factory was situated close to his home at Hertford and it was here that the record he had used for his 1918 election campaign had been pressed. He was also a friend of Louis Sterling,[1] the company's managing director and so it seems likely that he had also used Columbia for his early experiments and subsequent production of what was to become the very first 'constant speed', long-playing record, which he was to bring out in January 1922.

1. Later Sir Louis Stirling, who in 1931 became Managing Director of EMI.

As a 12-inch disc rotated at 80 rpm, with an outer groove speed of about 50 inches per second and an inner groove speed of 14—the former too fast and the latter too slow for good reproduction—he had figured that a greater playing time could be achieved by reducing the rate of rotation at the outside and increasing it as the needle traversed the record face. A special 'controller', attached to the average spring-driven gramophone, held the speed in check in the earlier part of the record but raised it constantly as controller and needle moved across the record. It is interesting to note that the 'constant surface speed' recording principle has, within the last few years, been revived in the production of compact digital discs, although the back-up technology is far in advance of PB's simple mechanical speed regulator.

When his record first appeared it created a tremendous amount of interest for it was claimed to be capable of playing three to five times longer than any other 12-inch disc then on the market. The *Daily Express* described it on 1st May as 'A Record Record' which the gramophone makers had been seeking for thirty years. The reporter claimed to have heard fifteen songs played on one small record—eight on one side and seven on the other—'all within the space of half-an-hour'.

Encouraged by the enthusiasm with which his latest invention had been greeted, on 19th May PB launched World Record Limited—with a nominal capital of £10,000 and an office in London's Piccadilly Arcade. Herbert White, a friend since his buccaneering days, was appointed co-director and it was his money that helped PB set up the enterprise. He also persuaded three other old acquaintances to join him at this time: Charles Gendle, Herbert Goody and Fred Mitchell. All were clever engineers who possessed additional skills which PB recognised would be extremely useful in the setting up of his company. Fred Mitchell was a trained aeroplane mechanic with a talent for building and design, Charles Gendle had experience of the business world, while Herbert Goody, originally a veterinary surgeon, had such an aptitude for chemistry he was the obvious person to oversee the preparation of waxes and the galvanic work of the production side.

With such a useful team, World Record Limited soon got under way and within a few months had bought up the patent rights of another gramophone company, Vistaphone, and in July acquired Cromwell House at Riverside, Mortlake, a hundred-year-old mansion, built on the site of Oliver Cromwell's home near the River Thames. PB planned to convert its forty rooms into recording studios, concert rooms, music library, stores and general offices and to have the very latest equipment installed so that eventually American and other overseas markets could be developed.

In September the American magazine *Talking Machine* reported that 150 titles, covering all types of music, were already in the process of being recorded at Cromwell House on 12-inch records capable of playing for twenty minutes non-stop. According to the report, with their controllers, these would

Hertford House, the home he built for himself

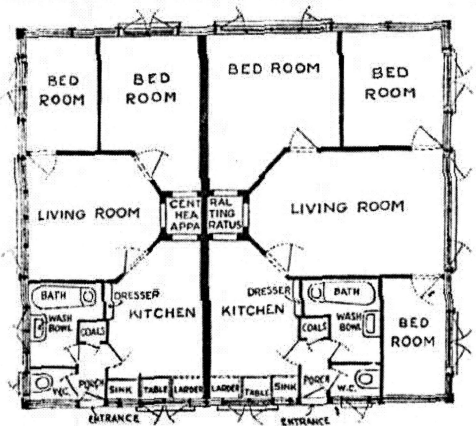

| BED ROOM | BED ROOM | BED ROOM | BED ROOM |

LIVING ROOM — CENTRAL HEATING APPARATUS — LIVING ROOM

BATH | DRESSER | KITCHEN | KITCHEN | DRESSER | BATH | BED ROOM

WASH BOWL | COALS | | COALS | WASH BOWL

W.C. | PORCH | SINK | TABLE | LARDER | LADDER | TABLE | SINK | PORCH | W.C.

ENTRANCE | ENTRANCE

HE CHEAPEST FLATS.—That on the left can be let at 4s. 9d. a week and the one on the right at 6s 9d

One of his five housing designs, 1919

MR. BILLING'S TREAT TO 12,000 CHILDREN.

"COME EARLY AND STAY LATE!"

BISHOP STORTFORD NEXT MONDAY, HERTFORD ON WEDNESDAY, AND CHESHUNT ON FRIDAY.

(left) Cartoon from *The Hertfordshire Mercury,* 1919

(below) Dot entertains a young guest.

Cromwell House, Mortlake, London. Recording studios and offices for World Record Ltd.

World Record label

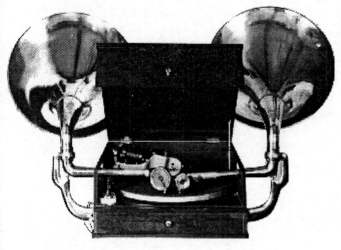

The *WORLD RECORD* CONTROLLER.

(above left) Dual horn gramophone

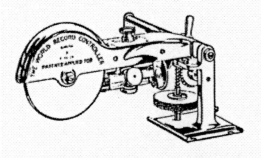

(above) Trinity gramophone

By use of this Controller "WORLD RECORDS" play from 3 to 5 times longer than any other Record in the World.

(left) World Record controller

PRICE :

Plated Model - - £1/19/6
Gilt Model - - - £2/19/6
(With Sapphire Bearing)

be on sale in England within the month at between 5 and 10 shillings a record, the price being dependent on the standing of the artistes or orchestras. When PB demonstrated his invention in New York that November, he claimed that one disc had played for an astonishing thirty minutes and on his return told the press that negotiations were in hand for records to be manufactured in the United States under licence by certain firms or sold direct to dealers there. This evidently happened for shortly afterwards the Fletcher Henderson Orchestra was recorded on one of PB's long-playing discs at a New York studio, specially fitted out for the process. Other countries also began to produce his constant surface speed records and controllers, including Japan, where the discs carried the Nitto label.

A big rush of orders during the latter months of 1922 caused temporary delivery delays, but production was later speeded up in time for there to be enough records and controllers available for the British Industries Fair at London's White City in February. The fair ran for several weeks and King George V was among the many who showed interest in World Record's exhibits, actually pausing for a while at the stand to listen to a record.

Although 1923 started on an optimistic note, by early summer the company's financial affairs were already showing signs of strain for, in setting up his ambitious new headquarters at Mortlake, PB had—not for the first time—overstretched himself. Added to which, instead of devoting himself to the consolidation of what he had already managed to achieve, with Herbert Goody and independent of World Record, he had been working on the production and marketing of yet another new type of gramophone record.

For some time Goody and he had been trying to formulate a strong base for making an unbreakable, flexible record and early in 1923 managed to achieve this by using fine circles of linen impregnated with a thermoplastic mix. They then set up a separate company to manufacture the new discs and registered it as the Featherweight Flexible Records Limited. The first Featherflex records, mainly of light classical music, were released in November 1923 after being pressed at the Clarion works in Wandsworth[2]—not at the Columbia pressing plant used by World Record Limited.

There is a family story that, during the early experimental stage of his unbreakable record, PB accidentally spilt some lacquer on his silk shirt and this seemed to produce exactly the texture he had been seeking. This prompted him to clear drawers and cupboards of all his specially-made shirts, which he then proceeded to cut up and throw into the record mix. Knowing PB, the essence of this story may well be true, but it is far more likely that if it did occur, it would have been at a much later stage, after the records had been on the market for some months and he and Goody were faced with solving a slight problem that

2. PB and Goody were also responsible for making Britain's last commercial wax cylinder record there.

had by then emerged.

At first the records had sold well but after a while they began to be returned with complaints that a 'piercing whistle solo' could be heard whenever the music stopped. It transpired that, after a few weeks on the shelf, the linen slowly reverted to its original pattern of warp and weft and, as this ran along the needle, a high-pitched hissing sound was created which hardly added to the listener's enjoyment of the record. Further experiments were carried out and the whistle was eliminated, but by the time this was achieved it was too late to save the dwindling finances of Featherweight Flexible Records Limited which, badly hit by the setback, was eventually forced into liquidation. As Goody later commented, this was despite the appeal of its record labels, which carried the motif of a scantily-clad, red-haired girl—'a real Pemberton Billing job'.

By 1923, two of PB's sisters, Hilda and Mary, were married and living with their children in Australia. This meant that he was the only member of his family still in England, his father, brother and remaining sister, Mabel, having all died during the War. He missed them greatly for both he and Dot were very family-minded and always enjoyed visits from their relations, most of whom viewed PB's antics with affectionate amusement. His sisters adored him and were extremely fond of Dot and, when they heard there had been no improvement in her health, suggested he bring her to Australia that autumn for a holiday. Both PB and Dot took up the idea with enthusiasm and he also saw the visit as an opportunity to set up a branch of his record company in that country. With this in mind, he registered his record patents in Australia and made plans to have business talks in Melbourne, where his World Record discs were selling well.

When they left England on the *Orsova* on 16th September, Dot was looking forward to the long voyage with pleasure but by the time the liner reached the Red Sea she had become too ill to leave her cabin. She recovered sufficiently to land at Adelaide, where the *Orsova* put in for a few days and Mary was waiting to greet them, but felt too weak to travel on to Melbourne with PB when the ship again set sail. Knowing her brother had business appointments in that city, Mary persuaded him to leave Dot in her care and he reluctantly continued his journey without her. But as soon as she felt able to do so, Dot insisted on joining him in Melbourne and it was there, on 29th November, that she died. According to her death certificate, she was fifty-four years old and had been suffering for some time from chronic lymphatic leukaemia which, within a matter of days, had suddenly exacerbated.

PB may not have been fully aware of how seriously ill his wife was, for her death certainly came as an horrendous shock to him. For weeks he was in a state of numbed confusion and distress and after her cremation, insisted on keeping her ashes in a small black box which he swore would remain with him wherever he went for the rest of his life.

Despite his extra-marital adventures and proclivity for a pretty face,

Dot's death meant the loss of the one woman he had always placed above all others in his affections. Six years earlier, in an autobiographical piece in *The Imperialist* he had written of their happiness together and at the same time had given an insight into the kind of marriage he shared with this gentle loyal little woman: 'In the years that have passed we have gone through many stormy waters—literally and figuratively—together. Doubtless there are many women as dutiful, as faithful, as loving, but none could be more so. Throughout my troubled career I have sometimes thought God hasn't been very kind to me—doubtless I didn't deserve it—but He has been in this instance.'

Mary, who was closest to him of all his family, had often accused him of expecting too much of his wife and of suppressing Dot's interests in favour of his own but even she had to admit that, despite her brother's generally selfish behaviour, Dot's love for him had remained steadfast to the end.

After the funeral, Mary stayed on with her brother for a while and did what she could to help assuage his grief by encouraging him to go ahead with his plans for opening a branch of his company in Melbourne. Initially his idea had been to set up a separate selling outlet for his records but when he discovered that there appeared to be no actual recording industry in Australia, he saw the potential such an idea presented and decided to take his plans further.

On 1st February 1924, the *Australian Musical News* reported: 'A factory is to be opened in May at Bay Street, Brighton, Melbourne, at which records of the singing, instrumental work and so on of Australian artistes will be taken and completed. The World Record (Australia) Proprietary Ltd. is thus initiating a new industry so far as Australia is concerned. This company controls the Pemberton Billing patents throughout the world.' Shortly after this announcement, PB returned to England for a few months with the idea of persuading some of his workforce from Cromwell House to join him in Melbourne to help set up the new factory.

Bert Goody was already in Australia, for he had travelled over on the *Orsova* with PB and Dot with the idea of introducing the Featherflex unbreakable record to Australia and he had already registered the company in Sydney. At that time the 'whistle solo' problem had not yet surfaced but when it did, early in 1924, he and PB were able to carry out further experiments at the Melbourne factory. Fred Mitchell was the next to appear on the Australian scene for PB had earmarked him for designing and building the new factory on the land set aside at Brighton. Gendle was the last of the team to leave England and his particular brief was to help PB set up the business side of the new venture.

During 1924 more patents were issued but it was not until November that the factory actually materialised. PB had a small bungalow built for himself behind it and this later became known as the 'Wocord Arms'. Following a temporary breakdown in her marriage, Mary and her eight-year-old daughter Rosemary went to live with him there and when his sister became ill PB showed how kind and caring he could be. Despite his busy working life, he somehow found time to collect Rosemary from her boarding school at Adelaide and escort her by train to Sydney, where her mother was then convalescing and while they were in New South Wales, he took them all for a memorable picnic in the Blue Mountains before returning to Melbourne. But such moments of relaxation were rare. Occasionally in the evenings at the Wocord Arms he would play a few tunes on the large pianola which occupied one complete wall of the small sitting room, but he never did find an opportunity to sail the small boat which Goody had helped him to build.

For him, time was always of the essence and he was forever looking for ways of cutting out what he considered to be unnecessary niceties. This is very evident from the memories of one of his Melbourne employees, Don Rankin. He recalled how PB, having bought a Douglas motor-bike, could not be bothered to follow the manufacturer's instructions to run it in over a set period of time and decided instead to set it up in the factory yard, switch on, and get one of his men to keep filling the bike's tank until the required number of hours had been reached. On another occasion Rankin witnessed PB's impatience on seeing a workman who had been instructed to make a doorway through a wall of the factory gingerly knocking out a few bricks. He became so irritated by the man's pathetic handiwork that he seized the sledge-hammer and with one blow demolished not only the required section but the whole wall itself.

In the summer of 1924, PB made national news in Australia with a statement that was also taken up by the British press. Speaking at a National Club luncheon in August, he startled the assembled company by declaring that he believed there would be another war within twenty years and that, as the next British Government would lean more and more towards a 'Little England' policy, Australia would be well advised to 'tie up' its fleet and spend money instead on an effective air defence. It was a country of great distances and the importance of mobility had, he said, been proved in the last war. Twenty million pounds spent on a naval air service would, he claimed, be an insurance against invasion and more worthwhile than building battleships and cruisers. It was possible to make hundreds of new aeroplanes within a few weeks and in peacetime these could be used to transport passengers and mail and to 'explore and prospect the whole of Australia for oil—or anything else'. Contrary to the derogatory comments this speech evoked among some of his political enemies in England, his motive was in no way intended as a signal that he was proposing to return to the aircraft industry for by that time he was far too occupied in getting his Australian factory under way.

On 31st December 1924, World Record Limited in England sold all its rights to the Vocalion Gramophone Company and Gendle, World Record's former company secretary, who had also helped PB establish the Australian company, stayed on to become Vocalion's general manager. Vocalion

World Record, Melbourne

3PB broadcasting studio at Brighton, Melbourne

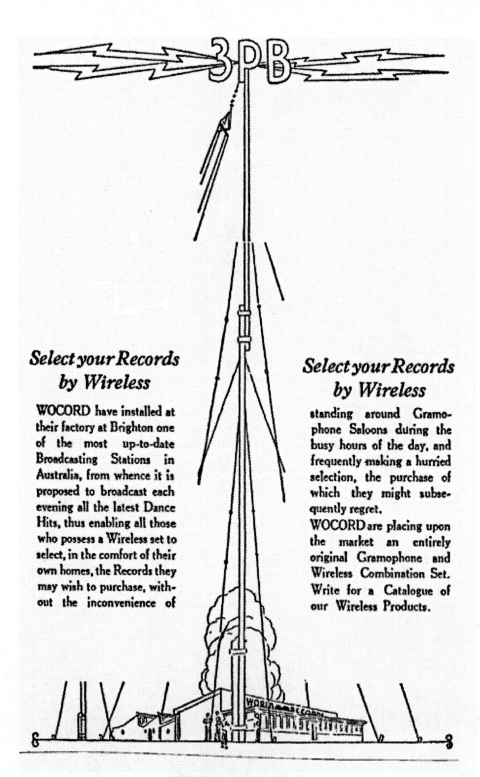

Select your Records by Wireless

WOCORD have installed at their factory at Brighton one of the most up-to-date Broadcasting Stations in Australia, from whence it is proposed to broadcast each evening all the latest Dance Hits, thus enabling all those who possess a Wireless set to select, in the comfort of their own homes, the Records they may wish to purchase, without the inconvenience of

Select your Records by Wireless

standing around Gramophone Saloons during the busy hours of the day, and frequently making a hurried selection, the purchase of which they might subsequently regret.

WOCORD are placing upon the market an entirely original Gramophone and Wireless Combination Set. Write for a Catalogue of our Wireless Products.

3PB broadcasting studio

Visiting the Blue Mountains with Mary and neice Rosmeary, 1924

Veronica, soon after their meeting in Australia

continued to produce PB's long-playing record and controller attachment and his special Trinity gramophone, a three-in-one affair consisting of 'a concert grand with sound doors', a full 'table grand to be carried about' or a 'Picnic Portable' with leather carrying handle.

Just how much PB was otherwise involved with Vocalion is not clear. He certainly went on to sell his long-playing records and controllers in Australia under that company's label and when he brought out his 5-inch Wendy discs for children in January 1925, these were also pressed at Vocalion's English factory, although they were sold only in Australia by PB's company. Why he chose to have these discs pressed in England is inexplicable for by the end of 1924 he was already pressing his own at Melbourne. The first of these were the cardboard-based, 'indestructible', Austral records and early in 1925 he brought out, under his Australian company's new trade name Wocord, his double- and single-sided flexible and very thin Wafer records.

As the year progressed, further distribution branches opened in other parts of Victoria and on 6th June it was announced in the Australian magazine, *Listener In*, that a new 'B' class radio station—3PB—to be run by World Record (Australia) Limited, had applied for a licence. The magazine reported that 3PB would broadcast dance records every night between eight and ten o'clock. These would include specially selected jazz and orchestral items from America, England and Europe which had previously not been heard in Australia and listeners would be given the opportunity to select these records in the comfort of their own homes, at 'cheapest on the market' prices.

PB's company had a stand for its records and machines at the Melbourne Show and began broadcasting (and simultaneously recording) most of the popular bands, vocalists and other entertainers then appearing at local theatres and dance halls. The company's record catalogue claimed that within twenty-four hours of a melody becoming popular, it could be issued on disc and there were also facilities available at the studio for those wishing to record their own voices or musical performances—something hitherto unknown in Australia.

Unfortunately, the enterprise PB had shown in setting up such an ambitious scheme was not matched by the organisation to back it up. Gendle had not been impressed by what he had seen at Brighton when he visited the factory in the early summer of 1925. He had initially thought that he and PB could work out a joint scheme with Vocalion in Melbourne, but came to the conclusion that the whole scale of PB's undertaking was too small to make any kind of reasonable profit. The factory building alone, which was only 450 square feet, seemed totally inadequate to house its studio, recording room, galvanic plant, pressing room and stores. The 3PB transmitter was not living up to its expectations either and was described by Goody as being 'just one enormous football of a valve which produced a signal barely audible across the street'.

Even the sales of records were not proving sufficient to counteract the company's other problems. Despite PB describing his Austral records as 'indestructible' they damaged easily and the new 10-inch shellac discs issued under the Condor label were not selling as well as he had hoped. There were difficulties, too, with distribution and strong pressures from larger gramophone concerns eager to open branches of their own in Australia. All these factors led eventually to the closure of the company in January 1926, but his foresight in founding—if only in embryo form—an entirely Australian-based recording industry had not been entirely wasted.

Gendle went on to build Vocalion's own large factory and separate recording studios at Melbourne the following year and, learning from some of his friend's mistakes, made it a profitable and well-run concern. Many of PB's former employees stayed on to work for the other firms which were later to take over the Brighton factory, including Fred Mitchell, PB's former manager, who in due course patented his own record designs and improvements. By that time, however, PB had long since left Australia for good.

At the beginning of August 1925, in an endeavour to find some way of salvaging his already ailing company, he had been persuaded by Gendle to visit America to investigate the new Western Electric system of recording and from there had travelled on to England. Waiting to greet him, having arrived some weeks earlier, were his sister Mary, her daughter Rosemary and Veronica Jones, the attractive auburn-haired woman who had left her husband in Australia in order to be with the man with whom she had fallen in love on their first meeting.

CHAPTER EIGHTEEN

PB first met Veronica in Melbourne, on 29th August 1924—a date she was always to celebrate as her 'true birthday', for she claimed her real life had only begun from that moment. She was born Elsie Veronica Farmer, on 9th February 1898, at Streatham in South London, the eldest daughter of a Greek mother and English father. At the age of twenty-one, she married a childhood friend, the kindly, reserved Owen Jones, and left with him shortly afterwards for Australia, where he had been appointed Chairman of the Forestry Commission for Victoria.

At the time of her meeting with PB, Veronica was twenty-six years old and recovering from a near breakdown following the death from meningitis of her baby son. As her husband's work had taken him away for a spell, friends suggested that she join them at a special ball being given in Melbourne and, somewhat reluctantly, she had agreed. PB had also needed some persuading, for such social occasions he regarded as a frivolous waste of valuable time, but as he was then setting up his factory he saw the occasion as a useful public relations exercise. However, on being introduced to Veronica, he found the obvious interest of such an attractive young woman appealing and spent the rest of the evening in her company.

Veronica was accustomed to the admiring attentions of her devoted husband and of most of the young men she met, so when PB appeared on the scene, she found his attitude towards her refreshingly different. Her coy, flirtatious manner, which men usually found so engaging, appeared to irritate him rather than amuse and during the course of the evening her self-esteem was further dented when he suggested she set about doing something constructive with her life. No one had ever spoken to her like that before and she resolved to win the approval of this exasperating, yet highly attractive man. The next day she enrolled for a secretarial course, having discovered that PB was looking for someone to help with his mounting business correspondence. She then sought him out, proudly told him what she had done and offered her services, which he accepted.

When Mary realised that Veronica had fallen in love with her brother she warned her that PB had still not fully recovered from the death of his first wife and that, in her opinion, it would be many years before he would commit himself seriously to any other woman. But this did not deter Veronica for by this time she was so infatuated by him, nothing could dissuade her from continuing what had become an exciting relationship. Her mother had shown the same dogged determination when, at the age of sixteen, she had left her parents in Cairo to follow her soldier lover to England and eventually marry him. Veronica had inherited much of her mother's looks and passionate temperament, together with the same thirst for adventure which, in the years that followed, was to prove a valuable asset.

On hearing that PB planned to return to England, she had no hesitation in deciding to leave her husband and join the man who by then had been her lover for some months. Owen Jones made it clear that he had no intention of divorcing her for he loved her still and was sure that one day she would return.

Exactly how PB felt about his relationship with Veronica at this point is difficult to gauge, but even if at first he viewed her merely as a convenient and attractive sexual partner, over the years she became increasingly more important to him as a devoted companion. To outsiders he seemed to treat her in an appallingly male chauvinistic way, expecting her to dance attendance upon him at all times and be ready to shelve everything at a moment's notice to satisfy a whim—even to the extent of exchanging one home or way of life for another. Yet Veronica never considered herself oppressed in any way. She once said she needed a dominant influence in her life, something she had lacked in her marriage to Owen Jones and had found in PB. She loved the sheer excitement that living with him entailed and fortunately had a healthier constitution than Dot to cope with its demands and a personality that accepted with equanimity their fluctuating fortunes—as well as his susceptibility towards pretty young women.

The couple's first home in England was on *Freedom*, still berthed at Twickenham. This suited PB at the time, for money was short and the quiet backwater location made it easier to keep the nature of their relationship secret. During the weeks following their return he tried to raise money for his Australian factory but without success and was finally obliged to agree to its closure. He nevertheless retained enough interest in the recording industry to register a patent for another disc a month after his return and, in June 1926, to become involved with the production of records at the newly-formed Duophone and Unbreakable Record Company based at Feltham in Middlesex. Although he was not registered as a director, his patented 'Burnt Off Flexible Records' were being produced by Duophone and were reported in the November 1926 issue of *Records* magazine as being of 'really good value' at 1s 6d each.

At the British Industries Fair at White City the following February, the disc was described as 'the record you can walk on and then play'. King George V and Queen Mary were said to have watched with apprehension as PB took a recording of one of their favourite singers, deliberately scratched across it with a pin and then tapped it with a hammer. When it was established that this treatment had no ill effect, the King was reported as saying: 'Other records can't stand that kind of treatment, can they?' Indeed they could not and the larger companies were already trying to find ways of either buying PB's patents or perfecting similar records of their own.

Reginald Cox, who worked as a record press man at Feltham, has vivid memories of PB working beside him on the presses, sometimes in his pyjamas, dressing gown and slippers, having been unable to sleep the previous night for thinking of ways to perfect his records. He employed a works manager but, according to Cox, this position seemed rather superfluous since PB still took most of the responsibility upon himself. There was also a foreman, two press-room charge hands, a works chemist, four pressmen and an inspector, most of whom regarded their eccentric employer with affection and respect, despite the uncertainty of their employment. On several occasions they were all sacked on a Friday evening, only to be sent an urgent telegram on Monday instructing them to report back to work immediately. Veronica was known to them all as PB's secretary, Mrs. Owen Jones, and none were given cause for thinking that she was anything other than that.

PB had his own attic room at the factory where he sometimes slept and Veronica travelled in each day, first from the boat at Twickenham and later from Chattern House, which PB had rented at nearby Ashford. Cox remembers the room above the factory as having three electric lights outside the door, the function of which was carefully explained to each new employee. If the blue lamp was lit it was the signal for a visitor to knock and wait; if green, it meant permission had been given to knock and walk in but if the red lamp was showing, anyone who entered would receive the rough edge of PB's tongue and probably lose his job as well.

In 1928 Duophone moved its works from Feltham to a disused tyre factory at New Malden in Surrey and PB supervised the conversion himself. According to Cox, the new building was large and 'even to us looked a bit too ambitious', which, sadly, proved to be the case. Within a very short space of time, the concern was taken over by the Decca Company and PB's patents were believed to have been sold to his old friend Louis Sterling.

Away from the factory, the private life of PB and Veronica had not been without incident during those years. In the spring of 1927, when the factory appeared to be running well, they had decided to take a holiday aboard *Freedom*, sailing through the French canals to the Mediterranean. Unfortunately, at the outset of their journey they ran into dense fog in the Thames estuary and struck the Nayland Rock off Margate. They were able to continue but ran aground in Pegwell Bay and had to wait for the rising tide to float them off before finally dropping anchor at Deal. Much to PB's annoyance, when he took the yacht into Dover harbour next morning he was met by the press, who had been alerted to what one reporter described as 'PB's series of thrills in the Channel'.

For once he seemed disinclined to talk about his experiences or to have photographs taken and was reluctant to let Veronica do so either. The newsmen had to be content with speaking to the 'dark-haired woman secretary' through a porthole, while PB, 'wearing a beret with a long pale blue tassel', would only say that he was cancelling his original voyage and taking his boat to Southampton. It was shortly after their return from this trip that PB rented

Chattern House at Ashford so that Veronica's life might be more comfortable, for by then she had revealed to him that she was pregnant.

As Owen Jones still refused to divorce Veronica, PB suggested he find a suitable house in the country for her, where she could bring up their child away from prying eyes and he could visit her from time to time but this did not meet with her approval. She feared that if she were not with him all the time, he would soon find someone else to take her place, so in the end it was agreed that she would remain with PB and arrangements would be made for the child to be looked after elsewhere—at least until such time as Owen Jones might be persuaded to give Veronica her freedom.

A daughter, Noel, named after her father, was born on 28th December 1927 and the circumstances of her arrival proved to be every bit as dramatic as other episodes in her flamboyant father's life. It was a difficult premature birth and Veronica nearly lost her life in the process. The nurse in attendance was sure the baby had not survived and it was only later, when a faint whimper was heard, that it was realised the discarded infant was, after all, alive.

Within a few weeks of her birth, the little girl was taken to a small private establishment in Kent—Hawkenbury Hall—where a Mrs Royals and her staff looked after a number of other children, most of whose parents were serving abroad. Sixteen months later on 5th April 1929 a son, Robin, was born and he, too, was quickly despatched to join his sister at Hawkenbury Hall. Here the two children were destined to remain for some years, growing up happily enough but totally unaware of who or where their parents were or, indeed, if they were still alive. Meanwhile PB and Veronica continued with their own busy lives, sending money to Mrs Royals for their children's keep and occasional lavish presents, which arrived without any message or indication as to who the sender might be.

During the summer of 1927, PB had been working on another project at the gramophone factory at Feltham, but it had no connection with records. He always loved the freedom a boat afforded, of being able to set sail and get away from the restrictions that living in houses imposed. Cars provided another means of escape from everyday living so, he figured, what could be better than some form of 'land yacht' that would incorporate both? With this in mind he designed and built a streamlined motorised caravan, the patent for which was accepted on 1st October 1928.

Early in that year the magazine *Autocar* gave a glowing account of this 'motor yacht on wheels'. It was eighteen feet long, had a saloon, two state rooms, an all-electric galley and a wash room: 'At every point the hand of an experienced yachtsman is revealed...no space is wasted and fitted lockers are to be found in the least expected places...The dining table is located over the engine casing, on the inner end of which is a very complete instrument board. When the 'yacht' is at anchor a short extension of the table folds over the instrument board.' Underneath the main table top was a large metal sink with an electric heater for warming the water and the 'yacht's other equipment included bookshelves, an electric fire, wireless set, gramophone, writing desk, wind-up windows, four electric lights, larder, china pantry and even a built-in cigar-lighter. There was also an ingeniously fitted 'toilet room,' a galley containing an ice box and an electric stove.

There was no end to PB's ingenuity. When a hinged panel was dropped in the toilet room a shower was revealed, complete with a metal floor tray, waste outlet and plug. *Autocar*'s only criticism was that the vehicle had a 'somewhat unconventional appearance, which would probably attract unwelcome attention where anchor was dropped'. The magazine also added that the builder might perhaps consider 'the feasibility of a periscope or other device which will enable the helmsman to see behind when going astern'.

A company was formed—Road Yachts Limited—and the motor caravan was put on display at the London showrooms of the distributor in Baker Street. When Decca moved into the factory at New Malden, PB and Veronica were all ready to ship the vehicle to America for a coast-to-coast sales promotion trip but he changed his mind at the last minute. At midnight on the eve of their proposed departure, Veronica was frantic with worry because PB had still not returned from what she had understood was to have been a short business meeting. When at last he did appear, it was with the astonishing news that the trip was cancelled because he had managed to get backers for a recently written play and that it was to be presented later that year under the auspices of George Grossmith, at the Strand Theatre in London.

The first performance of *High Treason* took place on 7th November 1928 amid a great deal of publicity. PB claimed to have written it within a week and, considering the speed at which he usually worked, this was probably true. Aspects of his own life and philosophy figure prominently in the play and it certainly provided a platform for his views on current affairs. It is not difficult, for example, to gauge PB's disapproval of the way the League of Nations was then functioning. In his view it represented the capitalistic interests of the respective governments and each had been unsuccessful in persuading the others to disarm for 'the world's land and mineral grabbers are the true mothers and fathers of wars'.

The leading character—a campaigning barrister, Stephen Deane—is a thinly disguised PB who 'had captured the imagination of a certain section of the public, though some thought him to be a madman'. The final act is set in the Old Bailey on the last day of a bishop's trial for the murder of the Prime Minister, with Deane, of course, defending him.

Almost all the critics, scathing as they may have been of the writing, called it a remarkable work and most agreed that, although the theories he propounded may have been misguided or simplistic, his sincerity was apparent. The play enjoyed a brief notoriety but this was not enough to keep it running longer than thirteen days in the West End of London, nor was its distinguished cast a sufficient draw. It included Ursula Jeans, H.A. Saintsbury, Reginald Bach (who was also the producer), H. St. Barbe West and George Bealby—whose role as Lord Rawleigh, a press peer, was so obviously modelled on Lord Northcliffe that more than one critic condemned it as bad taste. When the curtain fell for the last time, PB appeared on stage to make an announcement. Although it was by then close on midnight his charisma was such that his audience stayed to listen attentively to what he had to say and applauded him loudly when he had finished.

The striking outfit he wore caused almost as much comment as his speech: a double-breasted dinner jacket with velvet collar and watered silk lapels, wide trousers, a soft silk shirt with pointed collar and a diamond brooch in place of a tie. After briefly expressing his regret that the play was being taken off so soon, he used the opportunity to expand on his political views and wound up by informing his audience that, in order to bring these to the notice of those responsible for governing the country, he had decided to stand for Parliament at the General Election the following spring and he would be putting himself forward once again as an Independent candidate for his old constituency of East Hertfordshire.

Although *High Treason* was destined never to appear again as a play, it was revived the following year in a much changed form as one of the first British science-fiction talking pictures. The ninety-minute film was a Gaumont British production, directed by Maurice Elvey, and had a cast which included Benita Hume and Wally Patch. The script owed much to the producer, L'Estrange Fawcett, but PB's fertile mind at work is very evident. When it had its London premiere at the Marble Arch Pavilion in September 1929, it was billed as 'The Sensational World Talkie' and the *Daily Express* described it as 'not only the best talking film yet made but the screen's greatest achievement in imaginative construction'.

The film, set in the 1940s, had a background of futuristic sets and models. Men and women were dressed alike in what reviewers described as a 'type of boiler suit' and were portrayed as working together to prevent financiers from plunging the world into war. Television and radio had taken the place of newspapers, there was a Channel Tunnel in operation and London had 'towered into the air'. Aircraft and airports were 'as common as taxicabs and taxi-ranks' while motor-cars 'had completely changed their shape' and 'mechanical orchestras' had replaced human performers. Despite the prediction by one critic after the preview that 'fantasy is nearly always uncongenial to the box-office', the film was moderately successful when it went out on general release in February 1930.[1]

1. Recently, with a new musical soundtrack, the film has been shown with success at several cinemas around Britain and America.

CHAPTER NINETEEN

The General Election of 1929 was fixed for 30th May and, as with his previous campaigns, PB prepared for it well in advance. He knew that this time he had an even tougher battle on his hands for there were three other candidates standing for East Hertfordshire: T. Evander Evans for the Liberal Party, Dr Roger Edwards for Labour and Admiral Murray Sueter for the Conservative and Unionists. Sueter had managed to retain the seat through all four previous elections since his initial entry to Parliament as an Independent member, following PB's resignation in 1921. He had been an able representative and was once again considered to be a popular choice for the constituency. PB had no qualms about challenging his old friend for the seat as it had been a great disappointment to him when Sueter, some years earlier, had forsaken his Independent stance and allied himself to the party which PB felt had instigated so many underhand tricks against him in the past.

He opened his campaign in mid-March with a large meeting at the Corn Exchange in Hertford and acted as his own chairman. For over an hour, following his introductory speech, he answered questions in what the *Hertfordshire Mercury* reported as 'a calm, dispassionate manner—not at all like the electric Pemberton Billing his constituents had been used to in the past'. He still had many friends in the constituency and these were rounded up and pressed into service. Some accompanied him around the area in his red car, poster-bedecked van, or motorised caravan—soon to be nicknamed 'the Tank' by his constituents.

The van was fitted with a loudspeaker—previously used on stage for his play—and this transmitted a recording of his three campaign songs: 'Vote, Vote, Vote for Independence', another version of that used by him in the 1918 election; 'spell In-De-Pen-Dence', to the tune of 'Constantinople', another popular melody of the time, and 'send the Man Who Woke 'em Up to Wake 'em up Again', written specially for him by his friend Wolseley Charles. This began:

> Send the man who woke 'em up
> To wake 'em up again.
> Remember what he promised us, he did.
> Won't the politicians lie
> When the man they couldn't buy
> From off their box of tricks removes the lid?
> We're Socialists, Conservatives and Liberals
> Yet we're joining in this popular refrain:
>
> We're tired of party politics,
> We're sick of party lies,
> Macdonald, Baldwin and Lloyd George
> And all you other guys,
> To your scheming and your dreaming

PB will put us wise,
So we'll send him back to wake 'em up again.

Other verses referred to being 'tired of this tax-a-tion', which was 'the highest since Cre-a-tion', complaints against the Defence of the Realm Act (DORA), still in operation ten years after the war and, finally, a mild attack on Lloyd George and his policies: 'We won't be fooled by Welshmen...'

If some of the electors could not read or were not interested in his pamphlets, most at least knew the songs by the end of the campaign. This was particularly the case with 'send the Man who Woke 'em Up', as PB had the foresight to distribute free copies of the sheet music throughout the area. Many a family tried it out on the piano and local children quickly learned the words and sang them in the streets with gusto.

After the theme of his play, it is not surprising that 'World Finance versus World Peace' figured prominently in his electioneering literature and he claimed to have a plan for turning the League of Nations from a mockery into 'a powerful world force for peace'. He suggested that as every nation owed money to other nations or is owed by them, the League of Nations should be 'the Great Trustee, Clearing House and International Banker for the nations of the world'. Every country would make its payments to the League which would then distribute this money to the creditor nations.

Other subjects dealt with included the coal mines, roads, railways and canals (he advocated more use being made of cheaper canal transport) and a more benevolent Government participation in land usage in order to 'eliminate the middle-men who at present batten on the [farming] industry'. He also outlined plans for 'Municipal Nursing Homes", independent of the hospital system. Listed on the back pages of his election booklet were the subjects on which he had previously addressed the House of Commons and the number of speeches he had made on each. As the total came to an astonishing 2,082, this was the subject of some ridicule amongst his opponents, who queried whether it represented actual speeches or included his many famous supplementary questions.

It was Veronica's first experience of electioneering and she did what she could to help, but as Robin had been born only a month before, she was prevented from taking as much part in the campaign as she would have wished. However, when she did eventually join him at Hertford, she was not entirely at her ease, since most of those assisting PB had known and been very fond of Dot. She also had to accept that, in their eyes, she was merely his secretary with no claim either on him or his time. She disliked the proprietorial attitude which many adopted towards him, particularly the women who made no secret of his attraction for them and, knowing his weakness in that direction, she felt uneasy whenever he accepted invitations that did not include her.

Under the circumstances, perhaps it was just as well the couple did not after all have to make a home for themselves within the constituency. Despite a very creditable poll, he lost to Murray Sueter, though halving the majority. Naturally, he was disappointed at the outcome but he was also hurt by a rumour that had circulated during the latter part of the campaign which persuaded him to sue for libel the man who had once been his friend. He was told that Sueter had commented, at one of his election meetings that he had been PB's commander during the war and that he knew why he had left the Service and if this was generally known, the constituents would not vote for him. Sueter strongly denied ever having made such a statement but PB, feeling his honour was at stake, impulsively took him to court. Since there was no proof that he had suffered any material loss or, indeed, that the statement had actually been made, there was hardly a case to answer, his claim was dismissed and costs were awarded to Sueter.

Shortly after the election, PB and Veronica left Hertford for South Cornwall where he had bought a dilapidated farmhouse at St Just-in-Roseland with the intention of renovating and refurbishing it himself, as a relaxing antidote to the pressures of the past few weeks. Having failed to get elected to Parliament, he was even toying with the idea of making the farmhouse their permanent home for it had a perfect tranquil setting beside the estuary of the River Fal, several acres of land and its own private landing stage. He visualised himself building a workshop in which to pursue future inventions, using the farmhouse as a base for his sailing and, perhaps, writing more plays and books in the study he would create for himself. He already had an idea for another political drama and had even chosen its title: *Let us Prey*. Fired with such exciting possibilities he quickly set to work.

For the next few weeks he and Veronica lived out of their suitcases amidst utter chaos, while he worked furiously creating, with her help, what was soon to become a very attractive, comfortable home. When at last it was finished, Mary and some friends were invited to spend a weekend and were so charmed by what they saw that, over dinner on the first evening, one of the guests turned to PB and said: 'If you ever want to sell this place, please let me know for I'd be delighted to buy it from you—lock, stock and barrel'. He was as astonished as everyone else, not least Veronica, when PB replied: 'Are you serious? Because if so, you can have it—make me an offer. I find Cornwall too relaxing.'

As he had scarcely paused to draw breath since arriving, Veronica found this last statement surprising enough, but that he was quite willing to leave the house into which they had both put so much work understandably came as a great shock to her. She watched in silence as PB and their guest agreed on the price and shook hands on the deal—almost before the meal was at an end. She nevertheless accepted PB's sudden decision and agreed to leave the farmhouse within the week for a rented house in London at the Vale of Health in Hampstead. For her this was just another episode in the unpredictable life of the fascinating man whose varied fortunes she had chosen to share, but little did she guess at the time that he was already making plans for taking her even further afield.

The first week of August 1929 was spent at Cowes with yachting friends. While there he bought a 997-ton steam yacht, *Four Winds*, and, having engaged a crew of fifteen, astounded his friends at Burnham-on-Crouch by sailing the huge vessel up the estuary the following month for the annual Festival Week.

He had rarely missed this occasion at Burnham, where—with his flamboyant appearance and eccentric behaviour, he was a distinctive figure amongst the sailing fraternity. He had been a member of the Royal Corinthian Yacht Club since before the war and had just been elected to the Royal Burnham Club. When his friends saw *Four Winds* arrive and her owner being rowed ashore in a small boat, they thought it was yet another of the elaborate practical jokes for which PB was renowned.

Over the years these yachting friends had become accustomed to his fluctuating fortunes and many had been persuaded to back some of his ventures but few bore him any ill-will over the losses they usually incurred as a result. In their eyes he was always good company and generally well-liked. Most of them appreciated that, although he was not averse to asking for financial help to further one or another of his schemes, he made it a strict rule never to ask for money to tide him over any personal hardship, even if there had been times when this was desperately needed. When he sailed with such panache into the Crouch that day, there was much amused speculation as to what his current project might be and if the yacht was part of it. They were soon to learn.

PB's strongly-rooted patriotic feelings had not diminished over the years and it saddened him that Britain was still suffering, more than ten years after the war, from unemployment and economic problems. He knew enough of the business world to realise that, with the greatly-improved methods of production, the distribution and sales of various commodities were not keeping pace with the speed at which they were being manufactured. This problem had been highlighted for him during his recent electioneering and while he was in Cornwall he had mulled it over and come up with an idea. After buying the large yacht, his next step was to launch a company—the British Trade Crusades Limited—with the object of fitting out vessels such as *Four Winds* to travel round the world as floating exhibitions for British products. He even had a scheme to provide gramophone records describing the goods on view in the language of each foreign port of call.

It was an ambitious enterprise which had some backing at first but, through no fault of his own, the timing proved to be unfortunate. On 24th October Wall Street collapsed, American money suddenly ceased to flow and in the world-wide economic repercussions he was obliged to sell *Four Winds* and instead embarked on another idea, suggested by the boxer Jack Dempsey and other business friends. This was to set up a casino in Mexico—an 'American Monte Carlo' he called it—just over the United States border at Playa Ensenada. With this in mind, on 21st June 1930 he and Veronica set sail for New York on the *Mauretania* having, within the space of only a few days, thought up a way not only of getting himself across to the Pacific coast as cheaply as possible but at the same time giving a patriotic boost to at least one British product.

Two days earlier he had approached the car manufacturer Victor Riley at his Coventry factory with the suggestion that he should prove the reliability and durability of their cars by driving a Riley 9 Brooklands Model from New York to Los Angeles in an attempt to break the previous six-day record for a car of that class and capacity. Victor Riley willingly gave his backing and the Competition Manager for the company, Rupert St George Riley (no relation to Victor) agreed to accompany PB on the journey. As the *Mauretania*'s hatches were too small to allow the car to be loaded, arrangements were made for Rupert Riley to bring the vehicle over on the *Aquitania* a week later. The car caused quite a sensation on its arrival and PB and Riley had difficulty getting it away from the docks through the crowd of excited onlookers. When they at last managed to move off through the streets of New York, motorists craned their necks to stare in amazement as the powerful little car weaved its way through the heavy traffic with PB at the wheel.

After seeing Veronica off on the train to Los Angeles and making various arrangements for the trip, PB and Riley went to see Ray (Cannon-Ball) Baker, who was at that time America's best-known long-distance record breaker. He warned them that they had chosen absolutely the wrong month of the year to attempt such a journey for July was notorious for its sudden cloudbursts, overwhelming heat and flooded or impassable roads. Undeterred by his comments, they set out at ten-thirty on the morning of 9th July, having first obtained signed confirmation as to the date and time of their departure from the policeman on duty at the entrance to the Holland tunnel under the Hudson River.

PB was determined to begin the journey in style and drove off at great speed but the effect was rather spoilt when they shot out of the tunnel into bright sunlight and immediately took the wrong road at a fork. Worse was to follow, as Riley—who kept a complete diary of the trip—later recorded. They were to lose their way on several other occasions during the days that followed, adding many extra miles to what proved to be a long, hazardous and arduous journey. The heat at one stage was an intense 115°F and this was followed by a violent cloudburst, stinging rain, tearing wind, flying mud and surging water— three feet deep in places and 'running like a mill-race', according to Riley. They drove through Pueblo Indian territory and the searing heat of the barren desert lands of New Mexico, praying that the canvas bags slung on the sides of the car held sufficient water to see them through to their next supply.

With 1,000 miles still to go, they crossed the border into Arizona, passed through the Painted Desert, the Petrified Forest and miles of cactus and scrub where the potholes were frequently a foot deep. Loose sand piled high in the middle of the road by the wind also had to be negotiated and this caused the little sports model to rise off the ground and land with a terrifying crash several yards ahead, showering sand into their eyes.

The heat by this time was even more oppressive and wet rags had to be wrapped round the steering wheel, which PB had been clutching so tightly all the way that he was now having difficulty in straightening his fingers. In fact, his left hand never did recover and the little finger remained bent inwards to the palm for the rest of his life. After crossing the Blue Ridge mountains and in a temperature still over 100°F even at midnight, the intrepid driver and his companion arrived in California.[1]

Knowing he then had only 250 miles to go, PB took the rest of the route at a great pace, like a horse sensing the home stretch. He crossed Death Valley and, after a final spurt, drew up at the pre-arranged hotel, where Veronica awaited him, exhausted but triumphant. Despite all that had happened on the way, he had succeeded in beating the record and achieving his purpose—to prove the Riley's undoubted capabilities.

Rupert Riley wrote afterwards that he felt 'an unstinted admiration for PB and the car—4,000 miles in five days, 20 hours and 13 minutes calls for grit, determination and pluck. It was an amazing single-handed achievement by a man of PB's age'. (He was almost fifty years old.) PB hoped the gruelling journey would be well-publicised on both sides of the Atlantic but few newspapers took up the story, preoccupied as they were with the impending world-wide economic depression.

For the next three years, he and Veronica lived in varying degrees of comfort, either on the Pacific coast or travelling in the motorised caravan, which he had managed to get shipped over. The casino at Playa Ensenada was reasonably successful at first but when his colleagues sold out to some Mexican businessmen PB also decided to leave. He then spent time fitting out boats and applying for American patents on some of his unbreakable gramophone records. He also tried to find a market for his motorised caravan but the economic climate precluded the launch of any new business venture.

It was while he was in the United States that his creative mind began mulling over designs for a new type of camera. He had always been a keen photographer but found the average camera and its equipment cumbersome. This had become even more apparent to him when he and Riley attempted to make a photographic record of their trans-continental journey and the experience set him thinking about the feasibility of producing a camera small enough to fit into his pocket. Fate decided, however, that work on such a project would not be completed while he was in America.

On 4th March 1933, the US Congress suspended all banking for a week and PB suddenly found he and Veronica were without funds. They managed to make their way back to New York in the caravan, but arrived without a cent in

1. See Appendix VI.

their pockets. They sold the caravan for a ridiculously low sum, which was still not enough to get them back to England, so PB resorted to something he swore he would never do. He sent a wire to his old friend, Louis Sterling, asking for the loan of sufficient money to return home. Kind man that he was, Sterling sent such a generous amount that PB and Veronica decided to sail back in style on the same ship they had arrived on three years earlier—the *Mauretania*.

On their return, PB immediately offered his services to Sterling in exchange for his kindness and subsequently went to work with him on a device by which records could be played continuously one after another, the forerunner of today's jukebox. He was still without much of an income, however, and for the first time in many years had to forego owning either a boat—*Freedom* having been sold before he left England—or a car. His niece Rosemary always remembered with amusement how he was then forced to travel by public transport and would wait for 'a clean bus' to come along. But this state of affairs did not last long, for money began to come in from the sales of some his patents and he also found backers for several fresh ideas that he was confident would soon prove profitable.

CHAPTER TWENTY

By the autumn of 1934, PB and Veronica were once again living in some style. They had rented a large house at East Farleigh in Kent, as well as an apartment in London, and PB had bought a new car. He had completed the detailed designs for the pocket camera and other photographic equipment he had begun in America and applied for the patents. He was also involved with some friends in a business venture concerning the old Royal Court Theatre in Sloane Square, the top floor of which he had begun using for his London office and workshop.

On 28th September his nephew James Melrose (son of his sister, Hilda) flew into England from Australia, providing a proud moment for PB and an enjoyable interlude from his normally absorbing business affairs. Jimmy was not quite twenty-one years of age and had only begun flying lessons sixteen months earlier, yet he had distinguished himself by making a solo flight from Darwin to Croydon in the record time of eight days, nine hours, bettering by eleven hours the previous solo record set by Jim Mollison in 1931, but his achievement was not recognised as the flight had not been officially monitored. PB was so delighted by his nephew's exploit that he presented him with his own much-treasured RNAS wings, which until then had been a distinctive feature of his everyday attire, worn in place of a tie at the neck of his silk shirts.

Mixing with Jimmy's aviator friends must have rekindled some of PB's old enthusiasm for aeronautical matters, for within a month he had designed and applied for a patent for his 'Durotofin', an aircraft with rotary wing systems. This was an extremely advanced gyroplane with dual rotors mounted on outriggers extending from the sides of the fuselage. According to PB it was capable of going straight up, forwards, backwards and sideways.

The Aeroplane magazine of 28th November contained a full description of the *Durotofin*—a model of which PB had already made at his Sloane Square workshop. The article began: 'If one had not seen, in the course of some twenty-five years, the most improbable of Mr Pemberton Billing's inventions working quite satisfactorily in practice, one would have turned down this odd contraption without further thought. But so many of his odd ideas do work that one is never ready to disbelieve them...Thanks to our becoming accustomed to the Autogiro, it does not look so fantastic as it would have done four or five years ago.' After giving a glowing report on the ingenuity behind the design, the writer concluded: 'Now all we have to do is sit back and wait till Pemberton Billing invites us all to see the machine fly.' Sadly, despite the patent being fully accepted in 1936, the aircraft itself was never completed.[1] However, a year or so later a remarkably similar helicopter—a German Focke-Achgelis—appeared and was greeted with much approbation in aviation circles

---

1. See Appendix III for extra notes on this and subsequent aircraft.

because of its remarkable manoeuvrability.

There were no further patents registered in 1935, for PB was busy perfecting his pocket camera and supervising the conversion of the Royal Court Theatre into a cinema, with an unconventional back-projection screen. This required the renting of more land behind the stage and, since three different leaseholders were involved, negotiations took time. He was convinced that in the long run it would be well worthwhile, for the novelty of such a screen would, he told his backers, attract more customers, particularly in that sophisticated part of London. By the summer all seemed ready for the grand opening and he sent out invitations to a special private showing on 3rd July of *Dinner at Eight*—with cocktails afterwards on the stage.

Most of his guests were impressed by what they saw and vowed to return with their friends when the cinema was officially opened in a few days time. The original date fixed for this had, however, to be changed when the magnificent gold and silver curtains he and Veronica had chosen to cover the screen were found to be a fire hazard and had to be replaced. Consequently it was several weeks later, after the authorities had been satisfied as to its safety, that the cinema was at last allowed to open its doors to the public. Faced with the disposal of yards and yards of expensive disallowed material, PB made sure that none went to waste and, much to the amusement of his friends, for years afterwards gold and silver curtains, covers and cushions were to be seen in almost every room of his house. Another hiccup occurred over the proposed showing of the film *The King Steps Out*, when he had to make hurried alternative arrangements on discovering the booking coincided with the week of King Edward VIII's abdication.

Jimmy Melrose returned to England for a holiday in the summer of 1935 bringing Hilda with him. There was a great family reunion at PB's house in East Farleigh with Mary and her family joining them and one of the highlights for them all was a trip to Rochester to inspect PB's most recent acquisition, a 432-ton, two-deck schooner *Andria*. He had also bought himself a new car—a Rolls-Royce Alpine—for the cinema was now proving a success, his pocket camera was almost ready for marketing and for the first time in many years his financial future seemed reasonably secure.

In the late autumn he bought—almost at first sight—The Towers, a large house at Shepperton, on the western outskirts of London, with grounds overlooking the Thames. Here he met for the first time a young man who was destined to become an important member of the Pemberton Billing household. Bernard Reid was sixteen years old. His father had died some years before and, as his mother was not able to bring him up herself, he lived with his grandparents. He was working for the previous owners in the garden of The Towers when he saw a Rolls-Royce draw up and a large man heave himself out of the driving seat. As with most people on their first meeting with PB, Bernard was immediately struck by his awe-provoking presence and penetrating blue eyes, but the man approached with a charming smile, asked his name and said that he would like to see over the house.

When PB later came to know more of Bernard and his circumstances, he was convinced that the young man was capable of more than just helping in the garden and doing odd-jobs about the place and he went to see Bernard's grandfather to discuss this. The grandfather was delighted with PB's proposals which included teaching Bernard something about seamanship and engineering and training him to drive and maintain his car, and PB's generous offer was promptly accepted.

The young man spent the first few months of his new employment on board the *Andria*, learning all he could from the seaman in charge of PB's boats. By now, the yacht had been moved to Southampton and PB had acquired a second vessel—a streamlined, twin-screw hydroplane called *Voodoo*, which had originally been built with the intention of breaking the world water speed record. After this, Bernard returned to Halliford Court—as The Towers had been renamed—and, as he was now old enough to drive, soon became PB's regular chauffeur.

In May 1936 PB's patent for the pocket Compass camera was approved and he persuaded the Swiss watch making firm of Le Coultre et Cie to manufacture it. It came on the market in 1937, after almost six years of development and testing, but he was still adding refinements and making fresh accessories for it a year later. Of all his inventions this was the one of which he was most proud. Even today the small camera—measuring only 30 x 53 x 70 mm when closed and weighing 7¾ oz—is hailed as a remarkable photographic achievement, incorporating as it did an astonishing number of features. One contemporary writer described it as having 'more actual camera per square inch and per ounce than any other in history'. PB named it 'Compass' because he believed it encompassed everything a photographer might require and it certainly pointed the way towards many new ideas for future camera designers.

The f/3.5 lens pulled out on a telescopic tubular mount and the camera's design incorporated a 22-speed shutter (from 4.5 seconds to 1/500 second); a coupled range-finder which worked down to two feet; a visual exposure meter; three filters; straight forward and right-angle view-finders (for taking pictures to the right or left of the direction in which the camera seemed to be pointing); a ground-glass focusing screen; a panoramic head; an integral spirit level and a tripod socket for stereoscopic photography—a tripod being one of the many accessories available. Initially PB intended the camera to be loaded with small glass plates—each packed carefully in specially produced, individual cases made of heavy paper—but he later brought out custom-built, paper-backed rolls of film as an alternative. As these could only be obtained direct from the manufacturer, they were not easily available and operating the camera itself also proved a little difficult because of the minute size of many of its features—

winding the film required turning a tiny milled wheel. However, the resultant negative, measuring 1 x 1½ inches, was usually excellent.

His plans for another version of the camera, which he named the 'sextant', never reached fruition for while he was waiting for the patent of the Compass camera to be approved, he became involved in the design of another aircraft, which *Flight* described in April 1936. PB had telephoned the magazine to ask if they would be interested in an aeroplane that could be sold for £100, or for £125 including tuition. Within the hour, according to the article that followed, he had turned up at *Flight's* offices, explained his new aeroplane, produced from his watch pocket 'just about the neatest all-purpose camera in the world', persuaded *Flight* to photograph the model of his new aeroplane and departed, leaving everyone feeling slightly dazed.

His £100 aeroplane—'Skylark'—was certainly unlike anything seen before. It had the usual wings, tail, undercarriage, cockpit and engine, but these were all assembled in an extremely unorthodox way, without fittings and almost without bolts. The sheeting on the wings was fixed in place with self-tapping screws and all the joints were welded, without reinforcement of any sort. In fact the entire airframe was of welded steel bicycle tubing covered with sheet aluminium. Consequently the total weight—including the 48 hp Douglas engine, petrol tanks and pilot—was estimated to be only six hundred pounds. Instead of ailerons, the aeroplane was controlled by moving the tailplanes, which were independently hinged and so geared as to move separately or together. The cockpit, positioned below the swept-back parasol wing, was shaped rather like a bathtub.

PB intended to form a company to produce the aeroplane in quantity but because he was so involved with his other projects, this did not materialise, which was just as well for, as *Flight* remarked in its summing-up, a good deal of thorough testing would be necessary before the many unorthodox features could be considered 'welded (literally) into a trustworthy whole'.

Once the Compass camera sales were under way, PB was ready to branch out further. He rented an old motor-cycle sidecar factory at Norbiton in Surrey where he continued with experiments on his Durotofin and constructed his own version of a 'swash plate' engine. On hearing of a Bentley tourer about to be auctioned he had the idea of buying it, removing its engine and replacing it with his 'swash plate' but, fearing the bidding would be too high, on the day of the auction he arranged for one of his factory hands to walk among the crowd muttering something about the Bentley's cylinder head being cracked in a most inaccessible place. This ploy seemed to have worked for when it was the Bentley's turn to come under the auctioneer's hammer, PB was the sole bidder and managed to buy it at a bargain price. Delighted with his purchase, he towed the tourer back to his factory only to discover that the cylinder head really was cracked after all.

Throughout their early years at Halliford Court PB's home life with

Veronica had been settled and happy. To the outside world she was still Mrs Owen Jones, his secretary, and the couple continued, if only for appearances' sake, to occupy separate bedrooms—particularly when travelling. It is therefore not surprising that some of their closest friends were still not aware of just how intimate their relationship really was. As time went on, Owen Jones gave up any hope of Veronica ever returning to him and in 1934 decided to divorce her but neither she nor PB seemed in any hurry to alter their situation. By late 1937, however, changes were in the air.

PB was by this time not far off his fifty-seventh birthday and both the Royal Court Cinema and the Compass camera were continuing to prove successful. He had seen his sisters' children and those of his friends grow up and he seemed suddenly to grow conscious of the passing years. This may well have prompted him into thinking about his own children, tucked away in Kent, and to consider regularising his relationship with Veronica in order that they might both spend their remaining years with their own little family. He discussed the matter with his accountant, Ronald Yates—one of the few people who knew about the children—and came to a decision

On 7th December he casually mentioned to Veronica that they would be going to a wedding the following day. Excited by the news, for she loved such occasions, she asked, 'Whose?' and was astonished when PB replied: 'Ours.' He had somehow managed to arrange everything without her knowledge and, far from being annoyed at such high-handed behaviour, she was delighted at the prospect of at last becoming his wife. Their marriage took place the next morning at Chelsea Register Office, with only a few close friends and relations present at the ceremony and at the small luncheon party afterwards at the Piccadilly Hotel. Most of the national newspapers reported the wedding of the 'ex-MP and war-time airman... to his secretary, Mrs Veronica Owen Jones' and there were pictures of the couple leaving the Register Office—PB looking large and prosperous in a camel-hair coat and a smiling Veronica in furs and wearing an orchid.

Whether he had told her at this stage that he had already notified Mrs Royals that the children would be leaving her establishment is doubtful. What is known is that Veronica was anxious not to have her pleasant life disrupted too much by their presence. A special, self-contained nursery flat was prepared on the top floor of Halliford Court and a nanny was engaged in readiness for the children's arrival, which was to take place just before Christmas.

Meanwhile, at Hawkenbury Hall, Noel—not quite ten years old—and eight-year-old Robin were called into Mrs Royals' private sitting room, feeling slightly apprehensive, for such a summons was unusual unless there had been some misdemeanour. The kindly woman tried to put them at their ease but when she then imparted the astounding information that their surname was not—as they had been led to believe—Owen Jones but Pemberton Billing and that they would shortly be leaving Hawkenbury Hall in order to join their 'Mother and Father' the already shocked children looked at her in disbelief, for no further explanation was given.

The 'Road Yacht'

Sketch of the interior

A scene from Act III of *High Treason* set in the Criminal Court of the Old Bailey

"HIGH TREASON" was produced for the first time at the Strand Theatre on November 7th, 1928, with the following cast in the order of their appearance :—

PRIME MINISTER'S SECRETARY	Reginald Bach
BISHOP'S DAUGHTER	Ursula Jeans
PRIME MINISTER OF ENGLAND ...	H. St. Barbe West
THE ARCHBISHOP	Clarence Blakiston
LORD RAWLEIGH (a Press Peer)	George Bealby
STEPHEN DEANE, K.C.	Austin Trevor
THE BISHOP	H. A. Saintsbury
CHARLES FALLOWAY	James Whale
JAMES GROVES	Victor Stanley
JUDGE OF THE CRIMINAL COURT ...	J. Fisher White
COUNSEL FOR THE PROSECUTION	Eugene Leahy
FOREMAN OF THE JURY	York Challenor
USHER	Ronald Adair

MEMBERS OF THE JURY, POLICE AND COURT OFFICIALS.

ACT I

The Prime Minister's Study at 10, Downing Street.

Six Months Elapse.

ACT II

The Study of Lord Rawleigh's House at Hampstead Heath.

SCENE I : *Morning.*

SCENE II : *Evening of the Same Day.*

Three Months Elapse.

ACT III

Criminal Court, Old Bailey.

Cast list for the play

Electioneering booklet and song, East Herts, 1929

(above) PB with his nephew, James Melrose, 1934
(below) Drawing of the Durotofin, from *Aeroplane*, 1934

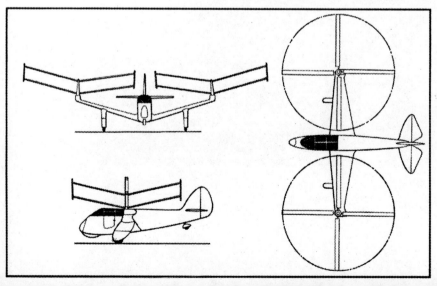

Halliford Court, 1935

The Compass camera

With the vicar at Halliford Court (a Compass photograph)

PB and Veronica on their wedding day, December 1937

Noel (aged 10) and Robin (aged 8)

Neither had any idea that their parents were even alive and had always presumed—as no-one had informed them otherwise—that they must have been orphaned when very young. Robin, in particular, had sometimes felt envious when the parents or relations of other children had come to visit but Noel, being that much older, did have dim recollections of two 'aunties' (possibly Mary and Veronica) coming once or twice to see them and leaving presents. Beyond that, neither could remember ever having had contact with anyone else outside the home. To hear now that they would soon be going to live with strange people who, they had just been told, were actually their parents, was a disturbing and frightening proposition. They had been happy and settled at Hawkenbury Hall. It was, after all, the only home they had known and the staff had always been kind. There had been only one nurse-cum-governess whom, together with all the other children, they had ever actively disliked and even she had left amidst great rejoicing a week or so earlier. It is hardly surprising therefore that more than a few tears were shed when they said goodbye to everyone at Hawkenbury Hall before setting off for London and their new life.

It had been arranged that Derek, Mrs Royals's son, should take the children to Victoria station, where Veronica would meet them. Noel, a normally happy and robust child, had insisted on taking the large Persian cat that, up to now, had been her dearest possession and this she clasped tightly to her all the way, deriving some slight comfort from the feeling of warmth and security its presence gave her. Robin sat throughout the first part of their journey glum and fearful, squeezed up beside his older sister. Up to now she had represented the only 'family' he had ever known and to him she was still the one safe refuge against the outside world.

On arrival at Victoria, Derek helped them off the train and put their meagre luggage beside them. Within minutes, a large woman in a fur coat swept down the platform towards them and introduced herself—somewhat perfunctorily—as their mother. Goodbyes were said to Derek and, feeling lost and unhappy, the pair then accompanied their newly-found parent across London to Waterloo station, where they all took another train to Walton-on-Thames. Here they were met by Bernard, in chauffeur's uniform, at the wheel of a Rolls-Royce, and whisked away to Halliford Court. In later years, neither Robin nor Noel could recall any details of that first journey with their mother or, indeed, if there was any conversation between them. According to Noel, everything that took place that day seemed unreal and they both felt they had been caught up in a strange dream, which did not end when they reached their new home.

Veronica led them through the impressive hall of Halliford Court and up the large staircase—with its frightening cast-iron monkeys on the newel posts at each turn—and told them that they would be living in their own quarters on the top floor. As they climbed the final flight, they almost stopped in their tracks for there, waiting to greet them, stood the very nurse whose departure from Hawkenbury Hall a few weeks before had been greeted by the children with such joy.

However, she welcomed the frightened children kindly, helped them unpack their few belongings and then suggested they tidy themselves up, for their father was waiting for them in his study on the floor below. Hand in hand they went downstairs and knocked on the door. A deep, intimidating voice bade them enter. Noel recalls what happened next:

'Father was standing in front of a blazing log fire with his hands behind his back and his monocle in his eye. As he peered down at us, he seemed so big and overwhelming, almost menacing—all six feet four inches of him—that my knees positively shook. Even the clothing he wore was strange: a kind of all-in-one velvet track-suit in bright red, blue and yellow stripes'.

He shook hands with them and said a few words but both children were so terrified they were glad to return to the nursery floor. It was a nightmarish end to what had been a traumatic day for them both.

To give Veronica and PB their due, they had engaged the nurse in the belief that she might provide some kind of continuity for the children. When they discovered how much Noel and Robin still feared and disliked her, she was given notice and replaced by an Estonian girl to whom the children very quickly became attached. Although they continued to be overawed by their parents, their first Christmas—and Noel's tenth birthday—at Halliford Court was memorable, if only for the abundance of food and presents heaped upon them.

Early in 1938, PB and Veronica went on a business trip to Switzerland but he seemed happy to return to his newly-acquired domestic lifestyle, with his loving wife, children and pleasant home—not that the children saw a great deal of either of their parents at that time for their meals were usually eaten separately in their own apartment. Each day they were taken by car to and from their respective schools and these, too, were daunting at first for until then their only education had been a few basic lessons at Hawkenbury Hall. Out of school they were expected to remain in their rooms but even here they were not allowed to play freely since PB disliked any disturbance when he was working in his study below and if he thought they were too noisy, pressed a bell which rang loudly upstairs.

Other than the period in Australia when his niece Rosemary and her mother had been living with him, he had had little experience of children and his attitude towards his offspring was Victorian. Children, he believed, should be seen but not heard; girls should be trained to become good obedient wives and boys to be strong fearless useful citizens, masters of their own affairs and households. It was, sadly, poor Robin who from the start did not fulfil the expectations of either his father or his mother. She hoped that he would be more like his father, both in appearance and character, while PB could not understand why a son of his should be frightened of anything. He seemed unable to understand the effect on this sensitive little boy of all that had happened since he and his sister had arrived at Halliford Court. At Hawkenbury Hall Robin had always received much attention from the staff, who found his large, dark eyes and engaging loving nature very appealing—attributes he had quickly discovered how to use to his advantage. Such tactics, however, had no effect on Veronica, who appeared not to realise that—at least in this respect— Robin had inherited some of his father's traits.

During the first summer together the family went to Poole in Dorset and the children had their first experience of sailing when they were taken out on their father's newly-acquired motor-launch, *Commodore*. PB was relaxed and happy on that occasion and the children consequently felt slightly more at ease.

In the autumn he set in motion the legal procedures for their official 'adoption' but it took several years for these to be completed and new birth certificates to be issued bearing the surname of Pemberton Billing.

Meanwhile, during that momentous year of 1938, international affairs had reached a crucial point. Events in Europe had gathered momentum since the mid-1930s—particularly after Italy's Fascist dictator, Benito Mussolini, and his counterpart in Nazi Germany, Adolf Hitler, sent military aid to General Franco and his rebel forces during the Spanish Civil War. In March, German troops had marched into Austria, having already occupied the Rhineland two years earlier and by September, Czechoslovakia was also threatened. Although Britain had no direct obligation to that country, France did, and Britain had pledged its support to France. This led to talks between Hitler, Mussolini and the Prime Ministers of France and Britain, Daladier and Neville Chamberlain, culminating at the end of the month in the famous 'peace in our time' agreement and the sacrifice of Czechoslovakia.

PB agreed with Churchill and his supporters that this treaty was a betrayal on Britain's part and so incensed was he at its implication, that on 7th October he published a twenty-eight-page booklet entitled 'An Open Letter to the Prime Minister'. In this he protested that Chamberlain's action presupposed an alliance that gave recognition to the 'ever-growing power of what can best be described as Hitlerism'. It suggested a partnership with a political organisation, which placed 'the aggrandisement of the State before the liberty of the individual and relies upon its military resources for the imposition of its will upon the rest of the world'.

He went on to allege that, should such a policy be pursued, Britain would disappear from the world as an influence for good and in so doing would be instrumental in consolidating four major powers of conflicting ideologies: Germany with its policy of Nazism, Russia with its policy of Communism, Japan with its military oligarchy and the United States of America, which would be forced to expand its sphere of influence in an attempt to maintain its system of capitalistic democracy. It would mean abstaining, he wrote, from interference in any political affairs in Europe, no matter what the German or Italian nations may decide to do to accomplish their European domination, 'even to the point of the massacre of Jews or others who do not come within the scope of citizens acceptable to their regime'.

His counter-proposal was that Britain and its Empire should present an organised front with a 'vast Security Air Fleet' to be used for purely punitive measures. PB was clearly back on his old hobby-horse. He felt the situation demanded combined national thinking, with no party politics involved, and with 'intelligent action taking the place of feeble hesitation'.

He circulated this booklet widely and sent a copy to his friend, Charles Grey, with whom he continued to have bitter arguments over their differing attitudes towards the situation in both Italy and Germany. Grey, in his capacity first as founder of *The Aeroplane* magazine and later as editor of *Jane's All the World's Aircraft*, had paid many visits to both countries and been greatly influenced by the propaganda machines of the Fascist and Nazi parties and PB had frequently tried to point out to his friend that he was being misled. Knowing that Grey was convinced Chamberlain's policy had been the right one, PB sent him a copy of his 'Open Letter' together with a short note:

> Dear Charles,
> You'll agree with this—like hell you will.
> Time alone will prove which of us was right.
> Yours sincerely, PB

By this time PB was sure that war was inevitable unless the Government radically changed its policy and, with the Spanish Civil War providing a tragic example of what might be expected in the way of civilian as well as military casualties, he set about designing a new form of mobile hospital. This included easily constructed prefabricated buildings, an ambulance and special collapsible stretcher units that could be stacked one above the other, with attachable wheels for greater mobility. He also made plans, in the early summer of 1939, to move his family out of Halliford Court should it become necessary.

Bernard had already received his call-up papers for military service and PB knew that, should war come, his other servants would also have to leave and the large house was likely to be commandeered for other purposes. He therefore rented a small furnished bungalow at Staines—The Kennels, off Chertsey Lane—and when war was declared on 3rd September, immediately transferred his family there. Much to Veronica's understandable distress, Halliford Court was then sold, complete with all the furniture and contents, and the staff dismissed.

CHAPTER TWENTY-ONE

While Bernard was waiting for his call-up to the Army, PB suggested he might like to help bring a recently purchased Brixham barge, the *Haughty Belle*, up river to Staines from its mooring near the Thames estuary. A tug had already been hired to tow the barge and PB had invited his accountant, Ronald Yates, to join them for the trip which turned out to be quite memorable for all concerned.

It began by *Haughty Belle* hitting Battersea Bridge, when the tug and barge went their separate ways. They next got stuck in a lock at Staines and on their arrival at The Kennels, PB lowered the barge's enormous mast so quickly that it hit the wheelhouse of the tug, demolishing it completely.

Bernard went off to the Army shortly after this episode. Meanwhile the family settled into a new routine to meet their much changed circumstances and the children began to see more of their parents—although even then their time together was limited.

As there were no servants at their new home, Noel and Robin were expected to help around the house. Noel enjoyed this for it made her feel that she was being a useful and much-needed member of the family, but it is clear that Veronica exploited this situation. Having had little experience of a daughter's role in a middle-class household, the twelve-year-old saw nothing strange in having to clean the whole bungalow and make her father's bed each morning before she set off for school. Nor did she think it unusual that, even when they were living at such close quarters with their parents, she should be responsible for all the cooking for Robin and herself or that they should continue to eat their meals alone. Veronica always prepared food for PB and herself separately, eating it alone with him afterwards.

Robin, too, was expected to help with the more manual tasks about the house and garden before leaving for school but he, unlike his sister, resented this. He was finding it difficult enough to settle down to his new life, let alone keep up with his classmates. As a result he became truculent and unco-operative both in and out of school, which scarcely helped to improve the strained relationship with his parents.

Although at this period of his life PB was extremely busy, involved in several diverse projects, he made a genuine attempt to get to know his children better. He set aside a full hour each evening which he devoted entirely to them and nothing, not even a telephone call, was allowed to interrupt it. However, getting them to talk about their doings and their future plans proved more difficult than he had envisaged for they were still not at ease in his company. As a result, most of the sessions ended up with him telling them about his own chequered life while they listened with rapt attention.

No doubt he felt that he and Veronica were now doing their best for the children; they were well-clothed and fed, were receiving a good education and had the security of their own home, but neither he nor Veronica seemed to provide what the children needed most at that time— the assurance that they were truly loved and understood. The only demonstration of affection either child experienced throughout those years was that which they showed to one another.

In the latter months of 1939, the Admiralty commandeered the *Andria* and Noel and her mother went to Cowes to remove some of the family's linen, china and other personal belongings that had been left on board. On their return, many of these items found their way into the now completely refurbished *Haughty Belle*, which was still moored on the river close to The Kennels. PB's original idea in buying the barge had been to use it as an air-raid shelter. He was convinced that his family would be safer on the water—barring a direct hit—than in most conventional shelters. The children enjoyed sleeping aboard the barge and during the winter of 1939-40 the whole family took up residence there, when heavy rains caused the Thames to overflow and the bungalow became flooded.

In the late summer of the following year, PB bought Rosebank, a house further along Chertsey Lane, and moved his family there from the rented bungalow. The barge went too and it was while living at Rosebank that his 'shelter' theory was put to the test for a bomb fell within fifty feet of where the family was sheltering on board. Most of the surrounding houses were damaged by the blast but *Haughty Belle* remained unscathed—as did the family— although the vessel rocked alarmingly for ten minutes after the explosion.

The Royal Court Cinema was also bombed that year, as was the flat in London where PB spent one or two nights each week. His apartment was on the ground floor of a building in the heart of the city and, although some of the upper floors disappeared altogether and his own doors were ripped off their hinges, he escaped unharmed after managing to struggle free from a bed strewn with plaster and broken glass.

He was involved in a variety of activities during the early years of the Second World War and tried to interest the Government in his earlier designs for a mobile hospital and for a special high-speed motor torpedo boat, incorporating a remarkable driving system for its propellers. He also embarked on a new series of aircraft designs; wrote two books, Defence against the Night Bomber and The Aeroplane of Tomorrow; patented a gadget by which razor blades, then in short supply, could be automatically re-sharpened and somehow found time to oversee the sale of his remaining Compass cameras.

It was unfortunate for PB that only five thousand of these were made by the Swiss watch manufacturer Le Coultre et Cie before the war brought a halt to their production and, of these, eight hundred were never recovered after a smash and grab raid at his London retailers in the Piccadilly Arcade. The War Office bought four hundred of those remaining and, because the Compass was easy to conceal, some were said to have been used by Secret Service agents. The camera was particularly sought after by American servicemen, intrigued by its size and the ingenuity of its design.

PB had begun experiments for his forty-foot high-speed boat, the *Multichine*, at the time of the Munich crisis and continued these, at his own expense, throughout the war. Before he joined the Army, Bernard had towed the original six-foot prototype, built at the Norbiton factory, to the naval experimental tank at Haslar, near Portsmouth. PB was at that time developing a drive system at the factory for the full-size boat which he planned to be powered by two Rolls-Royce Merlin engines, have a cigar-shaped housing and contra-rotating propellers on each tip. Few other details of this *Multichine* are available but a full-scale version was believed to have been built on the River Clyde at a reputed cost of £62,000—a sum which PB hoped eventually to reclaim from the Admiralty. The boat also underwent trials at Felixstowe for the RAF, who were interested in its potential for air/sea rescue purposes but for reasons that are not known, it was never taken up by the Services and PB lost a great deal of money as a result. It is interesting to note that many years later a Norwegian tug was built with a drive very similar to the *Multichine* and this continued to operate successfully for several years.

But the *Multichine* was not PB's only wartime project that failed to get official backing from the Services. In October 1940 an article in *Flight* stressed the need for more long-range, high-speed bombers. PB wrote to the magazine claiming that it was not necessary to wait five or ten years before such an aeroplane could be developed and built, as had been suggested in the article, for a test model of a bomber with just such capability—his PB.37—was already nearing completion at the works of F. Hills and Sons in Manchester. *Flight* immediately commissioned him to write two articles, the first describing the bomber and the second on the method by which such an aeroplane could be launched.

Before the articles were published, the Air Ministry was approached to establish whether PB's designs were of sufficient interest for them to be classified as 'secret', for he had told Flight that when he had originally submitted them to the Ministry twelve months earlier, the reply had been non-committal. Clearance was, however, obtained and the articles duly appeared. In the second of these, PB claimed to have already spent 'thousands of pounds' on his experiments and that he had concluded—from the Air Ministry's lack of interest—that the only course left open for him was to go ahead and publish his ideas 'in the hope that the general opinion of the aircraft industry might succeed where my own personal arguments have failed'.

His aim, he wrote, was to produce a bomber capable of carrying five tons of bombs for five thousand miles at four hundred mph and, to achieve this, he had worked on the principle that such an aircraft must have some form of assisted take-off to enable it to leave the ground with its heavy load and make a satisfactory initial climb. He therefore introduced what he called his 'slip-wing', which took the form of a glider positioned on top of the heavily-loaded bomber, so that the wing loading as a composite would be reduced to a normal figure for take-off. Having reached the required altitude, the glider could separate from the bomber and return to base with or without a small engine to assist it.

Full-scale plans were drawn up from his original slip-wing ideas but the resulting aeroplanes—PB.47, 49 and 53—never progressed beyond this stage. The PB.47 was a high-speed bomber fitted with a high strut-braced slip-wing with its own power plant. On releasing the glider, it became a streamlined monoplane with tail-mounted, contra-rotating propellers driven by an engine in the fuselage. Cruising speed was estimated at five hundred mph on seventy per cent power for two thousand miles with a maximum speed of five hundred and thirty mph. at twenty thousand feet. The PB.49 was larger and, like the PB.47, unarmed except for its bomb load. It had a sixty-one feet wing span, was forty feet in length and was powered by two 2,000 hp liquid-cooled engines, housed in nacelles in the wings, driving contra-rotating propellers. This aircraft had a similar slip-wing to the PB.47 with a 210 hp engine, an estimated cruising speed of four hundred mph and was designed to carry a crew of three. The third bomber, the PB.53, had a span of fifty feet, was thirty-three feet long and powered by a 2,150 hp engine in the fuselage. It required a two-man crew and was reckoned to be capable of carrying four 500 pound bombs for two thousand miles at a cruising speed of four hundred mph.

PB wrote two further articles for *Flight* in December 1940, this time on the subject of fighter slip-wings and how these could be fitted to some of the RAF's aircraft and mentioned his design for an unusual pusher biplane primarily intended for mounting on to night fighters. This was equipped with a searchlight in the nose and the idea was that, on sighting an enemy bomber, the main fighter would break away to attack, leaving the slip-wing to pick out the target with its searchlight. He was convinced, he told *Flight*'s readers, that the Hawker Hurricane fighter would be a suitably strong aeroplane to carry the simple slip-wing he specified but others could be similarly adapted.

It was to promote his ideas that he brought out two books in 1941. Charles Grey wrote the foreword to the first—*Defence Against the Night Bomber*—and told of his stormy thirty-year association with PB. Some of his ideas, he wrote, appeared fantastic, but there was still 'much sound sense in the book'.

One of PB's most bizarre proposals put forward in the book was that the black-out should be abolished and, instead, the whole country should be lit with searchlights pointing upwards so that the enemy raider would be presented with 'nothing but a confused and frightening mass of lights, behind which nothing can be seen'. Another suggestion was that all aircraft factories and airfield installations should be built underground.

He also included chapters on his designs for tow and slip-wing fighters and bombers, which caused the reviewer in the Journal of the Royal

Aeronautical Society to comment: 'The slip-wing fighter is really the Mayo Composite disguised, as is the slip-wing bomber of the next chapter.'

PB denied that his slip-wing designs were in any way derived from Major Mayo's 'Composite' aeroplane of 1935. His idea for a slip-wing had, he claimed, evolved from his endeavours some years earlier to improve the design of his 'bomb-wing' aircraft.[1] This was a small high-wing monoplane carrying below it a large bomb or torpedo with wings and tail of its own. This enabled it to be propelled through the air by a comparatively small aeroplane which, when it had released the bomb, would have a very high performance with which to escape. He then realised that because a normal aeroplane needed more wing area to get off the ground than to fly level, the wings on the bomb could be discarded once take-off had been completed. This led him to the slip-wing principle as being the only rational method of supplying a temporary increase in wing area.

In his foreword to *The Aeroplane of Tomorrow*, PB wrote that the book was the result of long and sometimes intense discussion between himself—'a disciple of empiricism'—and his technical assistant, Roger Tennant, whom he described as 'a disciple of theory'. The book contained a brief history of aviation, its current problems and his prophesies for the future. As was to be expected, his own designs figured prominently, the most interesting project being that for an entirely new form of fighter, the 'Porcupine', a heavily loaded single-seater with fixed guns pointing not only in the line of flight, but to port, starboard, backwards and 'possibly upwards'. These guns would be provided with mirror sights so that the pilot could alter his flight path slightly to bring the enemy into whichever sight he chose.

One of the major problems associated with firing broadsides with a large gun on a small aeroplane was the effect of the recoil. This, PB wrote, could be overcome by the use of the Davis principle. The normal Davis gun developed in the First World War was a shell-firing gun entirely without recoil. This was achieved by firing a blank cartridge in the opposite direction to the shell. In the case of the fixed gun fighter, the gun would fire out of either side of the fuselage, shells being fired in both directions at once, which would enable it to 'shoot on either side simultaneously when attacking a formation'.[2]

Another idea described in *The Aeroplane of Tomorrow* was a massive twin-fuselage transatlantic flying boat for post-war travel, the PB.43/47. In July 1939, PB had been one of the first Englishmen to travel on the maiden passenger service flight of the Boeing 314 Yankee Clipper from New York to

1. He presented this with his other ideas to the Air Ministry in 1940, but it was turned down. The first German version of a 'flying bomb' landed in England in June 1944.
2. Years later, Philip Jarrett pointed out in *Flight* magazine of 26th August 1978 that what in 1941 had been regarded as pure fantasy was apparently acceptable thirty-seven years later, albeit in a somewhat different form, for use in a Tornado fighter, enabling a barrage of projectiles to be fired at right angles to the line of flight.

Southampton and had later written an account of his journey in *Aeroplane* magazine under the title, 'Are We Too Proud To Learn?' This experience undoubtedly had some bearing not only on his own ideas for a similar civil aircraft but also on some of the features he incorporated in his wartime bomber designs. He visualised his own transatlantic 'Airliner of Tomorrow' as being a flying boat capable of carrying 500 passengers and a crew of twenty. Luggage, mail and freight, he suggested, could be lowered by parachute, prior to landing, in shock-absorbing containers. Powered by eight 2,000 hp engines, the machine would, he claimed, be able to achieve a cruising speed of 250 mph and, even if four of the engines should be out of action, the machine could still keep flying and have sufficient fuel reserve 'to reach the safety of some Atlantic shore'.

Other topics discussed—which at that time were dismissed as fanciful— were refuelling in flight, the use of rockets for take-off, pressurised civil aircraft, jet propulsion and the relative merits of the scrap- and slip- wings.

In addition to the writing and launching of his books and his attempts to interest the various Service departments in his ideas and designs he also managed, in that year of 1941, to fight four by-elections, for he firmly believed that as a Member of Parliament he had something of worth to offer the country. The first contest was at the North London constituency of Hornsey in May and, as was to be expected, he stood as an Independent against the Conservative candidate, Captain L.D. Gammans. In his election pamphlet he put forward his already well-known views on 'How to Beat the Night Bomber' and 'Aeroplanes Can Win Wars'. He also set out some of his 1929 ideas for running the coal mines, road, railway and canal transport, world finance and keeping the peace after the war.

Although previously unknown to most, as in the past, the electors found his colourful personality appealing and attended his meetings in their hundreds, listening with interest to what he had to say and waving to him as he passed by in his distinctive Rolls-Royce convertible with its yellow bodywork and royal blue upholstery. When PB first bought this car, just before the war from his actress friend Frances Day, one of his wealthier acquaintances had remarked that he could not understand how PB could have afforded to buy it, as even he would think twice about such a purchase. PB had answered, with a twinkle in his eye, that he could not really afford it either 'but, more important, I cannot afford not to have it'.

A few days before the election, *The Times* published a letter sent by Winston Churchill to Captain Gammans:

> I am sorry to learn that at this critical time...you find yourself opposed by a candidate who offers electors a war plan of his own. The national unity... should not be ruffled even for a moment by a frivolous by-election candidate. I am sure the electors will feel that this Government...is more likely to be able to choose the right course than Mr Pemberton Billing.

This immediately prompted a reply from PB which was published in the same newspaper the following day:

> Surely it ill becomes you—who, when rejected by all parties were obliged to stand as an Independent to gain re-admission to the House of Commons—to employ the same methods of derision towards another Independent as all other parties employed towards yourself at Epping...But even your present attitude does not detract from my admiration of you as a courageous and forceful leader.
>
> I cannot, however, allow your letter to pass without expressing my regret that in a moment of great national crisis...you should have seen fit to surrender your political independence, so essential to the direction of this country's destiny today, for a mess of political pottage—the Chairmanship of the Conservative Party.

Annoyed as he had been over the Churchill letter, it was as nothing compared with his feelings when he heard a loudspeaker on one of Gammans' electioneering vans proclaim that: 'A vote for Pemberton Billing is a vote for Hitler'. So incensed was he that at a non-party meeting the next day he refused to shake Gammans' hand and those standing nearby heard him say, curtly: 'Not after last night'.

Only 21 per cent of the electorate voted on polling day and of those only 4,146 supported PB. The remaining 11,077 votes went to Gammans. After the declaration, PB let it be known that he had taken legal advice with regard to 'certain illegal practices in this contest' and the outcome of this was an action for slander against Gammans, heard the following year before Mr Justice Birkett in the High Court. As on so many previous occasions, PB conducted his own case and began by saying that the words used over the loudspeaker implied that he was a traitor and that his only purpose in bringing the matter before the court was to clear his name. As he was unable to prove that it was actually Gammans who broadcast the alleged statement, the case was dismissed and costs were awarded to the defendant but the Judge complimented PB on having placed his grievances before the court with 'such propriety and skill'.

Two months after the Hornsey by-election PB tried once more to gain a seat in another straight contest with a Conservative candidate, Cyril E. Lord, in the Midlands constituency of Dudley. This time he fared much better at the poll which took place on 23rd July for, although he lost, only 1,365 votes separated him from the Conservative candidate.

Undeterred, he was back fighting a third by-election in September in the Shropshire constituency of the Wrekin. Here he was up against two other Independent candidates as well as the Conservative, Arthur Colegate, a previous Private Secretary to the Minister of Reconstruction. Most of the electors regarded the other Independents as 'freak candidates' but no-one put PB in that category. He made such a favourable impression that most of his meetings were well attended, despite the black-out and fears of possible air raids. This time he had his whole family with him as both the children were on holiday from school.

At Much Wenlock, during their tour of the constituency, Robin had to share a hotel room with his father and in the middle of the night the sleepy twelve-year-old was woken up by PB, given pencil and paper and told to take down an idea he had for an election pamphlet as he was without his dictaphone. Why he could not have made the notes himself was neither explained nor questioned. He was striding around the room, dictating as he went, when he happened to glance over to where his son was perched on the bed, notebook and pencil still poised, but with his eyes tightly closed. Not surprisingly, the young boy had fallen fast asleep, a transgression poor Robin was never allowed to forget.

It was a surprise to many when PB did not gain the Wrekin seat for he had won a great deal of local support. Once again the Conservative achieved the victory with 9,946 votes to PB's 7,121. Of the other Independents, one collected 1,638 but the third lost his deposit.

PB and his family returned home to Staines but the temptation to make yet another attempt to enter the House was too strong for him to resist when he heard that the long-standing Conservative M.P. for Hampstead, George Balfour, had died and a by-election would take place in November. Hampstead was, after all, his birthplace and he had lived there on many occasions since—a fact he quickly pointed out to his electors. His main opponent was already well-known in the area, for Flying Officer Charles Challen had been a member of the Borough Council for more than ten years and was the Conservative party's choice. He had served in the RFC and lost an arm in the First World War and could therefore speak with authority on the aeronautical matters which PB had so often used as his own platform. The other two candidates, an Independent Democrat and a 'Non-Party-All-Out-Aid-To-Russia' Independent, PB immediately dismissed as being unlikely to garner more than a few hundred votes each.

Knowing he had a tough battle on his hands and determined that this time he would win, he worked particularly hard on his electioneering pamphlet. This consisted of one large sheet, folded into four sections, the outer fold of which had the appearance of a legal agreement between himself and the Hampstead electors in which he pledged, if elected, to carry out seven promises set out in detail on the inner pages.

He first claimed that he would do all in his power to 'assist Winston Churchill in bringing the War to a speedy and victorious conclusion' and followed this with the pledge that he would 'fight for justice and equity for the serving soldiers, sailors, airmen, police, members of the Civil Defence and their dependents' for whom he would establish a local bureau to deal with their pensions, allowances and gratuities. He then promised that he would fight for the 'workers of England—men and women of all political parties, who by their daily efforts contributed to the welfare of all'. He would also fight for: 'the survival of the small shopkeeper against the vested interests of the multiple stores' and for the old age pension and other State aids to be raised commensurate with the cost of living. It was, further, his intention to issue a broadsheet of his Parliamentary and public activities and, in the event of being returned as their Member, he would remain permanently in the Borough in which he was born and thus be available at all times to his constituents.

Inside the document, together with his plans for the above, were quotes from his newspaper articles and books headed 'PB's Warnings through the Years', which aimed to show that the policies he proposed were not mere election cries but those he had consistently advocated from 1909 onwards. Many were concerned with air defence and aircraft generally, but he also quoted part of his Open Letter to Chamberlain in 1938, prophesying what had, in fact, happened after Munich. He re-stated the ideals he had set out in his play *High Treason* for a 'brotherhood of man' and he deprecated Hitler's policy of ruthless religious persecution.

The women, too, were not forgotten and he pledged that he would press for them to be given equal pay for equal work. Single women, particularly those who were unfit or elderly, received special mention: 'disregarded, struggling in many cases against poverty and privation to keep up a semblance of cheerfulness and respectability, here is a class which indeed needs a friend and champion in the House of Commons'.

Such statements won him a great deal of support but many people were upset by his forthright views. He claimed to be neither Conservative, Liberal, Socialist nor Communist, seeing both good and evil in all their policies. In his opinion, each could learn something from the other. He had strong views on trade unions and what constituted 'the workers' of the country. To his mind, workers comprised 'every man and woman who contributed to the general welfare of the community and country, no matter in what form'. He attacked those trade union members who refused to recognise that 'journalists, shopkeepers or those who pushed a plough' were just as subject to exploitation as coal-miners or boiler-makers.

His strongest attacks were directed at those who were 'parasites on the State', refusing to work without just cause. These people should, he suggested, receive no money but be 'kept above the bread-line by a system of rationing as regards both food and shelter'. Those genuinely unable to work through some physical or mental infirmity should be properly maintained by the State—not by charity.

The people of Hampstead listened in their hundreds to what he had to say and read his daring and unusual pamphlet with interest but on the eve of the poll, 26th November, *The Times* published a recent statement by Churchill in which he declared: 'The nation has no time for political privateers who sail from constituency to constituency flying fantastic flags of their own designing'. Beside this appeared a letter to the Prime Minister by PB, 'without whom,' according to *The Times*, 'no by-election would in these days seem complete'. It read: 'I feel it is my duty to place on record before the result is announced, that my victory on Thursday next, having regard to my avowed policy, must be accepted by our country and our Allies as a vote of confidence in yourself as the leader of this nation'.

He should have known better than to make such an over-confident statement before the poll for Challen, the Conservative candidate, won the seat with 7,630 votes to a mere 2,734 for PB. It was no consolation to him that the other Independents polled less than 1,000 between them and lost their deposits.

Veronica on board *Andria*, 1939 (a Compass camera photograph)

Lower portion of PB.37, a slip-wing experimental aircraft under construction in 1940

PB.43/47 Venturi. Proposal for a twin-hulled giant flying boat to carry 500 passengers, as shown in *The Aeroplane of Tomorrow*, 1941

Electioneering at Hornsey, 1941

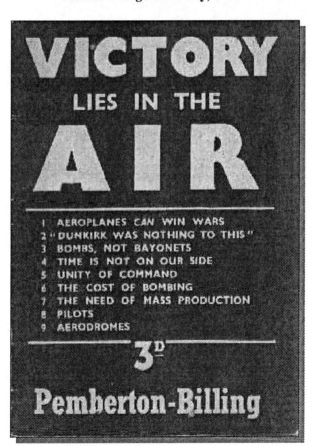

VICTORY
LIES IN THE
AIR

1 AEROPLANES CAN WIN WARS
2 "DUNKIRK WAS NOTHING TO THIS"
3 BOMBS, NOT BAYONETS
4 TIME IS NOT ON OUR SIDE
5 UNITY OF COMMAND
6 THE COST OF BOMBING
7 THE NEED OF MASS PRODUCTION
8 PILOTS
9 AERODROMES

3D

Pemberton-Billing

Victory lies in the Air, an electioneering booklet,
1941

Multichine undergoing trials at Felixstowe, 1940s

Commodore, 1948

(left) Noel and Bernard on their wedding day, September 1978

(below) Robin and his wife Maggie, 2002

CHAPTER TWENTY-TWO

After his failure to be elected at Hampstead, PB gave up any further idea of trying to return to Parliament. The main party machines, he told Veronica, had now become too strong for him to oppose successfully. Instead he decided to concentrate on helping the war effort and in December 1941, so as to bring all his interests together under one roof, he moved his family to Combe Leigh, a larger house on Kingston Hill. Here he converted the ground floor into offices for his Compass camera, together with dark-room facilities and a studio for his other design projects. Roger Tennant, his technical assistant and illustrator of his aircraft books, was also moved into Combe Leigh with his mother and brother Humphrey, whose job it was to develop the Compass camera films. PB's own family were housed in a large apartment on the top floor.

By this time Robin was a pupil at King's College, Wimbledon, and Noel attended a convent school at New Malden. As Charles Grey and his family lived nearby, during the holidays they often played with his two children. Games of cricket on the lawns of Combe Leigh during the summer were particularly memorable for they were usually accompanied by shouted instructions by PB from an upstairs window.

Organising the move to his new home proved more demanding than PB had expected, following as it did so closely on his exhausting electioneering campaigns. The family had barely settled in when he suddenly became very ill, with symptoms which at first the doctors found difficult to diagnose.

For some time he had suffered from chronic digestive problems but this was hardly surprising in one who, all his life, had considered food of secondary importance to an interesting project. Over the years he had got into the habit of eating at odd hours—if at all—and when he was away from home would snatch at whatever came to hand, more often than not eating it at his work bench. Veronica was a good cook and tried to coax him into more regular meals, tempting his appetite with all manner of delicacies, at the expense of her own and the children's wartime rations. Robin and Noel never had butter on their bread throughout the war years for their father refused to eat margarine and Veronica saw no reason why he should. Even on the rare occasions when they all ate out at a restaurant or hotel, Veronica saw nothing strange in his suggestion that everyone should order a different dish so that, when these were produced and subjected to his close inspection, he could decide which looked the most interesting and exchange it for his own.

It was not only his digestive disorders that gave cause for concern during those early months of 1942. He suffered frequent severe headaches, looked grey, tired and—even more distressing for those who knew him—seemed to be completely devoid of interest in anything or anyone. At the age of sixty-one he already appeared older than his years and to be suffering all the symptoms of a severe mental and physical breakdown. It was only after many weeks of enforced rest that he returned to anything like his former self. By the summer he had recovered enough to continue with his *Multichine* high-speed boat experiments and also tried to persuade the Air Ministry to adopt his idea for a bomber towing a fighter, but when little interest was shown in either, he soon relapsed into bouts of deep depression.

Towards the end of 1944 he suffered a stroke and his doctor told the distraught Veronica that he doubted if PB would survive. She tended him faithfully during his illness and, although his recovery was slow, he was eventually able to pursue at least some of his activities again. By now Noel was old enough to help her father and she was delighted to do so. She had already learned to drive and taken a course at a London secretarial college with this purpose in mind. PB sold his Rolls-Royce and bought a Humber Snipe which she enjoyed chauffeuring for him—despite his impatience when he felt the speed at which she drove was not fast enough for his taste. Over the years she had grown to love and respect her father. She was fully aware of his shortcomings and that he could be something of a martinet, always expecting the whole household to revolve around his every need but she realised, too, that in Veronica's eyes he could do no wrong and she willingly followed her mother's lead in pandering to him.

Robin's attitude towards his father was very different, having, from the first, been shown little love or understanding by either parent. In his teenage years he deeply resented what he saw as his father's unreasonable demands and his mother's constant criticism. Nothing he did ever seemed to please Veronica and her reports to PB on their son's behaviour invariably resulted in further upheavals in the household and unhappiness for Robin, who was never given a chance to put his side to his father. Fortunately, there still remained the same deep bond between Robin and his sister, even though he found it increasingly difficult to understand how, after their extraordinary childhood together, Noel could now view their parents with such love and respect. As the years went by he felt himself becoming more than ever estranged from the rest of the family and at the age of seventeen was glad to leave home to join the Navy.

At the close of the Second World War PB had still not regained his health and in the summer of 1945 decided the time had come for him to dispose of most of his interests and retire from any form of business life. He sold Combe Leigh and bought a twenty-nine-year lease on a large London house—66, Gloucester Place—rented out the two top floors and converted the ground floor and basement into a comfortable home for his family. He also had the idea of forming a trust with the property so that Veronica might benefit from it in future years, for he knew how quickly money slid through his wife's fingers. In this way, should he die before her, she would be provided with some form of income that would not disappear too quickly.

When Bernard was demobilised from the Army, he rejoined the family at Gloucester Place and was shocked to see the change in his former employer and benefactor. Since moving to the London house PB had suffered further illness, which this time put him in hospital. While he was there Veronica continued to cook his favourite dishes, which she took to him by taxi across London. He made a good recovery and soon afterwards helped to organise the wedding of his niece Rosemary who at that time was working as a teacher and living close to the family at Gloucester Place.

Early in 1946 he negotiated with the Admiralty to buy—at a favourable price because of the unpaid work he had done on the *Multichine* during the war—a 112-foot ex-service Fairmile 'B' Class motor-launch. This he intended to convert into a floating home for he had plans, should his health improve, to take the boat to warmer climes. A very nominal purchase sum was agreed and he and Bernard travelled to Chatham to sign the necessary documents and take possession of the vessel. PB then returned to London, leaving Bernard at the Naval Yard with the boat until it was ready to be moved.

In due course Noel drove her father back to Chatham so that they could take the *Commodore*—as PB had by then named the boat[1]—to its new moorings at Burnham-on-Crouch. The short voyage went smoothly enough but when PB began to manoeuvre the vessel into its berth, the real fun started. Within minutes there was chaos for dinghies and small boats were coming up, hitting *Commodore's* stern and then disappearing. The launch had picked up a mooring 'trot' and it was being wound in as though with a winch. The total damage was about £8,000 but PB was not unduly concerned because, as he smilingly said later, 'I was bad news to the insurance company—they didn't like paying out £8,000 for a £4 premium!' It was certainly a spectacular arrival and his exploit became the main topic of discussion at Burnham for weeks.

Bernard stayed aboard to oversee the craft's conversion and when this had been completed, the family moved in. Packing and unpacking PB's personal effects was quite an operation in itself, for into several large crates had to be carefully stowed all the early models of his aeroplanes in their individual velvet-lined cases; his drawings and models of his boats and motorised caravan; many versions of his Compass camera, films and accessories; books and electioneering pamphlets; newspaper cuttings; numerous patents and a wealth of other documents.

When the move had been completed and the family were happily settled in, PB thought it a good opportunity to invite some of his long-standing Burnham friends aboard for a drink. One of these remarked, after he had been shown round the motor-launch, that he had not seen a life raft anywhere. PB quickly replied, with a wicked smile: 'You won't. At sea, this boat carries 4,000 gallons of high-octane petrol—we hand out parachutes.' It was a flash of the old PB that many had known in the sailing club days before the war, but it was plain to all who saw him on that

---

1. After his last yacht, which he had sold that year

occasion that he was by then a very much changed and sick man.

Although Bernard ensured that the powerful engines of the motor-launch were always kept in perfect order, as though in readiness for an instant departure should PB fancy a change of scene, the *Commodore* was never to leave its moorings again. Noel in particular loved the life aboard, listening to the incoming tide at night lapping against the side. She spent hours each evening talking to her father and sometimes massaging his head to alleviate the pain he suffered from time to time. Long after her mother had gone to bed, they would sit into the early hours discussing what he termed 'the fate of the world' and she came to know a side of her father she had never encountered before. During the day he continued to demand the attention of all and even kept a foghorn beside him which he sounded if he thought he was being ignored. Yet when Noel and he were alone together, she found a thoughtful man who seemed genuinely to care about those whom the world had not treated kindly.

He told her then of his strivings to improve the average man's lot, his hatred of party politics and the dangers he felt were inherent in the policies of those who veered too far either to the right or left. He had wanted to do so much, to contribute something of worth to the world—particularly to his country, which he loved—yet he feared he had not, after all, achieved this. Although he had several times come close to being a millionaire, he had felt uncomfortable with too much money and always felt happier when he had put it to work on some new project. Acclaim and financial reward had, he told her, always been the least of his considerations. For him, the greatest satisfaction had always come from the actual process of creating.

PB's sister Mary often visited him on the boat and teased him when he petulantly protested if she, Noel and Veronica left him to go on a short shopping trip or to the local teashop to meet their friends. It seemed as if he hated to be left alone for long and Bernard would often chat to him when the others were away. On several occasions PB spoke of the bitterness he felt at not being adequately reimbursed by the Admiralty for all the money he had invested in the *Multichine*, particularly as he was now having to live entirely on his capital and had his family to consider. He was worried about how they would manage if he were no longer with them, knowing that they would have little but the Gloucester Place trust to provide for them and he told Bernard that he was relying on his accountants and solicitor to handle this carefully for him. He also spoke of the pleasure he felt at seeing his son settling down so well in the Navy, although he sometimes wished Robin had been more mechanically inclined, for then he might have been interested in following up some of his own dormant inventions. One of his greatest regrets, he told Bernard, was that he and his son had not achieved a better relationship.

On the morning of 11th November 1948, while Noel and her mother were out shopping, PB had called Bernard in for what he described as a 'discussion on a very serious matter'. He made Bernard promise that, whatever happened, he would stay with Veronica and Noel for as long as they needed him. Noting the intensity with which PB attempted to elicit the promise, Bernard could not help but agree. Mary was expected for tea that day and when she came aboard at four o'clock, Noel was despatched to her father's cabin to tell him of his sister's arrival. She could not waken him and realised, much to her distress, that he had died during his customary afternoon nap from what was later revealed as a coronary thrombosis. He was sixty-seven years old.

On hearing the news, Veronica, shocked and inconsolable, collapsed into an armchair, which she refused to leave for several days. In her eyes he had always appeared so strong and invincible that she was unable to consider any kind of life without him. Despite the knowledge that in the past few years he had been a sick man, she never doubted that he would recover and they would then spend a happy old age together. Without him beside her she felt utterly lost and disorientated.

The people of Burnham were also shocked to learn of the death of the colourful figure who in the past had contributed so much to their local sailing fraternity. Many grieved over the incongruity of his last departure from the *Commodore* for, unable to remove his large body through the hatchway, the undertakers were obliged to cut an opening in the deck to take him ashore. Even more bizarre was PB's final instruction: a vein was to be cut in his wrist, to ensure he would not be placed in his coffin alive and this his doctor duly executed. The cremation was at Golders Green and his ashes were then scattered at the estuary of the Crouch by Veronica, Noel and Bernard.

Some weeks later, while sorting out PB's effects, Veronica discovered the small black box that had accompanied her husband on all his travels since the death of his first wife, Dot. It was a mark of her understanding and love for him that Veronica decided once again to take a small boat out into the estuary and sprinkle the ashes the box contained, close to the spot where she had previously scattered those of her husband. Although she knew he had been happy with her, Veronica realised that she had always taken second place in his affections to Dot, the woman who had shared so many of his most creative and turbulent years.

In his will, PB left £13,000, the trust fund he had set up for his family and the *Commodore*. He also made a small bequest to a charity for down-and-outs run by the London church of St Martin-in-the-Fields—possibly at the instigation of an old friend, the journalist Hannen Swaffer, whose particular interest this had been.

After Veronica had carefully packed away for the last time all her husband's treasured effects, they were stored in a garage she had rented at Burnham-on-Crouch and here, for more than twenty years, they were to remain undisturbed. She ignored the many requests she was to receive for further information about his life and for his models to be placed in aeronautical collections.[2] Even the *Commodore* was left to rot. It was as if she wished to put firmly behind her any memories she may have had of PB and their years

2. See Appendix VII for one such letter.

together when, in the early 1950s, she decided to start a new life for herself and applied for a job as housekeeper to Stephen Joseph at his Theatre-in-the-Round at Scarborough. She soon became a well-loved friend to the whole company and it was at this Yorkshire seaside town that, in 1978, she died.

Noel emigrated to Canada after her father's death, married soon afterwards and became the mother of four children. Robin, who married during his service in the Navy, went on to raise four sons, study drama and later play a major role in founding the Octagon Theatre at Bolton in Lancashire. Bernard kept his promise to PB and remained with Veronica and the *Commodore* for as long as he was needed and then left Burnham to work at the Government's communication establishment near Cheltenham. He met Noel again after an interval of many years when she returned for her mother's funeral. By that time he was a widower and she a divorcee who had re-assumed her maiden name. They so enjoyed reminiscing about the extraordinary life they had once shared with PB that Bernard later visited her in Canada for a holiday. This led to the pair deciding to marry and live on Vancouver Island, where Noel had for some years run a successful boarding kennels and become closely involved in local politics. Not wishing to change yet again the name under which she ran her business, it was agreed that Bernard should relinquish his own surname and assume that of his late respected employer and friend—Pemberton Billing.

It is a sad fact that few people nowadays are familiar either with PB's name or the many projects and activities with which he was associated. He still gets an occasional mention in books and articles dealing with Parliamentary matters, recorded sound, pioneer airmen or the sensational trial at the Old Bailey in 1918 but somehow over the years the other aspects of his incredible life appear to have been forgotten. This might have been different had not the evidence of so many of his endeavours been hidden away for so long by Veronica at Burnham-on-Crouch and then—a mere three years before her death—been totally destroyed by a fire at the garage where they had been stored.

Fortunately, there remain sufficient accounts in official records and newspapers to shed at least some light on his mercurial life. The many patents he registered are still available for all to see[3] and it is probable that he acted as a catalyst for others to develop his original ideas. As has been shown, some of his inventions were very much ahead of their time and it is a great pity that he did not pursue these beyond their first experimental stages.

Shortly after he died, a letter was published in a national newspaper by a man who evidently knew his subject extremely well. The writer, Alan Tomkins, claimed that the obituary notices had not given due credit to PB's undoubted mechanical genius: 'This genius was often dissipated as his darting mind turned restlessly to new ideas. He would toil like a maniac on a promising idea, and then drop it cold for no reason save that it bored him'. After giving instances of this, Tomkins went on to write of how others had also agreed that

3. See Appendix IV.

it was 'a national disaster' that nobody could manage PB: 'If only we could have selected his inventions and exercised a little control over that brave, flashing mind, he would have ranked in the eyes of the world with Edison, Parsons and Fleming'.

His niece Rosemary and daughter Noel agree that, if he had concentrated on fewer things and brought more to fruition, his achievements would have been viewed differently. He was motivated, according to Noel, more by the sheer thrill of working creatively and finding fresh fields to conquer than by the need for either commercial success or public acclaim. As it was, once an idea came to him and he had tried it out, he would often lose interest and move on to something else. Rosemary added that she 'admired him for his "guts" and complete self-reliance. He never felt the world owed him a living but rather that it was open to be explored and discovered.'

But what of his status in the aeronautical world? Sir Thomas Sopwith was once asked if he thought that PB's efforts at aeroplane designing had been worthwhile, since few of his early machines actually flew. The old pioneer designer replied, with a chuckle: 'Neither did any of ours—at first.' However, some of PB's designs were feasible, as was later proved, although others were too ridiculous to be considered seriously. In 1941, reviewing PB's *Defence Against the Night Bomber* for the Journal of the Royal Aeronautical Society, the writer made these comments:

> As a pioneer of flying, as a constructor of aircraft with novel ideas which rarely went into second editions, and as one who has the cause of the country close to his heart, he must be listened to, with interest if nothing else...There are times when the author talks or writes such sound sense that it seems a pity to have it completely overlaid, if not smothered, by the nonsense which he noises abroad. Pemberton Billing has that knack of being exasperating when he is not amusing and of being amusing when he is not exasperating. It makes a man interesting, but it does not make him logical.

The same reviewer also noted, however, that despite his eccentricity, those who had had 'the astonishing experience of knowing him would realise how difficult it was not to listen to him'. Herein lies the problem of trying fully to assess this extraordinary man. How does a writer adequately convey on paper an almost hypnotic charisma possessed by someone long since dead? PB certainly had that indefinable something which drew people towards him— whether on the electioneering platform or socially. More important, he also had the gift of being able to encourage others to achieve success—Scott Paine and Gordon England are but two examples of this.

Inevitably he made enemies, particularly during his Parliamentary career, and many saw him during those years as an arrogant opportunist and fanatic, a bluffing intriguer, even a dangerous demagogue. He certainly ruffled more than a few feathers in political circles. Lord Robert Cecil is quoted as saying to Bonar Law in August 1918: 'I had rather sweep a crossing than be a member of a ministry at the mercy of Pemberton Billing and his crew.' Nor did his frequent appearances in the law courts, whether in the capacity of defendant or plaintiff, add to his public esteem.

Yet it is only fair to say that for all his worldliness in some directions, he was a poor judge of character and was often enticed into schemes formulated by others for their own, sometimes sinister, purposes. By playing on his vanity, his natural enthusiasm for a cause and his genuine desire to be of service to his country, he was undoubtedly used on occasions as a pawn in some very shady political games.

Without doubt, some of his crusades—such as that for better administration of the air forces in the First World War and the provision of adequate housing for returning servicemen—were worthwhile, and even his sternest critics could not but confess to a sneaking admiration for the panache with which he set about achieving some of his more reputable goals. Charles Grey, in his book *A History of the Air Ministry*, was one of those who gave PB full credit for bringing about the Air Enquiry into safer flying conditions and the subsequent founding of the Air Ministry. He also made the point that, historically, many valuable reforms had been initiated by men such as PB, whose over-zealous approach had at first rendered their ideas unacceptable but that, when all the shouting had died down, others of a milder-mannered disposition had stepped in to carry the reforms through and taken the credit for doing so.

He also acknowledged, in an obituary tribute, that PB had made life colourful and amusing for all his friends and despite the frequent—and often bitter—disagreements he had with him during the thirty-two years of their acquaintanceship, he considered that their friendship had been very rewarding. 'He lived the fullest life of any man I have known and had very good value for it. Also I fancy the world has profited by his existence and I cannot recall that he has done harm to any individual. May he rest in the peace with which he was never content in his lifetime.'

In recent years it has been suggested that PB had leanings towards Fascism or that, should Germany have won the last war, he would have supported Hitler. Nothing could be further from the truth—his 'Open Letter' to Chamberlain in 1938 surely discounts such a theory. He would never have given his support to any regime that involved the loss of free speech or freedom for the individual—he was, after all, a very Independent MP. A patriot he certainly was but to understand his attitude in this respect, it must be remembered that he was born a Victorian and grew up in Edwardian times when the nation was encouraged to take pride in the Empire and in Britain's achievements worldwide and many of his subsequent activities were focussed on this. Although he was often critical of the way the country was being run and travelled widely, he would never have countenanced making his permanent home anywhere else.

But perhaps the most appropriate tailpiece for this book is to be found in some lines written by PB that he used on his 1935 Christmas card, for they show not only his admiration for Rudyard Kipling but the principles by which he strove to conduct his life. He wished recipients:

'Just enough humour to face a new year
In a world that is patently mad.
Just enough sense to get on with the job
In a country which isn't too bad.
Just enough work to make leisure worthwhile
And stop us from getting bored.
Just enough cash to be able to buy
The things we can't afford.
Just enough faith to believe in a plan
Where no-one or nothing remains.
Just enough loving to soften our hearts
Without likewise affecting our brains.
Just enough guts to hang on in a fight
When everything's 'shot to hell'.
Just enough savvy when friends inquire
To answer them 'all is well'.
Just enough kindness to help us to see
The other man's point of view.
Just enough sense to judge all men alike
Whether pagan or Christian or Jew.
Just enough insight to regard worth not wealth
As a measure of all mankind.
Just enough knowledge to profit in full
By the wisdom it leaves behind.
Just enough wisdom to read in these lines
Philosophy's A.B.C..
Just enough humour to understand why
They were written by N.P.B'.

APPENDICES

APPENDIX I

PB's Maiden Speech, 1916

I ask the indulgence which I know this House always extends to a Member when he first rises, and I claim that indulgence because of the somewhat peculiar circumstances which are responsible for my appearance in this House. Within an hour or two of my taking the Oath at that Table I am on my feet, fulfilling what I know to be a duty to my Constituents and to the country. It would not be fitting, and I know it is not done, that I should drag the dust, or rather I should say the dirt, of a hotly-contested bye-election into the comparative calm and cleanliness of this House. I will touch one personal note. I left the RNAS because I felt that, unless someone came to this House with a weight of authority which only a constituency can give him, the Air Service would continue to be a byword among its members, and a subject of almost tragic mirth in its efforts to defend this country. I have listened with considerable interest to the right hon. Gentleman the Under-Secretary for War and to what he has said in regard to the Air Service, and I have but one remark to make now. I fancy—indeed I am sure—he is most grievously misinformed.

Eighteen months ago, when the material at the disposal of the RNAS was something like one-twentieth of what it is today, we succeeded in raiding Zeppelin bases and carrying the war into the enemy's country, proving thereby that although our material was lacking, our personnel was such that we were able to carry out these raids successfully. I therefore definitely join issue with the First Lord of the Admiralty in his statement that the lack of material is responsible for our present policy of masterly inactivity and deplorable delay in answering the challenge of the enemy in the air. For the first six months of this war our Air Service was rich in leadership and poor in material. During the last six months we have been somewhat richer in material, but infinitely poorer in leadership. The six months gap between these two definite periods was devoted to internal intrigue and consequent service bitterness. This deplorable condition of affairs is directly responsible for the present impotence and inefficiency of the service. We *can* strike now in the matter of aerial offence, and I say that we *must* strike now.

I quite appreciate what a mark a Zeppelin shed is—bigger than a battleship and more vulnerable than the Crystal Palace. We possess machines to reach these sheds, which house not only a pest of the night, but that which has proved itself to be the eye of the German Navy. We hear of a new Trafalgar and there are rumours of a coming naval raid. Is it too much to ask that our Grand Fleet should cease to be handicapped in its movements by this never-ceasing flow of information conveyed to the German Admiralty by these spies in the air? We must, and can, exterminate these Zeppelins. I assure you our people are ready to make any sacrifice in this war, but they are not prepared to remain in darkness while our rulers remain indifferent. It has been suggested by the Under-Secretary of State for War that we have not the machines and we have not the pilots. If the right hon. gentlemen tells me that we have not the pilots, I shall be very pleased to introduce him, within the next twenty-four hours, to a hundred of them. If he tells me we have not the machines, I am prepared to lead him to them by the hand. If he tells me that we have not the bombs, then, with your permission, I will put them on the Table of this House.

APPENDIX I

I would beg hon. Members to lend all the wealth of their imagination and their wisdom to this very momentous question of our supremacy in the air. I would ask them to remember that this country is no longer an island, that every city lies on the shore of the ocean of the air, open to attack by enemy airships and a prey to outrage at any moment of the twenty-four hours. Who will dare to plead the expense of a great air fleet when we realise that this war may possibly be eventually determined in the air, and when we consider that with the cost of two or three days' hostilities we could not only gain but could maintain supremacy in the air? It is a wonderful thought; and I am quite sure if this House lends any time to it we may yet live to regain for this country the supremacy which we held for a few brief moments owing to the priceless men who first went out with the rotten material they had at their disposal. This country is demanding that this material should be used. The men in the service are demanding that they should be sent out to fight instead of staying at home. I do ask the right hon. Gentleman the First Lord of the Admiralty to insist, not in six months' time, not in six weeks' time, but, if necessary, in six minutes' time, that the material that is now waiting shall be used, and that the bombs which are being stored and which are due for delivery in many places in Germany, shall be delivered forthwith and without further delay.

APPENDIX II
A MAN AND A PLAN

The Protection of England
A Dream that MUST Come True
from *Air War: How to Wage It* by Noel Pemberton Billing (Gale & Polden, 1916)

He is the man responsible for the air defence of England. His room in Whitehall is a large one. From where he stands with his back to the fire the distant wall is covered by a map of England, 15 feet square. It is painted on glass and cross-sectioned into a hundred squares varied in size. In the middle of the room on a large table is fixed a replica of the map, and in the centre of the sections indicating districts is a telegraphic key. Nearby sits a writer facing the chart, and having in front of him an outline map of England marked in squares similar to the others

It is a fine afternoon in late winter. No one is more conscious of this fact than the Commander-in-Chief, Air Defence; indeed, fair weather has for him a special significance. In answer to his ring, a messenger appears. 'Tell Dr Egerton I wish to see him.' When the meteorological adviser leaves the room, it is immediately evident that the Chief's impressions have been confirmed.

Stepping to the table chart, he taps on the key at the base of the map. The noise of a buzzer is heard—one long, three short. The writer is alert, pencil in hand, with eyes fixed on the wall chart. A few seconds' interval and suddenly the map is illumined by patches of light. The order has been received and answered; the message 'Weather conditions favourable to air raid' has radiated through England to the air defence stations of the country.

But the map is not wholly illuminated; there are three dark patches—N.E.York 48, W.Suffolk 8, E.Somerset 36. The Chief taps again, and notes that no writer is recording the defaulters. Three seconds elapse, and 8 lights up; in another two seconds 48 responds; 36 is still dark. Turning to another assistant, the Chief raps out 'Check 36 by trunk.'

In three minutes the one dark spot lights up, and all England is alert. But why the delay? The lamp in Somerset has burnt out; the call failed. 'Duplicate lamps everywhere before full station call tomorrow night,' is the Chief's order—a weak spot in the system has been discovered and remedied.

Wireless message: Origin, North Sea. 'Four Zeppelins, altitude approximately 6,000 feet, proceeding West. Time 4.45.' Reading this decoded message a second time, the Chief turns to the control board—three long and three short buzzes are heard. Immediately the chart flutters back into darkness. What has happened? In each of those hundred districts representing as many squares the officers in command now know that Zeppelins are approaching, and have received the call 'Stand to arms.' His next action when the chart satisfies him that in every case his message has been received, is to darken the whole of the coast by simply tapping the code word 'Darken' to all coastal districts. It must be understood that at the first alarm call district officers communicate with police and power stations, who, in their turn, by raising and lowering pressure, intimate to the inhabitants the contingency likely to arise.

How are these messages conveyed from the Commander-in-Chief in Whitehall by the pressing of a button, and what do these commanding officers do? Situated in each one of these districts is a room somewhat similarly fitted to that of the Chief's, but in place of the map of England on the wall is a map of his district, divided into five or more sections, according to its civil or military importance.

Situated in each of these five sub-districts, and in telegraphic connection with the commanding officer's map, are listening posts; that is, a wooden tower, about 100 feet high, surmounted by four microphones, capable of detecting the sound of engine or propeller at a considerable distance. They face N.,S.,E. and W. respectively. In the watch-room at the base of the tower sits the officer in charge. Under his control are a searchlight, an anti-aircraft gun, and at stations of strategical importance, one or two night-flying aeroplanes.

Together with the rest of the sub-stations through England, this officer in charge received the first warning call, 'Conditions favourable for a raid.' The searchlight was at once tested, aeroplane engines were run, the guns were examined, and time fuses set. In a word, *the station was on duty.*

On the receipt of the raid alarm the commanding officer picks up the microphone receiver and waits. Half an hour passes, the distant whir of propellers is heard proceeding from the north-east. The noise rapidly grows more distinct. The commanding officer taps his key, and his district represented on the district commander's chart lights up. A buzzer in a room sounds three times, and within ten seconds in the Commander-in-Chief's room in Whitehall his chart, in its turn, indicates the definite locality where enemy airships are heard.

The Commander-in-Chief decides in these circumstances to send up the aeroplanes of this district and three adjoining districts, and while at once darkening these sections gradually to darken contiguous sections.

To effect this he proceeds to his control board and by the mere tapping of the keys of the various districts his orders are automatically carried out.

Everybody is on the alert. Four districts are in action; the others are in darkness and awaiting orders; the rest of the country is so far unaffected. Normal conditions prevail everywhere else. But so complete is the control from Whitehall, so perfect the system of intelligence, that in a moment, should other counties be threatened, the pressing of a button will put in operation the same offensive and defensive plans.

* * *

The above has been written in narrative form in order to convey as simply as possible the principle of a system which, with the existing wireless, telegraphic and telephonic facilities, could be established within a few weeks. It will be noticed that this plan of mine concentrates on central control, without which any system of aerial defence will prove illusory. Not only is the introduction of some such system imperative, if we are to meet the existing situation calmly, but effectively, but it is on such lines that we can eventually guarantee protection against attack from the air.

The introduction of this system into England tomorrow would mean the allocation to this service of approximately 300 guns, 500 searchlights, 500 to 700 aeroplanes, and the erection of 500 listening station towers - wooden structures which could be built at a comparatively small cost.

As to the 'personnel', it would include a Commander-in-Chief, with a small staff,

THE PROTECTION OF ENGLAND.

The Equipment of each Sub-District.

and a hundred district commanders, with something like 35 officers and men to each district, including pilots, gunners and searchlight operators.

Let it be remembered that England is no longer an island; that every inland city lies on the coast of the ocean of the air, liable to sudden attack from the ships of the air. No one after reading this article can fail to realise that the Commander-in-Chief of the Air Defence of England will be no sinecure post. It will occupy all the ability, experience, and the application of the ablest man that can be chosen. It would be sheer madness to add this enormous responsibility and stupendous task to the work of some already over-burdened commander.

AIRCRAFT DESIGNS

Supermarine Type List

Original Type No	Revision No.	Engine(s)	Purpose	Remarks
PB. Glider	PB.0 --	Glider		First design
PB.Monoplane	PB.1	Valveless rotary	Pusher	Unsuccessful
PB.Monoplane	PB.3	Two-cylinder JAP	Pusher	Short hops only
PB.Monoplane	PB.5	N.E.C.	Pusher	Not flown
PB.1 PB.7		Gnome	Flying-boat	At 1914 Olympia
PB.1 (mod)	PB.9	Gnome	Flying-boat	As above but engine in hull
PB.2	PB.11	Austro-Daimler	Flying-boat	--
PB.3 --		Austro-Daimler	Flying-boat	Not built slip-wing
PB.5	PB.21*	Austro-Daimler	Flying-boat	Not built slip-wing
PB.7	PB.19*	Sunbeam Salmson	Flying-boat slip-wing	Two ordered by Germany
PB.9	PB.13	Gnome	Single-seat	Probably 1267 scout 'Seven-day bus'
PB.11	PB.15	Gnome		Pusher Gunbus Probably 1374
PB.13	PB.17	Rotary	Single-seat	Improved PB.9 scout
--	PB.19 --	--	--	see PB.7
	PB.21 --	--	--	see PB.5
	PB.23E	Le Rhone	Single-seat	No.8487 only scout
	PB.25	Clerget or Gnome scout	Single-seat	9001-9020 only Monosoupape
	PB.27	Inline	Submarine-flying-boat	Not built stowed
	PB.29E	Austro-Daimler	Quadruplane	one only 'Night-hawk'
	PB.31 --		Submarine-flying-boat	Project stowed
	PB.31E	(2)Anzani	Quadruplane 'Night-hawk'	1388-1389 only 1388 built

* Unconfirmed

LATER PROJECTS. Additional notes compiled by Philip Jarrett to information given in the text. References to books by Noel Pemberton Billing are: *AoT:The Aeroplane of Tomorrow; DNB: Defence Against the Night Bomber*)

PB.33 & 35 The type-numbering system used by Billing in World War One, which used only odd numbers, seems to have ended with the PB.31E quadruplane. Between this and the next known type number, PB.37, there are two known designs, and it seems logical to assume that these were probably the PB.33 and PB.35. The first of these designs, which appeared late in 1934, was the Durotofin, a rotorcraft which combined the features of the Autogiro, the paddle-wheel aircraft then proposed by Platt in the USA and Rohrbach in Germany, and the helicopter.

A 'well qualified authority on aerodynamics' spoke highly of the Durotofin, saying that it 'should have strong positive stability in pitch and roll, whether hovering or in forward flight,' and added: 'The machine is of very original and attractive conception and yet incorporates no features of questionable aerodynamic design.' He particularly pointed out the advantages of eliminating torque-reaction forces by the use of twin counter-rotating rotors, a feature that was to be conspicuous on the first truly successful helicopter, the Focke-Achgelis Fa 61 of 1936. Despite its obvious potential, the Durotofin was never completed. Because he was involved with so many other projects, the PB.35, the 'Skylark', was not pursued either, beyond the model for his initial design produced in April 1936. This was, perhaps, just as well for although it was very innovative it was questionable whether or not it was, in fact, airworthy. *Flight* thought that the main wheels were too far forward to allow the tail to be got up for take-off. A small tailwheel was fitted at the rear of the fuselage girder. The prototype was to be powered by a Douglas engine mounted just below and forward of the wing leading edge, but Billing envisaged a purpose-built PB unit for production machines.

Flight commented: 'One expects PB to have an amusing time with the Air Ministry airworthiness people in connection with his plain welded joints without reinforcing of any sort'.

PB.37 c.1940. Slip-wing flying-scale experimental aircraft ('Small naval dive-bomber'), apparently built by F.Hills & Sons of Manchester. The lower component was a single-seat mid-wing monoplane with a tricycle undercarriage and wooden wings, tailplane and twin endplate fins and a steel-tube box-girder fuselage faired to circular section and fabric-covered. A 290 hp in-line engine was positioned in mid-fuselage, driving two low-speed pusher propellers behind the wing trailing edges via shaft drives. Wing area 67 sq.ft. The upper component or 'slip-wing' was a smaller single-seat mid-wing monoplane with a tricycle undercarriage and a cruciform tail, powered by a two-cylinder 40 hp air-cooled engine driving a two-bladed propeller and having a wing area of 135 sq.ft. Estimated performance for the PB.37: carries a 1,000 lb payload for 1,000 miles at 240 mph at 10,000 ft. Top speed estimated by Aerodynamics Dept. at Farnborough as 265 mph. Cost of building both components £3,000. Upper component built in 5 weeks at a cost of £600. Lower component was nearing completion after 11 weeks' work. Work suspended about June 1940. Believed scrapped.
Refs: *AoT,* p.242; *DNB,* p.118 & Ch.VIII; *The Aeroplane*, 7 July 1944, pp.14 & 15; *Aeronautics*, Aug. 1941, pp.59 & 60.

PB.39 The only known source of information regarding this number is PB's personal Christmas card for 1936. It was an extraordnary amphibious Durotofin-type rotorcraft with a fully-enclosed hull and small sponsons with floats at their tips which also housed wheels. Attached to a pylon above and behind the cabin was an enormous deep-chord two-bladed rotor which had small fin surfaces about two-thirds of the way out to the tips. These had a feathering movement and were supposed to impart forward or rearward motion in the same manner as the Durotofin. Perhaps the most interesting feature of the design, in view of modern helicopter developments, is the stabilising tail rotor, which is shrouded in the fin, much like the modern 'fenestron'.

PB.41 Upper component (slip-wing) of composite patrol fighter. Twin-boom pusher biplane with searchlight fitted in nose. Could be attached to Hurricane or Spitfire or similar new type.
Refs: *Flight,* 26 Dec. 1940, pp.550-552; *AoT,* pp.132, 240-8, 249, 263-5, 269-70; *DNB, Ch.VII*

PB.43/47 Venturi Twin-hull giant flying-boat with powered biplane slip-wing. Lower component had two or four propellers mounted beneath centre section between the hulls in large-diameter ducts or 'venturis'. 500 passengers accommodated in hulls and wing structure. Cockpit located on top of centre section between the hulls. Biplane slip-wing flying boat had its two-bay wings mounted high on its hull and there were two stabilising floats, strut mounted beneath the lower wing at each half-span. Small engine mounted over cockpit, driving tractor propeller. Slip-wing used to get heavily loaded flying-boat lower component airborne. Designated PB.43 in *AoT,* pp.273-276, but PB.47 on PB's Christmas card c.1940.

Data: Span 220 ft; length 180 ft; wing area 6,000 sq.ft; wing loading 75 lb sq.ft; loading (landing) 45 lb sq.ft; Passengers 500; mail 35,000 lb; luggage 57,000 lb; empty weight 185,000 lb; disposable load 265,200 lb; gross weight 450,000 lb; max. speed 330 mph; cruising speed 280 mph; range 3,200 miles; max. power 24,000 hp; cruising power 16,800 hp.

PB.45 Not established. See drawings in *Flight,* 21 Nov. 1940

PB.47 Unarmed 'higher-speed bomber'.
Refs: *AoT,* pp.241,244,251-2; *DNB,* Ch. VIII

PB.49 High-speed, long range bomber.
Refs: *AoT,* pp.70,193,252-4; *DNB,* Ch. VIII; *Flight,* 14 Nov. 1940 pp.413-15; *Flight,* 21 Nov. 1940 pp.429-32 (with slip-wing).

PB.51 Not established. See *Flight,* 21 Nov. 1940.

PB.53 High-speed bomber. Ref: *AoT,* pp.250-1.

Projects to which no type numbers have been matched
(These might, of course, include the PB.39, PB.45 and PB.51 - though they might be different projects altogether.)

PB. Slip-wing fighter
Ref: *AoT,* pp. 263-5; *DNB,* Ch. XI, pp.151-3; *Flight,* 21 Nov. 1940 pp. 429-32 and 19 Dec. 1940, pp.524-5.

<u>Tow Fighters</u> (two proposed designs)
Ref: *AoT,* pp.265-7; *DNB,* Ch. VII (refers to both designs), Ch.XI, pp.153-4.

<u>Porcupine Fighter</u>
Ref: *AoT,* pp.261-2.

APPENDIX IV
PB's PATENTS

Year	Number	Description
1903	23127	Powder-puff attachment
1904		Removing cigarette from parcel
		Tilting (lamp) shades
1906	27850	Typewriters
1907		Powder sprinkling containers
	14096	Typewriters
	212000	Game-scoring devices
1909	9625	Balancing combustion engines
	7389	Game-scoring device
	8086	Door and latches
	9070	Calculating machines
	11692	Cigarette holders
	1693	Carpenter's plane
	11694	Toilet requisites
	11695	Card dealer
	12668	Calculator
	21279	Envelope holding apparatus
1913	24163	Aerial craft indicator
	24462	Flying boats,etc. (also 8223 in 1914)
1914	4310	Anchors
	7828	Aerial craft
	7829	Aerial craft
1915	4535	Ordnance (rotary bomb dropping)
	4537	Aircraft (witheld under Sec. 30 PA1907)
	15054	Aircraft
	17445	Aeroplanes
	17446	Gramophones
	164404	Motor vehicles
1920	137969	Walls
	142179	Heating and cooking appliance
	142582	Heating and cooking appliances (hotplate)
	142667	Heating and cooking appliances (stoves)
	174117	Golf practice machine
	173879	Golf practice trainer
1921	164404	Sound recording apparatus
	185188	Motion picture apparatus
1923		Talking machine
1924	210835	Sound recording apparatus
	220057	Sound records
1925	238300	Gramophone records
		Combined phonograph & picture projection apparatus
	239564	Continuation of above
1927	266443	Gramophones, records, etc.

	276065	Gramophones, records, etc
	266791	Gramophones, records, etc
1928	285584	Manufacture of sound records
	294696	Manufacture of sound records
	297881	Motor caravan
1933	428003	Camera support
	428454	Camera support
	428455	Camera shutter
	428511	Built-in exposure meter
	428515	Developing apparatus
	428516	Printing apparatus
1934	437945	Lens fitting & mounts
	463943	Photographic roll film gear
	465102	Photographic roll film gear
	467837	Spools
	469653	Film roll
	476614	Film-holding plate (metal)
	478342	Compass camera
	445611	as 476614 for film, not plate
	445784	Swivel plate
	447901	Film wind-on counter
	452013	as 476614, but cardboard
	480108	as 476614, but cardboard
	489557	Collapsible camera
	446509	Helicopter
1936	480108	Carriers for photographic film
		Support for cameras
		Photographic developing apparatus
		Photopraphic roll-film cameras
		Roll film & spools
		Tripod stands
1938/9		Carriers for photo-sensitised material
	484298	2-stroke engines
	493373	Means of stabilising marine vessels
	498214	Hulls for marine craft
1938	522529	Hospital stretchers
1939		Ambulances
		Mobile folding structures, etc.
1940	538482	Package of razor blades
	526070	Loading devices for vehicles
	551481	Propeller drive for marine vessels

This list does not include his American and Australian patents and those inventions or designs for aircraft he never bothered to register.

APPENDIX V

PB's YACHTS

From Lloyd's Register of Yachts

1908-11	*Violet*
1911-12	*Triton*
1912-13	*Hildegarde*
	Princess Alice
	Moira (previously known as *Clara*)
	Fiddlesticks
1914	*Hiawatha*
	Utopia (previously known as *Gleniffer*)
1915	*Dyack*
1919	*Magdelena*
1920-23	*Freedom*
	Indemnity
1924-28	*Freedom*
1928	*Pretty Lady*
1929	*Four Winds*
	Freedom
1930-32	*Crusader A*
1934-46	*Andria*
1937-46	*Commodore*

ACROSS AMERICA IN A RILEY "9"

Just as we are closing this issue for Press we have received news of another remarkable achievement put up by the Riley "9"—an achievement which constitutes further definite and conclusive evidence of the ability of the British Light Car to do that which the World has hitherto believed to be utterly beyond its powers.

Piloted by Mr. Pemberton-Billing, who is an enthusiastic Riley owner, and, as all the World knows, a constant champion of British cars, the car illustrated below has traversed the continent

A RECORD OF AN AMAZING PERFORMANCE BY
Mr. PEMBERTON-BILLING

of North America, covering a distance of over 4.200 miles in 5 days 20 hours and 13 minutes, averaging throughout the run 41 m.p.h.

Below we publish a copy of Mr. Pemberton-Billing's cable announcing his success.

For the nonce we must leave this to tell the story, but knowing our readers' interest in achievements of this nature, we shall return to the subject in our next issue when further and fuller details are to hand.

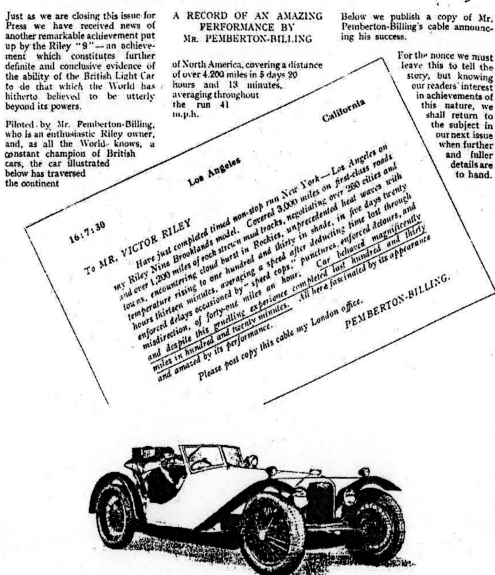

16:7:30

Los Angeles

California

To MR. VICTOR RILEY

Have just completed timed non-stop run New York—Los Angeles on my Riley Nine Brooklands model. Covered 3,000 miles on first-class roads and over 1,200 miles of rock strewn mud tracks, negotiating over 280 cities and towns, encountering cloud burst in Rockies, unprecedented heat waves with temperature rising to one hundred and thirty in shade, in five days twenty hours thirteen minutes, averaging a speed after deducting time lost through enforced delays occasioned by "speed cops," punctures, enforced detours, and misdirection, of forty-one miles an hour. Car behaved magnificently and despite this gruelling experience completed last hundred and thirty miles in hundred and twenty minutes. All here fascinated by its appearance and amazed by its performance.

Please post copy this cable my London office.

PEMBERTON-BILLING.

DIRECTOR
JOHN TANNER, MA, PhD

Telephone
01-405 6977 ext. 0258

ROYAL AIR FORCE MUSEUM
MINISTRY OF DEFENCE
TURNSTILE HOUSE
94-99 HIGH HOLBORN
LONDON W.C.1

Ref: RAFM/25/2

10th July 1967

Mrs Pemberton-Billing
119, Longwestgate
Scarborough

Dear Mrs Pemberton-Billing,

As you may know, the Royal Air Force Museum is in the process of formation and we are steadily amassing a collection of aircraft engines, equipment
armaments and documents and records of all kinds relating to the men and the
aircraft of the Royal Air Force and its antecedents, the Royal Flying Corps
and the Royal Naval Air Service. It is our aim to make this collection not
only a worthy monument to the achievements of Britain's flying services but
also the nation's aeronautical archives.

We are, of course, well aware of the enormous amount of invaluable work
that your late husband did during the pioneer days of British aviation and we
are well acquainted with his many revolutionary ideas about aircraft and their
employment in both world wars. Indeed, we have recently acquired all the
surviving aircraft drawings produced by the Supermarine Company and these
include several of the remarkable aircraft designed while your late husband
was still at the head of that very famous manufacturing concern.

My purpose in writing to you is to enquire whether you still have any
records, particularly photographs and documents, that would enable us to complete our picture of the early days of the Supermarine Aviation Company.
We should greatly like to add material of this kind to our collection and I
should consider it a great privilege to be allowed to see anything that you
may have. I should also hope that you might feel that the Royal Air Force
Museum is the appropriate repository for valuable material of this kind, but
if for the time being you feel unable to part with anything that you have I
should be very grateful if we might be allowed to borrow it for copying in
some appropriate manner.

We are, I assure you, most anxious to do full justice to all the wonderful work performed in the past by Britain's men of the air and, in this
connection, we must give due prominence to everything that your late husband
did. I look forward keenly to hearing from you and I enclose a franked
addressed envelope for your reply.

Yours sincerely,

John Tanner.

243

BIBLIOGRAPHY

Books by PB
Aerocraft (Edited by PB) March 1909 - March 1910 (11 issues)
Air War: How to Wage It (Gale & Polden, paperback, 1916)
PB, The Story of his Life (Imperialist Press, paperback, 1917)
High Treason (book of the play, privately published, 1928)
Defence Against the Night Bomber (Robert Hale, 1941)
The Aeroplane of Tomorrow (Robert Hale, 1941)
Victory Lies in the Air, (privately published, 1941)

Further reading
Hansard Parliamentary Debates: Commons 1916-1921.
Imperialist and *Vigilante* (London,1917) Verbatim report of trial of N.P. Billing

Andrews, C.F. and Morgan, E.B. *Supermarine*
      Aircraft since 1914 (Putnam, 1981)
Asquith, Lady Cynthia, *Diaries 1915-18*
      (Hutchinson, 1968)
Barker, Dudley,*Lord Darling's Famous Cases*
      (Hutchinson,1936)
Beaverbrook, Lord, *Politicians and the War*
      (Thornton Butterworth, 1928)
      Men and Power (Hutchinson, 1956)
Bennett, Daphne, *Margot: A Life of the Countess*
      of Oxford and Asquith (Gollancz, 1984)
Bruce, J.M., *British Aeroplanes, 1914-18* (Putnam, 1957)

Cole, Christopher and Cheeseman, E.F., *Air Defence*
      of Britain (Putnam, 1984)
Cooper, Diana and Duff, *A Durable Fire, Letters 1913-50* edited by
      Artemis Cooper (Collins, 1983)
Gardiner, Charles, *Fifty Years of Brooklands*
      (Heinemann, 1956)
Gilbert, Martin, *Winston Churchill (Vols.III and*
      IV) (Heinemann, 1971, 1975)
Graham, Evelyn, *Lord Darling and his Famous Trials*
      (Hutchinson, 1929)
Grey, C.G., *History of the Air Ministry* (Allen &
      Unwin, 1940) *Memoirs* (mss)
Hyde, H. Montgomery, *Their Good Names* (Hamish
      Hamilton, 1970)
Jerram, M.E., *Incredible Flying Machines* (Marshall
      Cavendish, 1980)
Kettle, Michael, *Salome's Last Veil: The Libel*
      Case of the Century (Granada Publishing, 1977)
Lloyd George, David, *War Memoirs: Vol. V* (Nicholson & Watson, 1936)

BIBLIOGRAPHY

MacMillan, Norman, *Tales of Two Air Wars* (Bell, 1963)

Miller, H.C., *Wings over Brooklands* (Angus & Robertson, 1968)

Pakenham, Thomas, *The Boer War* (Weidenfeld & Nicolson, 1979)

Pound, Reginald and Harmsworth, A.G.A., *Northcliffe*
(Cassell, 1959)
Read, Donald, *Edwardian England* (Harrap, 1972)

Rose, Kenneth, *King George V* (Weidenfeld & Nicolson, 1983)

Roskill, Stephen, *Hankey - Man of Secrets: Vol.1* (Collins, 1970-4)

Scott, J.D., *Vickers, a History* (Weidenfeld & Nicolson, 1962)

Searle,G.R., *Corruption in British Politics, 1895-1930* (Oxford University Press, 1987)

Smith, C.H.G, *A Brief History of Flying* (HMSO, 1967)

Symons, Julian, *Horatio Bottomley* (Cresset, 1955)

Taylor, A.J.P., *English History 1914-45* (Oxford Universlty Press, 1965)

Taylor, Joseph Crabtree, *Memoirs* (mss)

Whitehouse, Arch, *The Zeppelin Fighters* (Hale, 1968)

INDEX

Printed in the United Kingdom
by Lightning Source UK Ltd.
104850UKS00001BA/1